TALLAHASSEE
LIBRARY
COMMUNITY COLLEGE

D1593512

Singleness and the Church

Singleness and the Church

A New Theology of the Single Life

JANA MARGUERITE BENNETT

OXFORD
UNIVERSITY PRESS

OXFORD
UNIVERSITY PRESS

Oxford University Press is a department of the University of Oxford. It furthers the University's objective of excellence in research, scholarship, and education by publishing worldwide. Oxford is a registered trade mark of Oxford University Press in the UK and certain other countries.

Published in the United States of America by Oxford University Press
198 Madison Avenue, New York, NY 10016, United States of America.

CIP data is on file at the Library of Congress
ISBN 978-0-19-046262-8

1 3 5 7 9 8 6 4 2

Printed by Sheridan Books, Inc., United States of America

This book is for my sister, Elissa Brine, a most wonderful single mom.

Contents

Acknowledgments

FIRST AND FOREMOST, I want to acknowledge the lives and witnesses of the numerous single Christians I have met—some in passing, some who have become lifelong friends. They are too numerous to name without inadvertently omitting someone, but not a day goes without my encountering and remembering particular people who have shown Christ to me by their lives. That there are so many reminds me how full life is, and how bereft the church would be without the lives of single adults. I hesitated to write this book now—as a married woman and mother of three children. But so many people convinced me that something ought to be said and that maybe married people ought not be silent about single witness.

I also owe many thanks to the following people who had read parts of the manuscript, talked with me through the writing of this book, and otherwise provided helpful critiques and ideas: Margaret Adam, Elise Erickson Barrett, David Cloutier, Holly Taylor Coolman, Dana Dillon, Amy Doorley, Neomi DeAnda, Dennis Doyle, Marva Gray, Stanley Hauerwas, Meghan Henning, Kelly Johnson, Bill Johnston, Beth Felker Jones, Brad Kallenberg, Jason King, D. Stephen Long, Emily McGowin, Vince Miller, Benjamin Peters, Bill Portier, Julie Hanlon Rubio, Mark Ryan, Myles Werntz, Celia Wolfe, and Sandra Yocum.

Thank you, as well, to Cynthia Read, Theo Calderara, Gina Chung, and all the other wonderful editors at Oxford University Press. Thanks for seeing this project as something important enough to publish.

I am especially grateful to my graduate assistants over the years who helped find books, make copies, critique parts of the manuscript, and copy edit the bibliography: Christine Dalessio, Anthony Rosselli, and Tyler Campbell. The interlibrary loan staff at the University of Dayton were amazing in getting me references I needed.

This book would not have been possible without the support of my chairperson, Dan Thompson, Dean Jason Pierce, and Provost Paul Benson at the

University of Dayton. I am also grateful for Ramon Luzarraga with Benedictine University-Mesa, for hosting a series of lectures on parts of this book in Mesa, Arizona. Anne DeRose, with St. Stephen's Parish in Sun Lakes, Arizona, and Steve and Becky Greene with the radio show, "The Catholic Conversation," provided additional hospitality and airwaves for discussing this book. My mother, Ann Bennett, provided nannying for my baby so I could get to these gigs! This book goes as far back as ideas shared at the 2006 New Wine New Wineskins conference of Catholic moral theologians, and a 2009 presentation to a students' group at the University of St. Louis. Thanks to them for being guinea pigs for a very early draft of some of these ideas.

Finally, of course, Joel, Lucia, Gabriella, and Theodora Schickel: I am so very grateful for you.

Jana Marguerite Bennett
Feast of the Archangels,
September 29, 2016

I

Loneliness: The Character of a Single Life?

THIS BOOK IS mostly about single adults and what it means to be a disciple of Jesus Christ in singleness. By saying "single adult" and "singleness" I mean a whole range of living patterns that involve being unmarried in American culture. Being never married, single parent, engaged, divorced, widowed, cohabitating, and same-sex attracted and single, all find voice in this book. This is a simple definition, broad enough to include a whole range of ways people live as single people, though I do not pretend to be making anything like an exhaustive statement in these pages. Christian thinkers are not often so inclusive in thinking about being unmarried—yet there is some Biblical precedent. In Paul's famous 1 Corinthians 7:32 passage, where he extols single life as an ability to be "anxious about the things of the Lord," he describes being never-married, engaged, divorced, widowed, and possibly even some form of (non-sexual) cohabitation, though that last is debated.[1]

My hope with this book, and with my simple but broad definition of singleness, is to tell expansive stories about singleness that show how singlenesses contribute to the life of the whole church. Singleness in the context of Christianity is rich in variety and complexity. Thus I include a wide range of states of life that count as unmarried, but each have their own characteristics. I name this range of singlenesses as impermanent ways of living singly. I will also use the phrases "state of singleness" and "single state of life" to refer to different ways of being *im*-permanently single. When I mean to refer to a state of life that is permanent, I will name marriage or vowed religious life specifically.

There is one way of being single in Christian life that is noticeably not a direct focus in this book. I am not *particularly* addressing the vowed religious life of a monk or nun, or the celibate life of a priest taking holy orders, especially as practiced in the Roman Catholic Church. Vowed life is distinct from other singlenesses. For example, vowed life involves making a public witness in front of a community; it also involves a commitment to permanence. Vowed ways of being single certainly deserve more focus than they often get from Christians as a whole (and would be worth a book-length discussion as well). Yet vowed religious life does receive specific support from church officials and Catholic institutions in ways that impermanent states do not.

Christians often overlook or ignore impermanent singlenesses. Pope Francis recent Apostolic Exhortation on family (*Amoris Laetitia*) reminded Catholics that they have often forgotten single, non-vowed people in their midst and need to be far more supportive. He calls on Catholics to

> provide love and support to teenage mothers, children without parents, single mothers left to raise children, persons with disabilities needing particular affection and closeness, young people struggling with addiction, the unmarried, separated or widowed who are alone, and the elderly and infirm who lack the support of their children.[2]

This book is directed toward remembering some of the people Pope Francis identifies.

The church's own way of speaking about singleness is a reason why Christians forget single people in their midst. For example, impermanent states of singleness are simply collapsed into a discussion of baptism. The Roman Catholic document *Lumen Gentium* suggests that in baptism, all people are called to a life of discipleship, though each person has a distinctive role.[3] This view of baptism is similar to that in a number of Christian traditions.[4] A Catholic view goes further by saying that as baptized adults, we must choose a form of life that is lifelong and includes vows—that is, either marriage or in vowed religious life.[5] Marriage and vowed religious life offer further proclamation to the Body of Christ because of what those states of life entail: the importance of stability and lifelong fidelity, children in marriage, and deep, lifelong non-biological relationships in vowed religious life. By contrast, the impermanent states of singleness have often not seemed to have a particular character or wisdom to impart. Rather, they simply take on the general vocations Christians have in baptism.

I remain unconvinced that there isn't more to be said about the particular character of single baptized people who live in impermanent states—similar to how marriage and vowed religious life are understood as connected to baptism. Christian tradition hints at further thinking about singleness. For example, the scriptures hint at a community of widows in the apostolic church (as I'll discuss in more detail in Chapter 6). Similarly, Paul himself makes some distinctions between impermanent states of life, distinctions that might well be developed and considered in more detail and depth. I want to explore in more detail what is in the Christian tradition regarding impermanent states of singleness.

The very impermanence of single states discussed in this book means a kind of flexibility. People may fall in and out of many single states of life, just as they may enter and exit marriage and vowed religious life from impermanent singleness. I am currently a married woman with three children, but I was once never-married with no view even toward getting married; I was once engaged; I can assume that someday I may be widowed or (hopefully more improbably) divorced; if I am widowed or divorced early in my children's lives, I can expect an extensive bout of single parenting. In other words, people need to assume the likelihood of having more than one season of singleness in a lifetime. The flexibility and impermanence of these states of life does not negate that members of these states of life provide an important witness to the church. As a married woman, I am writing this book not only because I have been and may one day again be single; I am also writing this book because I think it is intensely important that Christians—all Christians—take singleness seriously as part of Christian community.

A side effect of our refusal to look particularly at impermanent states of life is that Christians treat singleness primarily as a waiting game or a kind of purgatory on the way to marriage. Despite Paul's celebratory words about singles being able to be *anxious for the things of the Lord,* singleness makes many Christians anxious. More than that, a broad examination of singleness in American Christianity reveals a whole host of troubling and often contradictory ideas, stemming both from culture and Christian community. Perhaps the difficulty can best be described in the following prominent cultural example.

"Marriage responds to the universal fear that a lonely person might call out only to find no one there. It offers the hope of companionship and understanding and assurance that while both still live there will be someone to care for the other."[6] These are the mincing words Supreme Court Justice Kennedy wrote in his majority opinion for the *Obergefell v. Hodges* case that made same-sex marriage legal in the fifty United States. While many marriage equality supporters lauded the decision, some unmarried people found themselves slighted by Justice Kennedy's presumption that a life without marriage was a life of loneliness and no hope of companionship.

In a *New York Times* op-ed piece commenting on Justice Kennedy's words, writer and English professor Michael Cobb exclaims, "[a]s I read that bit alone in my apartment, I choked on my coffee."[7] Cobb strongly questions the marriage equality movement when it aims to be a part of the legal marriage institution that already exists. He would rather call into question why the government ought to be scrutinizing peoples' relationships in the first place.

> Why can't I put a good friend on my health care plan? Why can't my neighbor and I file our taxes together so we could save some money, as my parents do? If I failed to make a will, why is it unlikely a dear friend would inherit my estate?
>
> The answers to all these questions are the same: It's because I'm not having sex with those people.[8]

Kennedy's description and Cobb's derisive discussion of that description display well three commonly presumed characteristics of a single life: no significant (romantic) relationship, especially as enshrined in marriage; no sex, especially in a Christian context; and abject loneliness. Of course, singleness is more complicated that any one of these characteristics. For each of the three characteristics, there are also strong alternative narratives that operate, too. The flip side of not being in relationships is that one has freedom; the idea that one doesn't have sex outside marriage is contrasted with the more enticing and popular proposition that singleness involves more exciting sexual escapades than can be had in marriage. Loneliness need not be a part of single life.

Christian theologies have assimilated and amplified the common cultural assumptions about singleness as well as the alternative narratives. This turns out to be troubling for living a Christian life well. In the rest of this introductory chapter, I will discuss more fully how people describe singleness in terms of no (romantic) relationships, no sex, and loneliness, especially in the American context.[9] Therefore, the arguments I recount are representative of secular American discussions as well as Christian thought. I suggest that these common ways of looking at singleness are inadequate for good Christian theology. Loneliness is not, in fact, *the* character of a single life, nor do the other two common assumptions about singleness adequately describe single life. I conclude this chapter with my own proposal for going forward in this book: a development of a theology of singleness.

No (Romantic) Relationship: An American Cultural Presumption

When friends (both in and outside the academy) heard about this book, I typically got two responses: (1) Why would you write about that? No one cares about marriage anymore. Everyone knows now that families are broad and diverse, to the point that singleness is no big deal. Or, (2) Oh, thank goodness! I feel like no one cares about us singles.

Both responses make sense in American and Christian contexts. For example, to look at the decline of the current marriage rate might suggest that we live in a culture that fosters, supports, and appreciates, being never-married. The marriage rate continues in a slow rate of decrease from the height of marriage relationships following the post–World War II boom (72 percent of adults were married in 1960, compared to 50 percent today; the never-married rate has doubled, 15 percent in 1960 to 30 percent today).[10] Moreover, people are getting married at later and later ages, leading to larger numbers of never-marrieds in their 20s and 30s.[11] When the number of never-married adults is added to the number of divorced, widowed, and cohabiting adults, unmarried adults comprise about half of the United States population. Surely this is a situation, population-wise, that might make for a strong sense of singleness as an important way of life for adults.[12]

Increasingly, authors like Michael Cobb strongly defend and extol single life as beneficial, especially compared to marriage. In his book *Single: Arguments for the Uncoupled*, Cobb paints an image of a desert as a beautiful place, an icon for what it means to be single. Deserts aren't often beneficial images, but as someone who grew up in a desert climate and saw the desert as a place of rainbow colors and amazingly beautiful vegetation, I get what Michael Cobb sees. He describes a place where a person can stare at a broad horizon line which "opens up an extremely important panorama on the grand, distant, oceanic, deserted world."[13] To be single, in other words, is to have endless horizons—to be free of the stratifications that coupledom places on life, but also to be freed for that unending horizon where anything might happen.

Other authors join Cobb in making articulate arguments in favor of unmarried life, though most authors writing about singleness write about single *women*. There is Kate Bolick's discussion of contemporary spinsterhood, which emphasizes independence and freedom, much like Cobb. There is Rebecca Traister's discussion of the kind of power single women have wielded in American politics in spearheading suffrage and abolitionist movements, precisely because they have been unmarried and free to do so.[14] Anthea Taylor critiques numerous portrayals of single women in popular culture (such as the books and movies about Bridget Jones). Taylor wonders why there aren't more positive portrayals—especially since there are numerous single contemporary women who want to celebrate being single and who don't appreciate the heavy-handed narrative of coupledom. Taylor finds that even feminists are not inclined to celebrate the single woman, choosing instead to be "recuperating marriage" against earlier feminisms that were suspicious of marriage.[15]

In a cultural context, it is notable that authors who note singleness positively do so by extolling the values Americans love: freedom, autonomy, independence. Single life can be narrated as an extension of what it means to be American. Relationships can be entered, or left, on the basis of one's own needs and desires. Such an argument is seen as the best antidote against words like Justice Kennedy's, which likewise trade in freedom, autonomy, and independence—most especially the freedom and autonomy to marry against the loneliness of single life. For example, Michael Cobb wonders whether he ought to provide an "exhaustive account of centuries of muscular American individualism...? Singleness must be shaped by the legacies of Emerson and Thoreau (and countless others)."[16] That is to say, in other times and places in American culture, singleness might not have elicited the kind of strong sentiment Justice Kennedy expressed. As another example, Thoreau's famous solitary sojourn in the woods, which he depicts in his book *Walden*, intimates that a person is more alone in a crowd than he is when living out of step with the crowd.

In spite of all I have said describing how singleness is becoming normalized in American culture, marriage still remains the point for many people. Anthea Taylor suggests, "The relentless privileging of this form of relationship serves to undermine other forms of affect and non-familial bonds...."[17] In a recent Pew Forum study, a large majority of Millennial never-married adults (69 percent) hope to be married someday,[18] despite the fact that Millennials have been described as a generation that is refusing to get married.[19] Across the whole American population, 61 percent of never-married adults hope to get married. This is in great contrast to other groups of non-married adults, such as those who are divorced (21 percent) or widowed (8 percent).[20] Despite the fact that attitudes about the necessity of marriage are changing so that many, especially in younger generations, find marriage less necessary than in the past, I suggest that cultural views on never-marrieds have gotten worse, not better, in the intervening years. Jillian Straus, author of *Unhooked Generation: The Truth about Why We're Still Single*, notes a constant buzz about romantic relationships: "These people [my single friends] have full lives—busy jobs, close friends, and passionate interests. Yet I couldn't help noticing that the topic of our failing relationships dominated almost every conversation."[21]

Singleness and marriage as being about freedom and independence particularly reflect dominant white culture, but it is important to recognize how a story of singleness changes when looking at other cultural markers in the United States. Briallen Hopper, a white author who proudly claims the term "spinster," narrates her gradual realization about singleness as it relates to race—and that singleness need not be all about the individual:

> When I was first learning how to be a spinster, my mentors were three straight African American women, 10 or 20 years ahead of me, who spent long years of their youth in a small mostly white town in suburban New Jersey. All of them had lives full of friendship, faith, family, community, political purposefulness, significant caregiving responsibilities, dazzling professional success, and, occasionally or eventually, real romance. But they also had lives marked by the demographic reality of blackness in America. None of them had the standard story of most of their white peers: pair off in your 20s or 30s; marry; have kids. From these women I learned to measure singleness in years or even decades, not months. As one of them quipped when I asked about her love life when she was my age, "I know why the caged bird sings."[22]

The "demographic reality of blackness in America" Hopper speaks about is the 1.5 million black men who are missing from the United States. Early deaths from homicides, medical conditions like heart disease that disproportionately affect African American men, and years behind bars have claimed the lives of many African American men—a reality that becomes even starker with every police shooting death that becomes public. One group of journalists comments: "Perhaps the starkest description of the situation is this: More than one out of every six black men who today should be between 25 and 54 years old have disappeared from daily life."[23]

So, being unmarried can also be symbolic of the pain of missing people. That's one of the arguments that comes across in Ralph Richard Banks' noted book, *Is Marriage for White People?* Banks' book tells the story of missing black men alongside what he sees as dashed hopes for marriage among black women: "black women may accept solitude, but most of them don't choose it."[24] In Banks' view, low rates of marriage lead to distrust in African American communities, which occurs alongside the woes of children who live in single-parented households. More than that, Banks is among many scholars[25] who narrate the low rates of marriage in connection to the United States' racist past of slavery, segregation, and other forms of racism. Slavery prevented black families from forming at all. The famous 1960s Moynihan Report named "single-parent black families as a 'tangle of pathology.' Moynihan reasoned that while the black family's troubles may be traced to slavery and economic inequality, the tangle of pathology had perhaps become so entrenched as to be self-perpetuating."[26] The very fact of singleness demonstrates perpetual racist systems that prevented African American families from becoming the best of what family can be, especially in its role of raising children who are equipped to be full participants in society.

Banks' work is controversial, in part because it presumes marriage to be definitively desired, the event that would most benefit the single black women's lives that form the backdrop for his questions. Marriage is also the event that would, *en masse*, change the face of African American culture and fortunes. Yet as one reviewer caustically says: "The pressing public policy issue is not the black marriage decline, interracial marriage, or whether marriage is for white people. Rather, it is whether marriage should be the normative ideal for intimate life and the vehicle by which we confer a range of important public and private benefits."[27] Depending on context, then, marriage can be even more heightened as an all-important state of life and the main relationship (apparently) worth having.

On the other hand, marriage and singleness can become collapsed into each other. Briallen Hopper negatively reviews Kate Bolick's book *Spinsters* because singleness, especially the spinsterdom reserved for women, ends up being a blank canvas for everyone. Hopper writes: "Bolick defines spinsterhood as an identity available to any woman, married or single, who sometimes feels suffocated by conventional cohabitation and who has decided to prioritize *me-time*: 'For the happily coupled [...] *spinster* can be code for remembering to take time out for yourself.'"[28] *Marriage*, in her view, can champion freedom and independence from other relationships, just as we assume singleness does. Singleness can be everyone and everything so long as a person is independent and celebrating the kind of individualism that Cobb and Bolick both love. Singleness simply becomes at one with American proclivities for being autonomous, independent people.

Hopper calls into question Bolick's and Cobb's views of singleness-as-blessed-individualism with no relationship attachments. For one thing, Bolick's and Cobb's views actually reinforce the idea that the only relationships that really matter are romantic ones leading toward marriage. Yet what if singleness' contribution is not its individualism but its broader relationality? Hopper learns from her African American friends that to be single is to be integral to a community. What would it mean to think about singleness primarily in terms of other kinds of relationships, and not solely as unattached individuals or non–romantically inclined people?

American Christians emphasize the importance of marriage and romantic relationships, to the point that single people feel overlooked and unwanted. One of the books still often noted in discussions of Christian singleness is Albert Hsu's 1997 book, *Singles at the Crossroads*. Hsu noted: "Many singles have felt out of place at churches. One single man was very turned off by the compartmentalizing of singles in the church. 'Before I was just a Christian and now I'm a single,' he said."[29] Yet Hsu imagined something different, as he combed through scripture and Christian tradition. Church communities have rarely reflected a rising population of singles in their demographics and instead emphasize marriage and family in their programming. By contrast, Hsu dreamed about "Singles who see their singleness as an opportunity instead of a curse... Churches that are sensitive to the needs of singles... welcoming them as full partners in community and ministry."[30]

A few other books have followed, focusing on single Christians and attempting to rethink what singleness looks like, both from the church's perspective and from the view of single people. Nondenominational pastor Barry Danylak has written *Redeeming Singleness: How the Storyline of Scripture Affirms the Single Life*, a scriptural theology that examines the whole of the Bible to show how singleness is simply part and parcel of the life of God's people.[31] Danylak is a rarity; most Christian singleness books are more like self-help books. They provide discussions about how to endure and even thrive in singleness, such as *Whole in Christ*, a collection of essays from several authors with chapters addressing topics related to contentment, chastity, and envy.[32]

Still, many Christians do not really like the idea of singleness, tending to be at best dismissive and at worst suspicious. For example, Dr. Al Mohler from Southern Baptist Theological Seminary stated, at a conference devoted to discussion of singleness, that a main difficulty with singleness is that "The more you, as an adult, define yourself as an 'I,' the longer you do so resiliently, the harder it's going to be to become a 'we'."[33] As in the first section, some of the underlying assumptions about singleness hinge on questions about independence and freedom, although from many Christians' perspectives, that American focus is unhealthy (at least in some cases). Marriage is the right way to become a "we" and to cast off selfish singleness. Gary Thomas highlights how Christians see singleness as troubling, precisely because of its perceived autonomy:

> If you want to be free to serve Jesus, there's no question—stay single. Marriage takes a lot of time. But if you want to become more like Jesus, I can't imagine a better thing to do than get married.

Marriage is the way to a cruciform life and, Thomas hints, the better way to be a disciple of Christ.[34]

No wonder singleness appears as lonely, because for Christians it often is. In addition to the suspicion cast on single lives, church culture promotes marriage and coupledom even to the point that some singles stop attending church. Two authors writing together about singleness, Christine Colón and Bonnie Field, suggest that for most evangelical Protestant congregations, singleness seems only "a 'season of life' to be endured before marriage" rather than a positive state of life.[35] In other words, people are *supposed* to be pining for marriage relationships. The evangelical group Focus on the Family developed a singles group called "Boundless" that caters to helping people get married. Its website proclaims that Boundless is primarily for young adults "who want to grow up, own their faith, date with purpose, and prepare for marriage and family."[36] It is a singles' ministry targeted at a particular group of unmarried Christians, with a presumption that marriage is what makes us adults and is the task that young adults who own their faith ought to be preparing for. No wonder, then, that the authors of *Singled Out* also note that while 50 percent of American Christian adults are single, single people are less likely to attend church (38 percent compared to 50 percent for married people).[37] Even if a church has a singles group, that group has a negative impact because separates singles from the rest of church, rather than incorporating people into the full life of the church and allowing the church to more fully recognize and appreciate the gifts of singleness. The dichotomy that exists between the independent, unattached, single person and the attached married couple points to the same assumption I mentioned in secular cultural singleness: the only kinds of relationships that truly matter—at least, the only ones that people tend to discuss—are the ones that involve romance and love.

Yet in Christian life, a negative discussion of singleness is not the best way to understand either states of singleness or the relationship marriage and singleness have with each other. The New Testament advocates *both* singleness *and* marriage. For example, we have Jesus' words in the Gospel of Matthew where he speaks about people who might be "eunuchs who have made themselves eunuchs for the sake of the kingdom of heaven" (Matthew 19:12). That passage about singleness stands in the same chapter as Jesus' strong words about marriage. In Matthew 19:4–6, Jesus speaks strong words against divorce and quotes Genesis in order to describe the significance of marriage: "Have you not read that the one who made them at the beginning 'made them male and female,' and said, 'For this reason a man shall leave his father and mother and be joined to his wife, and the two shall become one flesh'? So they are no longer two, but one flesh." Jesus further asks people to consider marriage as a strong part of living a godly life: "What God has joined together, let no one separate" (Matthew 19:7).

Jesus also has words against idolizing marriage and family above all other relationships. One often-cited passage is Matthew 12:46–50, where Jesus names his disciples (the ones who do the will of his Father in heaven) as his mother and brothers. His family, in other words, are not necessarily his blood relations. This is a fact that becomes very important for Christians over the centuries. Christian communities have often encouraged seeing even unrelated others as family. Some Christian traditions call each other "brother" and "sister" or name their ministers and priests "Mother" or "Father" for that reason, regardless of whether people were married or not. Paul, too, gives Christians a sense of the interrelatedness of singleness and marriage in several of his letters. One of the most significant is his first letter to the Corinthians, which I discuss at length in the second chapter of this book. Here, I will simply note: Paul states that marriage is a good, but he advocates for singleness as a better way of life.

It is also significant that Jesus names himself as the bridegroom of the church, the bride. In the New Testament, marriage takes on a new understanding: our relationship with Christ is understood (in part) as a marriage. In a sense, all of us Christians, whether married to another person or not, become married to Christ because we are members of Christ's church. There is also the reverse understanding: in a sense, all Christians are single, too, even if some are physically married, because Christians are the Body of *Christ*, who is unmarried. The fifth-century bishop Augustine of Hippo presses the point further when he writes, "the Church as a whole, in the saints destined to possess God's kingdom, is Christ's mother spiritually and also Christ's virgin spiritually."[38] As members of the church, all Christians have spiritual "virginity" (which is one of the primary ways Augustine speaks about singleness) even as they also have spiritual motherhood and, by extension, marriage.

When we look at scripture as a whole, marriage and singleness belong together and must be discussed together. Because singleness and marriage are interrelated, because all of us are interrelated by being members of the Body of Christ, Christians should not conceive of singleness as standing opposed to marriage, or vice versa. I think this is the case even for Christian traditions that do not have a particular vowed single state of life like monasticism. On the whole, Christian tradition calls for more expansive views of church and family that are capable of understanding marriage and singleness as necessary for each other and as important for rightly understanding what it means to be church.[39] For example, Pope John Paul II wrote about marriage and vowed celibacy his Apostolic Letter "On the Family":

> Virginity or celibacy for the sake of the Kingdom of God not only does not contradict the dignity of marriage but presupposes it and confirms it. Marriage and virginity or celibacy are two ways of expressing and living the one mystery of the covenant of God with His people. When marriage is not esteemed, neither can consecrated virginity or celibacy exist; when human sexuality is not regarded as a great value given by the Creator, the renunciation of it for the sake of the Kingdom of Heaven loses its meaning.[40]

It is significant that John Paul II describes that if either state is not present, the "Kingdom of Heaven loses its meaning," especially since prior to the Second Vatican Council (1962–1965) Catholicism often privileged celibacy over marriage to the point that marriage seemed incapable of being a place where Christian discipleship could happen.[41]

Theologians from other traditions have made similar remarks, though without the emphasis on vowed celibacy (as vowed celibacy is often a Roman Catholic category). Protestant theologian Stanley Hauerwas writes: "both singleness and marriage are necessary symbolic institutions for the constitution of the church's life as the historic institution that witnesses to God's Kingdom. Neither can be valid without the other."[42] The evangelical Christian and executive director of the magazine *Christianity Today*, Andy Crouch, argues that Christians see both marriage and singleness as subversive witnesses to the reign of God: "Life in a household undermines any idealization of marriage even while it enables both married and single people to live joyfully and faithfully together."[43] This last comment is important because it emphasizes households as broader than either marriage or singleness. What this does is de-emphasize a focus on romantic relationships as the only kind of relationship that Christians tend to recognize. Instead, relationships in households can encompass parent–child, friends, acquaintances, and other family relationships.

Some Christian theologians have articulated that perhaps such a vision already exists in some subcultures within the church, though still with some limits. Nicole Flores writes about the ways Latino/a families in the United States include extended family members as well as biologically unrelated people, people who are sacramentally included in family. When a child is baptized, the godparents become members of that family too, named as *comadres* and *copadres* of their godchildren. Flores aims not to romanticize this family structure: she is well aware that isolation, abuse, and adultery happen in marriages and families. Yet she also notes that the broad view of family in Latina/o culture offers "a sense of solidarity with people and communities beyond one's particular scope of interest...."[44] These kinds of extended families *can* create networks that engage and include unmarried people far more than the privatized, individualized nuclear family so often emphasized in American culture, and especially in white American culture.[45] That said, Flores also describes how an often patriarchal Latino/a culture misses opportunities to be the kind of church she describes.

I agree that the church needs both singleness and marriage if we are to rightly understand what it means to be the church. Pope John Paul II, Stanley Hauerwas, and Nicole Flores are all describing mostly hoped-for possibilities, or lived realities in small communities. Much of what people encounter today is instead what Cólon and Fields described above: a church that favors marriage and family while ignoring singles. Perhaps worse still, Christians reduce talking about singleness to a "no sex" prohibition. It is to that description that we now turn.

"No Sex"

As if to assert, again, that romantic relationships are the point, Christians are frequently guilty of emphasizing that single people should not have sex. (This teaching is true for many Christian groups, though not all.) Much of the literature on Christian singleness provides scriptural meditations and prayers intended to help people gain power over their sexual desire and activity. While most such books emphasize the importance of chastity and of waiting, they do not display knowledge of Christian traditions of celibacy in vowed religious life. Some have been self-help books, aimed especially at women who are wanting and waiting for marriage. One such popular Catholic book is by Emily Stimpson: *The Catholic Girl's Survival Guide for the Single Years.*[46] Stimpson especially aims away from vowed religious life, which is the main way Catholics think about singleness, and emphasizes how a person might look for love but avoid some of the temptations of sexual activity.

Thus, authors like Christine Colón and Bonnie Field denounce the lack of support they feel from their Christian communities regarding the mandate to stay sex-free. As they note about contemporary Christian conversations, the implication is always that

> [O]ur focus must be on guarding ourselves from sexual temptation until God grants us the blessing of marriage. But what if our thirties, forties, and fifties arrive, and we aren't married? And where does this leave those who are no longer virgins but seek to live a God-honoring single life? Discussions of virginity in particular often leave those who

were once sexually active feeling like they are damaged goods undeserving of God's forgiveness.[47]

Colón and Field find themselves frustrated by the single-minded emphasis on "no sex" with no corresponding community to provide support. Their conclusions ask for a church community that moves away from the nuclear family model, with its own versions of freedom and independence, toward "A church that intentionally creates a community based not on biological ties but on spiritual ties...."[48]

In addition to the kind of negativity that Christian singles might feel within churches, the surrounding culture also has issues with Christian thinking about sex and singleness. Practices of sexual asceticism, including celibacy, are some of the specific reasons Christianity is a suspect entity in American culture. For example, "none" is much-vaunted category of "religious" identity in American culture, referring to people who do not claim any particular religious tradition, though they may profess belief in God. "Nones" are not necessarily atheists or agnostics but can often be people of faith who are frustrated with so-called organized religion. Two of the reasons "nones" say they have dropped "Christian" from their identity are clergy sexual abuse scandals and Christian teachings about homosexuality.[49] In a culture where marriage is such an ambivalent (even though much-desired) practice, restricting sex and sexual desires only to a marriage relationship seems silly.

In fact, sexual relationships are one way to mitigate the kind of loneliness that singleness is—especially in an era of social media. At least that's one of the arguments Emily Witt's new book, *Future Sex* makes. Witt's book explores sex as a way of broadening an understanding of what it means to be single. In one interview, Witt says, "Part of the reason that I wrote the book in the first place was that all these articles about single women felt like a dead end. They described the confusion that I was feeling now that my expectations for my adult life might not turn out the way I wanted because the world had changed. But they didn't describe a way out of it. They only lamented the decline of the date followed by the engagement followed by marriage."[50] Witt tries to get beyond the marriage/family presumptions by simply embracing a whole range of sexual explorations and practice. She reduces marriage and family to the presence of sexual activity, so that the antidote to the cultural obsession with marriage is to bypass those relationships and head straight for the sex (with which our culture also has an obsession!). That's a curious move, though, for in reducing marriage and family to sexual activity, singleness too becomes reduced to sexual activity. In the end, sex is what it's all about. Witt's book doesn't change much in perspective through its pages: the point is to encounter, explore, and have sex. As she says, "We organize our society around the way we define our sexual relationships. And when you pretend it's about other things—that it's about liking the same books, or that it's about getting married—and that the sex is secondary, that's when you end up risking a lot of unhappiness."[51]

I'm making a very different argument in this book than Witt's. I think Witt is wrong and that there are a whole range of possibilities about life that don't have to be about sex and, in fact, that shouldn't be about sex. I'm getting ahead of myself, though.

I think it's important to know that Witt is not alone in her obsessions. Christians obsess about sexual activity too, though often in more negative ways. In obsessing about sex, Christians miss very important, positive theologies that tradition has often had regarding singleness. For example, Christians have a long tradition of glorifying singleness, especially in the form of vowed, chaste, religious life. Catholics, Orthodox, and Anglicans are the best known for having institutionalized singleness in the form of vowed religious life, though many other Protestant and non-denominational communities also have examples of religious life. I have encountered Methodist Benedictine monks, Protestant Franciscans, and nondenominational professions of consecrated chastity. These permanent states of life are typically characterized by public professions of lifelong vows before a gathered Christian community.

The specific vows made for vowed religious life include chastity, poverty, and obedience, as a way of following Christ's call to "be perfect therefore, as your heavenly Father is perfect."[52] That is, chastity, poverty, and obedience are seen as ways to live the love of God in one's own life as perfectly as possible. Celibacy is meant to be a position of strength, a way of directing one's focus toward things other than sexual desire. Thus one of the strong themes in Christian literature about celibate life is its source of empowerment for men and women alike. Saint Anthony of the Desert resists sexual temptations and becomes a spiritual founder of Christian monasticism. Saint Catherine of Siena's celibate life forms the basis from which she becomes a great preacher and speaker in the thirteenth century. Historian Elizabeth Abbott describes the "liberating celibacy" of religious life for women, because in nunneries women could seek leadership roles and do services for their communities that might be prevented in quotidian married life.[53] Indeed, Abbott extends her argument to later figures like Mother Ann, the founder of the Shakers, and Father Divine, an early twentieth century leader of the Peace Mission. Abbott argues that while the Shakers and Peace Mission did not last they "were not failed experiments.... What has endured are their legacies of a courageous celibacy that dared to challenge society's underpinning of women's inequality and racial subjugation."[54]

Christian prohibitions of sex have become connected to contemporary American politics in ways that actually undermine any articulation of positive Christian thinking about singleness and sexuality. Secular author Benjamin Kahan provides such an analysis of celibacy in relation to American politics: "Hymenoplasties, True Love Waits, Promise Keepers, and abstinence-based education: we live in a moment when celibacy has become a public, political topic"[55] on the American political Right—which has had uneasy but longstanding relationships with prominent Christian groups. "No sex" is so identified with conservativism that politically Right-minded Christians have taken up making arguments against certain sexual practices as almost the sole standard for what it means to be a real Christian.

Kahan's book *Celibacies: American Modernism and Sexual Life* seeks a more positive, mostly secular, story for celibacy. Kahan uses celibacy to mean unmarried, as well as "abstaining from sexual acts."[56] He begins by telling stories about singleness in the nineteenth century, especially how celibacy initially enabled economic and political freedom (especially for women) and activism in reform movements like women's suffrage. Kahan discusses the "Boston marriage," a nineteenth-century term for a long-term relationship between two women, which sometimes is linked to contemporary lesbian relationships. Kahan, however, thinks (along with other scholars) that Boston marriages likely did not include lesbian sex as commonly understood today[57]. Rather, Boston marriages are part of some of the several ways celibacy was lived in the nineteenth century, among people who had strong agendas for reform and protest. Celibacy was thus a political activity, especially on the left—a protest against marriage and family as the dominant forms of life. Such an active vision of celibacy has more in common with earlier Christian visions of celibacy that it does with the contemporary practice of the "no sex" rules. Celibacy is an active way of life that positively impacts society.

In Kahan's view, by the mid-twentieth century, celibacy begins to be narrated as a synonym for homosexuality, and therefore celibacy becomes as suspect as homosexuality was. Kahan mentions the example of the 1952 McCarran-Walter Act, which prohibited queer immigrants from becoming citizens; to state that one was celibate, however, became a way to circumvent the restriction on homosexuality, to find "kinds of national belonging, strategies for transforming national spaces, and solitary disguises...."[58] The raging national debate about homosexuality relates to a decline in positive views of singleness and celibacy; celibacy becomes a code word associated with sexual repression and not being free to be one's own self. Kahan overplays this argument a bit, for it is the case that the Sexual Revolution of the 1960s and pop psychology both identified sexual activity as healthy and good, and repression of sexual desires as bad. Thus popular thought regarded Christian teachings against sex as unhealthy, and was surely at least as much a factor in a decline of positive thinking toward celibacy.

Yet, if sexual prohibition has seemed almost universally repressive, especially against single Christians, one Christian response from Left-minded Christians has been to argue in favor of premarital sex and other sexual practices—or even (and perhaps more often) simply to stop discussing sexual activities at all. Such arguments stem from a view that Christianity does not have to be linked quite so closely with the sexual norms that figure in contemporary culture wars. One single Christian describes her upbringing in a church that prohibited premarital sex, and she finds that the church's views don't seem to respect her as a person. She writes,

> Sex is a form of creative power. And it is in the literal fact of its creative aspects that we feel alive, fully human, and connected. I think God wants nothing less than this for us, and that requires regular, intimate connections of bodies, or at the very least a very regular, intentional and unapologetic intimate connection with our own body. So sex is back on the table for me in an emotionally safe intimate connection with another person. Because marriage or no, I am clear about this one thing: celibacy is not for me. I need connection. I need intimacy. I need sex. Period. That's why I'm unapologetically single, saved, and sexin'.[59]

Some of the most well-argued books include Jennifer Knust's *Unprotected Texts: The Bible's Surprising Contradictions about Sex and Desire*, in which she shows that scripture is not universally against premarital sex and that perhaps in some cases, premarital sex might be acceptable. Adrian Thatcher has written a few books asking whether there might be some occasions when premarital sex might be permissible (i.e., that there are differences to be made between casual sexual relationships and committed relationships of those who are engaged to be married).[60] Thatcher tends to make his arguments advisedly; that is, he's not making blanket statements about the permissibility of sex, and sees that there are some kinds of relationships that aren't reflecting Christ.

In my view, both Christian impulses—to emphasize "no sex" as what singleness *means* in Christian life, or to argue in favor of (some) sexual activity outside marriage—serve to bypass the importance of singleness in Christian tradition. Simply saying, "No sex" isn't a very deep discussion of singleness; simply permitting sexual activity (even if only for, say, more committed couples), on the other hand, reinforces coupledom without really having to negotiate the particularities of Christian singleness.

Those Christian traditions that have religious communities still do provide (some) support for vowed celibate life, but do not have much support for the less formal states of singleness I am writing about in this book. In addition, most Protestant and non-denominational Christian traditions hold prohibitions against premarital and extramarital sexual activity, but likewise do not have a sense of the importance of community for supporting the celibacy that they often mandate of single people. As with the discussion of "no (romantic) relationships" I am left thinking there is more to be said about single people, and more that churches can and should contribute to the flourishing of single life.

Loneliness

Loneliness is another characteristic frequently identified in discussions of singleness. News media often presume singleness equates with loneliness.[61] Psychological studies on loneliness often focus exclusively on single people.[62] For example, in research on elderly widows (a typically presumed lonely population), some researchers have described loneliness even as an "epidemic" in contemporary America, noticing links between loneliness and a person's health.[63]

Single people frequently describe their own loneliness. The popular Christian author Lauren Winner, popular Christian author, describes the loneliness in her book *Still*. As a newly divorced person, she compares notes with a divorced friend: "the loneliness he experienced in his marriage was more devastating than anything he has experienced since. . . . I happen to feel differently. I find the loneliness of no one knowing if your plane lands on time, of no one to call if you lock yourself out of your house or your alternator dies—I find that loneliness worse."[64] One could and should make the case that loneliness is available to everyone, including those who are married and those who live in community. Yet Winner's description of loneliness captures important distinctions about what it means to experience the human condition of loneliness as a single person—what she names "everyday loneliness" versus "loneliness of estrangement." There is a difference in having someone constantly present, without having to contact a friend and make special arrangements. The quotidian nature of marital relationships is part of the point of marriage. Loneliness extends to other states of singleness that I address in this book. One single mother says, simply, "Guilt, and loneliness, is the companion of most single mothers."[65]

Loneliness is also a problem that people might wish to avoid. One scholar suggests: "the very word 'lonely' carries a negative connotation...signaling social weakness, or an inability to stand on one's own." [66] So, too, singleness becomes a problem, partly because of its association with loneliness. Some secular commenters have therefore resisted the associations made between singleness and loneliness. Psychologist Bella DePaulo, whose research focuses on singleness and its effects, suggests that "people think that single people are miserable and lonely and they don't have anyone."[67] In her research, DePaulo shows that the case is quite the opposite; single people thrive—but DePaulo also points out the ways in which the stereotype persists. DePaulo's research highlights all the myths she believes we have about being single, but then shows how it is often married people who are lonely, or bitter[68]. So, rather than seeing single people, especially never-married people, as the lonely ones, we ought instead to see them as the decisive, independent, autonomous ones.

Michael Cobb thinks that it's not just a case of redescribing singleness as strong, decisive, and independent, as DePaulo does. Rather, he thinks that contemporary society has a use for seeing singleness as loneliness. "...[A]n openness to couple love and connection is increasingly considered prerequisite for personhood in a form of government (say, the US government) that has striking resemblances to other totalitarian regimes of the last century."[69] That is, couple love, especially sexual couple love, becomes the main way to be part of contemporary culture and be seen as normal. Couple love is rewarded by government, sustained by tax benefits, and fostered by a continuous stream of cultural narratives (especially romantic comedies) that promote couple love.[70] We cannot imagine a world without romantic love or a person who has not been loved romantically. Even our visions of a person's soul involves being loved. This is a problem for singleness, which seems lonely and therefore loveless. For example, poetry, movies, politicians' biographies, and more suggest that the loneliness of singleness is terrifying. Michael Cobb notes such examples as *Bridget Jones' Diary, Sex and the City*, even President Barack Obama's autobiography and description of meeting his future wife.[71] Singleness is scary, and simply not the way things are done in this world. Singleness may even seem anti-human.

Hence, in Cobb's view: "Singleness is currently not compatible with a society in western Europe, North America, and probably other locations that wants people to feel desperate, lonely, fearful of death, and ready for toxic forms of sociality."[72] Society therefore encourages people to fall into couple love by playing on fears and promoting terror about singleness. Society benefits, in turn, because it is fundamentally based on coupledom. Promoting loneliness as a major characteristic of the single life perpetuates coupled society as it currently exists, and tamps down any revolutionary resistance to coupledom. Cobb's own response is to bring to light intensely isolated, single figures and to show how, in fact, being single opens us to possibilities that a life of coupledom can't perceive.[73] Singleness and isolation are the best ways to vivify culture and invigorate social life, as he sees it.

Cobb's and DePaulo's methods of approaching singleness are either to deny or to completely reconstruct what loneliness means. I do not think trying to sidestep loneliness in this way is truthful. While I do think being more positive about singleness is important, and that loneliness is certainly not limited to states of singleness, it does not do to pretend loneliness is not present nor that isolation might be promoted as a good way of being in the world.

In Christian tradition, loneliness cannot be sidestepped or ignored. Marilynne Robinson, author of the novels *Gilead, Home,* and *Faith,* all of which explore Christian theological themes, discusses loneliness in Christian tradition:

> I am not sure religion is meant to assuage loneliness. Who was ever lonelier than Jesus? "Can you not watch with me one hour?" I think loneliness is the encounter with oneself—who can be great or terrible company, but who does ask all the essential questions. There is a tendency to think of loneliness as a symptom, a sign that life has gone wrong. But it is never only that. I sometimes think it is the one great prerequisite for depth, and for truthfulness. [74]

Simply following Christ will mean loneliness—not only for single people but also as a condition of being called into Christian discipleship. Dietrich Bonhoeffer is one of the better-known authors writing about loneliness, in his book on Christian community called *Life Together.* "Many people seek fellowship because they are afraid to be alone. Because they cannot stand loneliness, they are driven to seek the company of other people."[75] Aloneness is part of Christian life: "Alone you stood before God. . . ."[76]

Yet at the same time, loneliness is never the last word for Christians. As Bonhoeffer reminds his readers:

> Let him who is not in community beware of being alone. Into the community you were called, the call was not meant for you alone; in the community of the called you bear your cross, you struggle, you pray. You are not alone, even in death, and on the Last Day you will be only one member of the great congregation of Jesus Christ.

For Bonhoeffer, being alone interplays with being together. Christian community is crucial, but not to the point that community becomes idolized over God; too, people are at their best in community when their loneliness is not idolized, when they do not have to idolize human attention and relationships, precisely because the relationships are already present. "We recognize then that only as we are within the fellowship can we be alone, and only he that is alone can live in the fellowship."[77]

All things considered, "no (romantic) relationships," "no sex," and loneliness each suggest troubling presumptions about singleness. These presumptions reduce singleness to a few constrictive ideas that speak mostly to singleness as a negative state of life. I worry that Christians have also often accepted the narratives of singleness offered by secular American culture, which does not celebrate the history and tradition of Christian singleness.

The Organization of This Book

In this book I focus on impermanent states of life by arguing that Christians across a range of times and traditions have developed a variety of theologies of singleness. I draw together some of the range of that thinking in order to promote a theology of non-vowed single life that I think is in keeping with Christian scripture, tradition, and witness over the centuries.

Each chapter focuses on a different impermanent state of life. I begin every chapter with a discussion of the main cultural and theological presumptions associated with that state of life, and sort some of the problems that arise from thinking about that state of life. Most importantly, I suggest why Christians particularly need to be concerned for how that state of life relates to the Gospel and what it means to be the church.

In each chapter I also bring in a guide, someone from the Christian tradition broadly construed who inhabited that single state of life and who commented on it. For example, John Wesley appears in Chapter 4, on engagements and committed relationships; Dorothy Day appears in Chapter 8, on single motherhood. The theologians selected for the purposes of this book are selected because they are relatively well-known Christian thinkers, though their particular writings may not have been brought together in the ways I bring them together here.

My inclusion of these guides is not only about the fact that they are representatives of these impermanent states of singleness. It is also that each one of these guides comments on what it means to follow Christ. I intertwine their views on Christian discipleship and what it means to be church, with their views of marriage, family, being unmarried, divorced, and so on. Scholars have written on the theologian guides in this book, either for their views on marriage or singleness or Christology or ecclesiology, but have not typically drawn all these together. I aim to bring together each thinker's thoughts about singleness, Christology, and marriage. I find that in bringing these themes together, the guides offer wisdom to all of us Christians, not just the single among us.

I have found, in the course of my research on the cultural and Christian debates as well as the writings of single people in the tradition, that particular (though not exclusive) characteristics emerge for each state of life. For example, my examination of Paul on being never-married suggests a particularly Christian view of making choices. My discussion of divorce emphasizes the importance of grace. After I have discussed the life and theology of each guide, I conclude each chapter by offering better approaches to singleness and discipleship for Christian communities and single people both.

I am aiming specifically not to focus on the "no romantic relationships," "no sex," and loneliness presumptions that I've discussed in this chapter. Instead, I want to discuss how impermanent states of singleness integrally relate to Christian life and witness as a whole. That said, I will still discuss "no romantic relationships," "no sex," and loneliness as the occasion warrants, but when I do mention them I hope to frame them in much different ways than they have appeared in this chapter. The most visible example is "no sex." In Chapter 3 I discuss casual unmarried relationships; the characteristic I highlight in that chapter is the importance of sexual desire for Christian life. "No sex" is present as part of the discussion about casual relationships and why Christians worry about them, but I have endeavored to make desire the positive focus for that state of life.

I focus on one characteristic per state of life in the meditations that follow, though I think much more could be said of each state of life. My hope overall is to *jumpstart* a conversation. I am not beginning something new. As I hope becomes clear in the pages that follow, I think that Christians have thought more deeply and richly about states of singleness in other times and places than they tend to do now. I am gathering up some strands from tradition that have been dropped. The church at large has not benefitted from the varieties of singlenesses in its midst. In fact, in the chapters that follow, readers will see how often it is the case that discussion of particular states of singleness dropped out of theological circulation decades ago, or have been almost entirely avoided.

A Few Additional Notes on My Usage of "Singleness"

Some readers may find my description of states of singleness to be too broad. After all, why bring together never-married people with people in committed relationships? The latter would seem to be in romantic relationships and therefore not really "single." It is true that in some ways my decision to include a range of states of life that are *not* marriage merely because they do not involve a contract, is too legalistic, too much trying to set a clear line where there should be blurry line instead.

There are valuable benefits for bringing together all these single states of life in a single book. One benefit is that, for all the differences that potentially exist between cohabiters and never-married people, when others have written on these states of life the central question is pretty nearly always about that state of life in contrast to marriage. As I discuss in much more detail in my chapter on cohabiting and other, more committed single states of life (Chapter 3), cohabiting appears as a problem for many Christians precisely because the couple have not made a lifelong permanent (read: official, legal marriage) vow. Being never-married, too, presents itself as a problem for many Christians (though not all) because the never-married adult has also not made a lifelong permanent vow, especially a vow of marriage.

Second, and related, these single states of life share at least one characteristic—the fact that they are flexible. One reason is that states of singleness discussed here might become part of a person's life in an instant, regardless of vows people have made. The prime example is widowhood, which often takes people by surprise. This flexibility isn't necessarily easy nor always appreciated, but it is a fact. That flexibility may be one reason why the states of life in this book have been discussed far less than vowed states of life.

Another point I want to address is whether my definition of singleness gives too much authority to the definition of marriage as determined by the nation state—that is, as a contractual, legal arrangement. Yet to say that the singlenesses I discuss here involve not-being-married is simply to narrate what is already the crazy case of marriage (and therefore singleness) in American Christianity. Most of the time (in American culture) legal and church marriages are seen as one and the same. A clergy person celebrating a wedding simultaneously makes a marriage legal as well as recognized by that Christian community. On occasion, the legal and churchly understandings of marriage do not quite coincide, and the same is true of being unmarried. A prominent example is how the Catholic Church understands divorce. Divorce is a legal matter for the state, but divorce is not a pronouncement that the Catholic

Church will make about any marriage between two Christians. The Catholic Church recognizes that the government facilitates divorces. Yet two divorcing people will still be considered married in the church, unless that couple also seeks an annulment—an in-church process by which a marriage is declared not to have had the elements of a sacrament from its beginnings. On the other hand, engagements in the United States are not typically legal matters (though engagements in other times and places have been legal matters). No contract changes hands when people become engaged, but engagement does have a strong place in Christian life and marks an important way of being unmarried. Some Christian churches celebrate liturgies of engagement or betrothal.

People typically experience both the legal and ecclesial sides of things all together. So, too, I want people to be able to see a variety of singlenesses in this book and to readily recognize states of life that they encounter in daily life. Thus in this book I use both legal and Christian (ecclesial) ways of understanding what it means to be a single adult, while also paying attention to the distinctions between "legal" and "ecclesial."

Another question about my use of singlenesses here is that some people find it wrong, from the start, to speak of "singleness" in relation to marriage, since that merely seems to emphasize singleness as negation, lack, and absence. Singleness can become the "antithesis" or the contrast point to marriage:

> the meaning of any category is derived through explicit or implicit contrasts, with positive definitions resting on the negation or repression of something represented as antithetical or oppositional. Thus, the apparently fixed opposition of singleness and marriage will never be uncontested, but is always open to challenge. These terms are also interdependent, because they derive their meaning from an 'internally established contrast' rather than from 'some inherent or pure antithesis'.[78]

When singleness is understood and discussed primarily as a contrast to marriage, that merely heightens the negative connotations that singleness tends to carry.

Yet, I suggest that it is the very flexibility and impermanence of non-vowed single states of life that enables good discussion, not only of singleness, but also of marriage and vowed religious life. That is to say, in this book I would rather say that singleness is not the antithesis of marriage but instead the state that helps form marriage and vowed religious life. Rather than being defined by a lack, flexible states of singleness demonstrate their immense presence and importance for marriage and vowed religious life. Thus, marriage and vowed religious life will show up on occasion, because I will show how impermanent single life affects and shapes them. Readers will see this especially in Chapter 6, where the widow Elizabeth Ann Seton also becomes the founder and mother of the religious order named the Sisters of Charity.

One final note is that it is important for readers to know that I am writing this book as a Roman Catholic theologian who loves the church deeply. I also grew up United Methodist, and was formed and influenced by both progressives and evangelicals in that tradition. The guides I have chosen reflect that wide background. There are surely many others I could have chosen here. I invite readers to consider the single Christians with whom they may be familiar as they read this book.

As I said in the beginning, this is a book about American Christian singleness primarily; my hodgepodge background is perhaps especially representative of the craziness of American Christian life. Listening to a range of voices is helpful for thinking about single states of life, though, because, as we shall see, different Christian communities have emphasized different states of singleness both in history and in contemporary discussion. So if one tradition has remained silent, there is usually another that has spoken. This book aims to make these voices present to each other, for the good of Christian life and witness to Jesus Christ.

2

Choice: Never Married and Paul

IN THE INTRODUCTORY chapter I hinted at some of the ways that American ideals of freedom and independence figure in contemporary thinking about singleness. In this chapter, I develop the relationship between how Americans think about autonomous freedom, and never-married singleness, by discussing the concept of "choice" as it relates to human relationships.

To be able to make choices about the life one lives—that is a bulwark of American social ideals. Singleness, however, messes with the concept of choice. Consider the following two discussions of singleness and choice. In an article called "Single by Choice," Janelle Nanos complains that her friends simply don't accept that she wants to be single:

> In the past decade, increased public support for gay marriage and a growing acceptance of domestic partnerships has helped to redefine what it means to be a couple—and a family—in this country. *But what do we make of a person who remains single by choice?* Our politically correct culture keeps us from voicing our judgments about people based on skin color, ethnicity, gender, or orientation. Yet we're quite comfortable telling people that they'll be better off when they've found someone to share their life with. That's in part because we're constantly being told that happiness and success come through our partnerships.[1]

For Nanos, romantic relationships get public acceptance because people have made the right choices—that is, to be someone's life partner. The wrong choice, to be single, is not a supported choice.

In contrast, Jessica Keating writes "Single by Default: When a Vocation Is Not a Vocation." Keating voices problems with the impermanent single lives I'm describing in this book, particularly in the way that "single life" sometimes gets treated as a distinctive vocation, a particular call, like the call to marriage and vowed single life:

> But I did not discern a call to single life. In fact, I am deeply skeptical that unconsecrated single life is a vocation at all, any more than infertility is a vocation, or chronic illness is a vocation.[2]

Keating discusses the loss of her own will: that the married life she so desires has not manifested, and that, in fact, it is not something she can "choose" of her own volition. She puts her concerns into theological language: she must follow God's will, not her own. Keating's impulse is right, I think, in how she develops what it means to follow God's will. She mentions that people often don't encounter life the way they hoped it would turn out—spouses die, jobs are lost, such that any choices we think we're making can change in an instant, regardless of state of life. Still, the way Keating describes the permanent vocations of marriage and vowed religious life makes them seem to be decisions *chosen*; being never-married, by contrast, can be merely a non-choice.

Choice and not-choice—being never-married puts a person in the center of debates about what it means to choose one's own life. In contemporary culture, to be able to choose makes one seem to be fully an adult, yet never-married people find their choices belittled, or taken away, or not even present. This chapter explores being never-married and choices in detail, with particular attention to theological concerns with choice.

The guide for this chapter is the Apostle Paul, author of several letters contained in the New Testament, and himself a never-married man. In his writing about marriage and singleness, Paul, too, grapples with questions of independence, freedom, and fulfillment of desires, though in starkly different ways from contemporary questioning. Paul provides contemporary Christians with one way to re-envision what it might mean to be never-married—to make a choice—and how being never-married comprises an important and distinctive life of discipleship for the whole church. I conclude this chapter with concrete suggestions, drawing from Paul, about what being never-married offers as a witness to the Church, and ways Christians need to be better ministers to the never-married people in their lives.

My argument in this chapter, especially through my reading of the Apostle Paul, is that the way we describe what it is to be human and be part of human relationships should not highlight independence and singleness. Instead, I argue that Christians' views of love should much become broader than the cultural story about love. The dominant cultural story is that it is necessary to desire and choose romantic love, even in the absence of relationships where romantic love makes sense.

Choice

Conflicting messages about being never-married and having choices have a rather lengthy history. For example, the English language has a number of not-so-nice terms and phrases to denote singlehood, especially never-married singlehood, which have been passed along through the centuries. Samuel Johnson uses "bachelor" in 1750 to describe an "unsettled and thoughtless condition,"[3] an allusion to someone who lacks the gravitas of one who has made a settled choice. Richard Allestree writes rather unkindly in 1673 about old maids and the fact that they have not chosen "voluntary Virginity":

> But this is a case does not much need stating in our Clime, wherin women are so little transported with this zeal of voluntary Virginity, that there are but few can find patience for it when necessary. An old maid is now thought such a curse, as no Poetic fury can exceed; lookt on as the most calamitous creature in nature. And I so far yeild to the opinion, as to confess it so to those who are kept in that state against their wills: but sure the original of that misery is from the desire, not the restraint of Marriage: let them but suppress that office, and the other will never be their infelicity.[4]

Historian Howard Chudacoff notes in his book, *The Age of the Bachelor*, how choice affects whether or not single people are seen as virtuous or filled with vice: "[i]n the minds of some observers, bachelors exhibited arrogance and selfishness, because they stubbornly refused to marry. To others, bachelors were simply misfits, misanthropes who purposely rebuffed all civilizing influences. . . ."[5] Another historian, Mary Beard, even blamed Hitler, the rise of the Nazi Party, and peoples' participation in that party on bachelor culture.[6]

Chudacoff points out that in decades when the marriage rate boomed (as in the post–World War II years) there was a corresponding decline in bachelor culture and a corresponding rise in in literature against singleness, such as the 1949 essay collection called *Why Are You Still Single?* featuring authors who argued that a life of singleness necessarily led to greater anxiety.[7] The title strongly indicates that its authors presume people can and should make choices to be married rather than single. On the other hand, decades when the marriage rate is in decline (as in the 1970s) show a stronger culture of living alone and stronger support for singleness as a choice, often in gendered ways.

For example, the 1970s single man was buoyed, to an extent, by the *Playboy* culture that developed around the same time, in a way that single women were not buoyed—a fact that highlights singleness as a man's good choice but a woman's negative choice that makes her clearly at odds with the rest of society.[8] Regardless of how being never-married played (positively or negatively), the ability to make choices about being never-married becomes a central part of the story.

Singleness and choice has also been studied in a psychological context, to see how cultural assumptions affect people's well being and sense of self. In 1995, psychologists Natalie Schwartzburg, Kathy Berliner, and Demaris Jacob authored *Single in a Married World*, in which they describe some of the several problems they observed in their never-married patients, including depression, anxiety, and the sense that they were not fully adult.[9] For these authors, part of the reason for the particular psychological angst of their single patients was that having a life of marriage and family was seen as a sign of independence, signs of being able to leave one's family of origin and make an independent adult decision. Remaining unmarried, however, reeked of dependence and a lack of adult formation. More recently, some writers have suggested that in an age like ours, with its shallow social media relationships, choosing marriage and family relationships provides the means to foster deep relationships and thus to develop a deep sense of self. That is to say, there is a link between a person's relationships and his or her ability to become a self.[10]

Kate Bolick's 2015 book, *Spinster: Making a Life of One's Own*, also clearly plays on making choices. One way to read the book, in fact, is as a coming-of-age memoir. In Bolick's view, becoming an adult steadfastly means being able "to take care of" oneself, which in turn means independence without relationships. Bolick observes:

> as a woman, I wasn't required to take care of myself—ever. Here in the year 2000, the future itself, men were still expected to be breadwinners and providers. No matter how hot my ambitions burned, I always knew, deep down, that if I couldn't make it as a writer, I could create personal meaning and social validation through getting married and having children. I had an escape hatch; men didn't.[11]

Bolick's view is that she has the ability to *choose* relationships, but that making that choice would cause her to lead "the life of a child."[12] What Bolick describes is an extension of Chudacoff's argument: American culture usually supports single men in ways that it doesn't support women. In fact, American culture especially promotes women in dependent relationships, not women as independent, free, singles. If a woman dares to choose singleness, that fact is itself evidence of adulthood, of resisting a dominant culture that wants to care for women in patronizing ways.

Being never-married, as I have presented it so far, seems merely to be a matter of choice, deciding for, marriage or singleness. Yet of course, making choices is more complex than simply asserting my own will and choosing in favor of what I want. In American culture, choice is also linked to freedom/ independence, as well as consumer desires. Both freedom and consumerism shape understandings of choice, especially in the way being never-married is understood. I shall discuss these in the next two sections.

Not So Simple: Choice, Freedom, and Independence

One contemporary assumption is that making proper choices requires freedom and the independence to choose. This is one of the reasons why being never-married offers something of a contradiction: being never-married often appears as an independent state of life, and yet there is the sense that one cannot or did not choose that state of life (which in turn leads to unhappiness, as the psychologists I mention above discuss).

The connection between freedom, independence, and choice becomes clearer if we examine a tangential question—what it means to "choose" religion in contemporary America. The dean of religious life at Stanford University, Reverend Scotty McLennan, once wrote a book for college students called: *Finding Your Religion: When the Faith You Grew Up with Has Lost Its Meaning*. McLennan assumes that most of his readers are "no longer happy with the religion of [their] childhood"[13] and in his book exhorts them to take a risk, to venture out and explore something new, but whatever they do, to *choose* something that helps them be better people! Freedom, choice, and independence go hand in hand with religious exploration—a person can't explore and venture risks without freedom. Moreover, McLennan's view of independence and freedom has strong moral connotations: a religion might feel right for us, while it may feel wrong for others. The purpose of being free to make choices is to become authentically oneself, so that one can be a strong, robust, independent person, perhaps much like Kate Bolick above, or Michael Cobb from chapter one.[14]

The view that choice links to freedom is compounded by collaborative social media like Wikipedia's entries regarding religious freedom. The fact that Wikipedia is a collaborative medium has the benefit of displaying (to some extent) what a great many people think about a given concept, and it provides a certain kind of consensus about what contemporary people, working together, might think about the idea of "freedom of religion." That kind of collaborative understanding is helpful here because it underscores again how important individual choice is in the concept of freedom, especially religious freedom. Wikipedia's description reads:

> Freedom of religion is a principle that supports the freedom of an individual or community, in public or private, to manifest religion or belief in teaching, practice, worship and observance; the concept is generally recognized also to include the freedom to change religion or not to follow any religion. The freedom to leave or discontinue membership in a religion or religious group... is also a fundamental part of religious freedom....[15]

Wikipedia's definition could be broken into two parts. The first part describes freedom of religion as individual or communal, public or private. In the first part of the definition, we are invited to think about religious freedom both in terms of individual freedom to worship and practice, as well as in terms of religious groups. Yet this broad sense of freedom is belied in the second part of the definition, which emphasizes the *individual* aspect of freedom of religion, and particularly on the individual's right to *choose* his or her own religion or to choose not to be part of a religious tradition at all. And when we take a close look at the overall story that is told in the Wikipedia article, it emphasizes this point about individual choice.

What is the Wikipedia article's overall story? It goes something like this: while there may have been times and places where religious freedom has been demonstrably appreciated in the absence of the modern nation state (for instance in ancient Hinduism), it is really only due to the modern nation state that humans have a guaranteed, consistent, freedom of religion, and hence are able to make individual choices for their own lives. Wikipedia claims that medieval Catholicism, and later the Protestant Reformation, were eras particularly hostile to religious choice, but that philosophies developed about economics and nation states in the eighteenth century are, by contrast, very warm and open to religious freedom and individual choices.

One of the eighteenth-century philosophers mentioned is Adam Smith, author of *The Wealth of Nations*. Smith is often named as one of the fathers of modern-day capitalism, an early proponent of free-market economics. This fact is important for my discussion in the next section about economies of desire. Smith also discusses the need for people to be able to choose their own religion because when they can choose, they thereby avoid "civil unrest." Freedom of choice prevents any civil unrest that might disrupt economic activity. Smith writes that it is best, in fact, to have two hundred or three hundred small sects, so that each group is faced with many people who disagree with them and no one can thereby amass enough power to fight the others. That is to say, in Smith's view, religions are part of the open market in just the way food and clothing are; it is necessary to have a free-market account of religion in order to ensure economic prosperity.

Following this opening with Adam Smith, Wikipedia's article goes on to discuss different religious traditions' views of religious freedom: Hinduism is "one of the more open-minded religions when it comes to religious freedom. It respects the right of everyone to reach God in their own way." Christianity and Islam are the only other two religious traditions mentioned in this section, and they are described as having many restrictions on religious freedom: for example, changing religion is impossible in Islam. For Wikipedia, the not-so-hidden message throughout this story is that humans are happiest and most prosperous when the following two conditions are met: (1) we have an infinite number of options for practicing religious freedom, and (2) each one of those options is seen as equally valid and true. Furthermore, the article continues, these commitments have particularly been met in contemporary democratic states, such as that of the United States of America. It is important to know that there are all sorts of ways in which this Wikipedia article is overgeneralizing or simply omitting information that may be inconvenient to its overall narrative about freedom and choice. It is not worth the space here to work through the whole of Wikipedia's entry, so I'll just mention a few. When it comes to history, for example, the article massively emphasizes the religious intolerance of Catholics in relation to Protestants, Jews, and Muslims, while de-emphasizing persecution in other places and times. Violent anti-Semitism at the hands of Christians is a true and important part of the Christian story, one that shouldn't be ignored and one for which Christians ought to be seeking forgiveness. But it is not quite truthful to so wholeheartedly name Hinduism as a tolerant, peaceful religion over and against Christianity and Islam.[16] The entry also does not detail a whole range of traditions that we might name religious, but which might also mess with the main narrative. Wikipedia nudges readers toward the "correct" choice for a particular American conception of religion, even as it makes claims about freedom and choice.

Thinking about human relationships demonstrates some similar trajectories about freedom and choice, especially for how nation states undergird freedom of choice in human relationships, and also for how even when it comes to human relationships, the individual's choice is the most important. Just as the category of things seen as religion must seem broad enough to offer a range of apparent choices, so too for human relationships. The modern nation state has the charge of legally ensuring (or restricting) our choices about relationships, especially romantic relationships. Public discourse often narrates religious traditions as putting limits on the kinds of choices humans can make about relationships, including practices like adultery, divorce, and premarital sex, to name just a few. The nation state has become a clear means of protecting individual choices for many of those relationships, and is one of the main avenues people take toward advocating for changes in both legal and social approval of changes in human relationships. Even as short a time as a century ago, divorce was legally difficult to do, but also received high social disapproval. These days, divorce is simply part of the American landscape, but religious communities that prohibit or otherwise restrict divorce seem quite odd.

In addition, choices about human relationships are mainly understood as an *individual's* choice. Kate Bolick's view of marriage as an "escape hatch" makes it seem that marriage is even a possible fallback choice to make if things don't work out. In her imagination she has had immense freedom to make whatever kinds of choices she wishes with her state of life. Choosing a religion ought to be a matter of vast and open possibilities, so too, choosing a relationship ought to be part of her vast array of options. This thinking is strange, especially when we realize that there are all kinds of reasons we cannot simply make choices as individuals when it comes to relationships. Sometimes love is unrequited; sometimes the other person or people involved want different kinds of relationships than the others.

The emphasis on *individual* choice (even though we are speaking of *relationships*) also shines through in contemporary concerns about consent, especially as seen in debates about campus sexual assaults. Though I will discuss casual sexual relationships in more detail in Chapter 3, it is important, here, to consider how the individual choice is emphasized over the human relationship in question, however fleeting that relationship may be.

Consent as a Particular Kind of Choice

In recent years, college campuses across the country have found themselves arbitrating the notion of "consent" in relation to sexual activity as a means of determining whether or not sexual assault has occurred. Frequently, when alcohol and drug use is present, colleges and universities have tended to see that a person's ability to make choices about entering into sexual relationships is at risk, so some universities (as well as states like California) have developed rules stating that consent means a deliberately spoken "yes".[17] When students have filed complaints alleging that they were unable to give consent, the other person in that relationship (however brief the relationship was) have been suspended, expelled, or, much more rarely, prosecuted in the judicial system and sent to prison.

The consent debate is important; advocates for sexual assault victims on campus are right to push a "yes means yes" view of consent. Yet other questions, perhaps better questions, get overlooked, such as why are students seeking intimacy in very short-term relationships? Why is the ability to choose the most important point young adults ought to consider in their relating to each other? Professor Jonathan Zimmerman argues that the questions we've been avoiding are questions about intimacy in relationships because we are so focused on choices and enabling people to have the freedom and independence to make choices concerning their state of life.[18] The public debate about consent discloses our cultural priorities: the *relationship* is less the point than the freedom to be an independent, choosing agent. Consent is about each individual person saying, explicitly, "yes" without particularly worrying about the relationship itself and the other person involved.

Christians sometimes play into this particular confluence of freedom and choice as prioritized over particular relationships with particular people, especially in relation to freedom for premarital sex. Lauren Winner describes how she understood and encountered sexual relationships in one Christian community: "what God really cared about was that people not have sex that might be harmful in some way, or that was clearly meaningless, loveless, casual. Yes the context for sex mattered, but marriage might not be the only appropriate context."[19] Freedom and independence to determine whether, when, and how sex and romance are engaged was part of Winner's initial encounter with Christian discussions of romantic relationships. Theologian Rusty Reno describes the way he thinks Christian discussion about relationships occurs: "Sex is like the public library: we want our children to feel free to explore their interests. In this way we can reassure ourselves that our commitment to sexual *freedom*...is just a sensible revision of traditional Christian moral strictness."[20] The less strict we are, and the more we emphasize choice, Christians think, the less likely it is that our children will leave the faith. Theologian Scott Paeth confirms that mainline sensibility in a comment on evangelical Christian concerns about premarital sex in his theology blog:

> I have to admit, I find the entire conservative evangelical conversation on this [premarital sex] to be very alien. It was not the way that these topics were dealt with during my mainline Protestant adolescence. We didn't dwell on the evil of premarital sex...we simply ignored and avoided the topic.[21]

In fact, many fewer mainline authors write about premarital sexual relationships than evangelicals, for a variety of reasons. The lack of the discussion implicitly offers freedom and independence in peoples' sexual choices and descriptions of their relationships.

Christians also emphasize marriage as an important choice an *individual* must make, especially because marriage is the main way people live as disciples in contemporary Christianity. As I have described in detail elsewhere, the Religion, Culture and Family Project, in which numerous theologians and others participated, emphasized the importance and necessity of "stable, equal regard" marriages and families for strengthening both the church and society.[22] Marriage becomes the commonplace, yet important, choice an individual must make. *The Catechism of the Catholic Church* also offers a sense of choice that can be easily construed in the ways I have described above State of life is about individual choice: "when they become adults, children have the right and duty to *choose their profession and state of life*."[23] State of life, for adults, seems open-ended, a state where all is possible. It is all too easy to read that notion of "choosing" a state of life in the way that Kate Bolick does: as a free and independent choice that one person can make simply by willing it. *I* choose to be married; in making my choice to be married, or in deciding that I am *called* to be married (to use a common Christian description), whether there is someone I am in relationship with that I might marry matters little if at all. Christians therefore frequently speak and write of being bewildered that they've been "called" to be married but they're getting older and haven't found that person they know God has in mind for them.

I do think that all Christian adults need to take seriously their responsibility to discern vocation, including when marriage is not, or will not, be part of that vocation. Yet, as I shall discuss later, such discernment needs to be grounded in one's own contingent life and the relationships one has and is cultivating, and not in the open-ended freedom of individual choice that American life celebrates.[24]

Fulfilling Desires (To Be Part of a Couple)

In this section I discuss how the matrix of independence, freedom, and choosing to be in relationships (or not) that I discussed above, are fueled by consumer choices, especially desires for choices. Several observers of changing American views on marriage and family in recent decades have noted important connections between the marital state, desire, and the economy. Such desires especially become related to sexual desire, and therefore to romantic relationships—to the detriment of thinking well about being never-married.

Wendell Berry suggests in his essay, "Sex, Economy, Freedom, and Community," published in a collection of essays that bear the same title, that the "community"—as contrasted with the more private "family" and the more public "nation state" and "marketplace"—has been disintegrating slowly over the past couple centuries, victim of contemporary cultural emphasis on individuality, freedom of choice, and autonomy. Berry sees community as distinct from private and public life, and very important to humanity: community has a kind of power "to enforce decency without litigation. It has the power, that is, to influence behavior. And it exercises this power not by coercion or violence but by teaching the young and by preserving stories and songs that tell (among other things) what works and what does not work in a given place."[25] Berry continues his description of community by noting that community is formed via informal "arrangements" between people—arrangements of marriage and family, work, and education.

The community's more informal arrangements affect and interplay with private life and "public life. Berry writes:

> Community life is by definition a life of cooperation and responsibility. Without the discipline of a community's arrangements, private life and public life, without the disciplines of community interest, necessarily gravitate toward competition and exploitation. As private life casts off all community restraints in the interest of economic exploitation or ambition or self-realization or whatever, the communal supports of public life also and by the same stroke are undercut.[26]

As Berry goes on to argue, the disintegration of community, including family and children, is linked to the rise of industrial economies, economies in which anonymous people and machines make the goods we buy.

In contrast, local *communities* provide faces, names, and relationships to go alongside our purchases. In Berry's view, economy and community are tightly interwoven—and they are simultaneously interwoven with sexual love, with marital and familial relationships forming part of the network that makes local communities and economies work. As those local communities fall, so too fall the small interwoven institutions that make up local communities, like families, education, care of the sick and the old, and most especially in Berry's view, respect for love.[27]

Once economic desire becomes broad, global, and largely anonymous, the human connections that are inherent in the things we buy disappears. We mostly do not know who made our shoes or who helps us with our technological problems, which in turn means we cannot practice love in any kind of recognizable form toward the people who provide us with things. More intimate human relationships become affected too, as we see in various marketing tactics employed in media. The distance between things we can buy, and things we can't (like human relationships) becomes blurred. William Cavanaugh notes, "Goods that cannot be commodified, such as self-esteem, love, sex, friendship, and success, are associated with products that bear little or no relationship to those goods."[28] For example, *Huffington Post* features regular blog posts about women in advertising that have noted sexual messages and sexed-up women in relation to the following products: M&Ms candy, Kia automobiles, Skinny Cow ice cream sandwiches, nearly any video game recently released, Bratz dolls, Curel body lotion, and more.[29]

Desire for human relationships can ultimately become part of our attempts to commodify life. Marriage is not simply available for the taking—but not for lack of trying. Mail-order brides and Vegas weddings might make it seem that we can simply pick up marriage off a shelf and use it if we want to, and discard it when we need to via divorce. More darkly, the rise of human sex trafficking makes it seem that human relationships, especially sexual relationships, are available for the taking, just as though we were choosing between types of crackers on a grocery shelf.

Theologian David Matzko McCarthy develops the connection between our views of relationships, choice, and fostering desire further in his book, *Sex and Love in the Home*. He notes the number of automobile commercials and advertising schemes that feature bikini-clad women. As he states, we are not dumb: "Few of us are tricked by the image of a woman in a bikini sitting on the hood of a sports car. Few men imagine that sexy women would fall all over us if we were to own a particular automobile."[30] What is happening is both more complex and more subtle: "an 'otherworldly' commercial can conjure up desire for an experience, rather than a guarantee for the experience itself."[31] The job of the commercial is to create desire for an experience "so that we will be a little less satisfied with our own lives, with our old dirty trucks or mind-numbing minivans."[32] In turn, our unfulfilled desires about sex and relationships become partly filled through our buying and consuming other things, activities that are about freedom and choice.

McCarthy goes on to suggest that "this 'economy of desire' corresponds to widely accepted sexual habits and basic social attitudes about sex."[33] Good sex is unmarried sex, single sex, free sex. Marriage cannot sustain the fiery passion that single sex brings with it. Kate Bolick describes a similar distinction regarding long-term committed relationships, the freedom of singleness, and desire in her memoir. In the middle of one rather serious relationship with "R," Bolick notes: "I wasn't a 'not-sexual' person, but I'd become one. I'd noticed that I was less interested in having sex than I used to be, but I thought that's just what happens after a few years. It was part of growing up, making compromises, settling down."[34] Bolick's initial panicked reaction to her anxieties about settling down into coupledom is to choose another person—to have an affair with someone who isn't R. Human relationships are simply there for the free choosing, relative to a person's own desires.

One result is that people (especially women) and sexual relationships become objects meant to foster consumer desire of products. Sexual desire drives consumer desire; consumer desire in turn shows up in the descriptions we have about wanting to get married. "I want to find The One," as though the perfect person could be selected off the shelf just as the perfect cut of meat might be chosen at the meat and deli counter.

Another result of this relationship commodification is that romantic (and necessarily sexual) love becomes the *main* desirable option, to the detriment of all other options in relationships. It is striking that authors like Bella DePaulo, Michael Cobb, and Kate Bolick each presume that singleness is a synonym for "has no romantic relationships," and that's a good thing in their view. It is striking, too, that such relationships get in the way. Bella DePaulo, for example, derides the "seemingly innocent question about having a family." While she rightly points out that answering the question "Do you have a family?" presumes coupledom and children, rightly points out that this question is unfair, and rightly notes many other kinds of relationships that could also be considered family, ultimately DePaulo wants to be able to answer "*no, I do not*" have a family without feeling ashamed or made to feel weird.[35] Indeed, DePaulo wants her readers to recognize that "having a family" can and should be seen as seriously detrimental to many other jobs and responsibilities.[36] Yet presumably DePaulo does have a family of some kind, and grew up in a family. It is just not the kind of family that most of us envision. For example, not envisioning family broadly enough means that caring for ill parents, or taking family leave to raise adoptive children (among many other kinds of examples) can be more difficult to justify in the workplace than taking maternity leave—an obvious aspect of romantic love. Depending on how a person's workplace is affected by the Family Medical Leave Act, it may mean a person can't take leave at all. Coupledom and its romantic, sexual love is our de facto family most of the time.

Loss of respect for nonsexual relationships itself fuels a desire for sexual relationships, whether that is seen in terms of marriage and family or in terms of a free-swinging single life that is distinct from marriage and family. We overemphasize marriage and family to the detriment of other relationships: friends, parents, siblings, acquaintances, and others. As historian

Stephanie Coontz has written, Americans' current view of marriage as a person's main relationship is a very recent phenomenon, coinciding with the changes we have seen in economies and communities.[37] A century ago, over 30 percent of the population remained unmarried. This number decreased to between 10 and 20 percent in the post–World War II years, while today a little under half of the population is unmarried.[38] Cultural nostalgia tends not to notice late nineteenth and early twentieth century norms about marriage and family that demonstrated far broader and more numerous relationships than sexual relationships—rather, we have nostalgia for the mid-century *nuclear* family.

In her writing about being single, Kate Bolick merely writes a common-sense conclusion based on cultural norms about independence and freedom: she can and should make free choices. Michael Cobb and Bella DePaulo, described more fully in Chapter 1, draw some similar conclusions. In American context, their arguments that of course the life of a single person—one who can fiercely embody the very notion of independence from any other person, who can make free choices—should take center stage, makes great sense. Yet Bolick's view of adulthood as solely the purview of autonomous, rational, independent thinkers is detrimental to both the married and the never-married. It is also detrimental to the holistic sense of community that Berry suggests. It creates a false sense that romantic relationships, marriage, or remaining never-married are clear, free consumer choices that we can make in absence of others.

Thus, I take issue with the ways Bolick, Cobb, DePaulo, and others describe what it means to become "yourself," to become an adult as a single person, which means self-actualization on one's own. The title of Bolick's book captures this nicely: *Spinster: Making a Life of One's Own*, and so does the following statement of Michael Cobb's: "simply being yourself—your single self—is already the fundamental form of dignity."[39] The emphasis in their writing about singleness highlights and prioritizes ideas of desire, choice, and freedom—and it is no accident that choice and freedom are precisely the values that American culture prizes in all of its adults. If, as some psychologists have suggested, being single implies being un-adult or not-yet-adult, then it makes sense that single people might choose to highlight the choice, freedom, and independence that are hallmarks of adult life as a means of countering those assumptions. However, I suggest that the contrary actually happens: emphases on desire, choice, and freedom only serve to emphasize never-married life as a problem and provide exactly the right context for Justice Kennedy's misguided and unfortunate comments that I quoted in Chapter 1.

The Apostle Paul: "Be As I Am. . . ."

In this section, I suggest that an antidote to our misshapen desires leading to unhealthy images of being never-married are best tempered by examining some writing of the Apostle Paul. In particular, what would it mean, as Christians, to think about both marriage and being never-married as adult ways of living as disciples of Jesus?

Some readings of Paul might suggest that he, a never-married man, wrote letters that contain justifications for independence, freedom, and desire—exactly all those ideals I have been calling into question. I admit as well that Paul is a controversial figure to turn to with respect to marriage and singleness. His discussions of marriage and sex have led to some Christians dismissing Paul outright, seeing in his writing invectives against women and against sexual pleasure. For some, Paul's words seem outdated and hold the Church back from better, healthier understandings of sex and sexuality.

Paul also is intriguing on questions of marriage and singleness because he clearly prefers and advises in favor of singleness. People who are unmarried do not have the anxieties associated with having families but can serve God with single-hearted purpose. Paul's view that singleness is better because it enables a person to serve God more closely only works if, in fact, being never-married is a state of life that fosters being unconcerned. Yet, as I have suggested above, being never-married carries with it any number of anxieties (especially about independence, freedom, and desire), all of which, I suggest, get in the way of being a disciple of Christ. My hope, therefore, is that Paul helps Christians rethink what it means to be never-married, and what it means to be independent, to have choice, and so forth.

Precisely because Paul is controversial and so clearly at the center of debates about marriage and sexuality in Christian tradition, I choose Paul as the central figure for consideration in this chapter. It is also because Paul's letters are scripture, part of the Bible that Christians hold as holy and crucial to living Christian life. By deepening our reading of Paul, we can begin to understand the place and importance of remaining unmarried in Christian tradition.

I will refer to several passages from Paul's letters, but one passage takes center stage. Paul's first letter to the Corinthians, chapter 7, focuses intently on marriage and singleness and has affected Christians' discussions about marriage and singleness down through the centuries. Some have read Paul's letter as being entirely supportive of marriage and see celibacy as a state of life that Paul meant *only* for the church at Corinth and only in their particular time and place.[40] More often, Christians have read Paul as advocating singleness, sometimes to the exclusion of married life. Some have even suggested that Paul sees marriage as an evil, over and against singleness as a good life.[41] This passage is therefore very evidently at the center of debate about Christian states of life.

Before I turn to a more in-depth discussion of the first letter to the Corinthians, and to chapter 7 in particular, I think it is important to know Paul's story as a Jew, as a citizen of Rome, and as part of a Middle Eastern world that bore the marks of heavy Greek philosophical influence due to the conquests Alexander the Great had made three centuries before Paul lived. Of particular importance is how Paul's several contexts might perhaps relate to his views of marriage and singleness as expressed in his letter to the Corinthians.

Paul's Historical Situation—Jewish, Hellenistic, Roman

Prior to his conversion to Christianity, Paul was Saul, a Pharisee and persecutor of Christians.[42] Pharisees were well known for upholding laws of purity found especially in the Torah (the first five books of the Bible: Genesis, Exodus, Leviticus, Numbers, and Deuteronomy). Pharisees privileged other writing that is now contained in Hebrew scriptures as well as oral teaching, and they developed commentary on those oral and written teachings. The Pharisees emphasized purity, as determined by the degree to which a person upheld God's law; by some scholars' accounts we even still see evidence of that Pharisaic focus on purity in chapter 7 of his first letter to the Corinthians, where he discusses the children of mixed (Christian–pagan) marriages. He writes that such marriages are holy, and the children are holy and not "unclean," a word Pharisees sometimes used in contrast to being "pure."[43]

Several Biblical scholars have examined Paul's texts to see whether and how his Jewish roots affect his teachings on marriage and singleness. Scholars seem fairly united in understanding Paul not to be rejecting his Jewishness but to be developing his Jewish roots in the Christian context, including for people who had not grown up Jewish. The Corinthian church, for example, was a church mixed with both Greeks and Jews. Jewish Biblical scholar Daniel Boyarin writes that Paul's view of marriage agrees with standard rabbinic Jewish thought of the day. While Paul clearly prefers a celibate state in 1 Corinthians 7, he does not outright deny marriage as a possibility for Christians.

Boyarin further suggests that Paul holds a standard "two-tiered system of thought regarding sexuality: celibacy as the higher state but marriage as a fully honorable condition for the believing Christian."[44] This two-tiered system is dualistic, a separation of two concepts, body and spirit, which Boyarin sees as a common philosophical frame of reference in first-century Palestine. Very often, the separation that dualism creates results in a rejection of one of the two concepts in favor of emphasizing the other. In the first century, some groups related to Jewish and Christian thought rejected bodiliness in favor of spiritualism, especially by living very ascetic lives that punished bodies (e.g., fasting, celibacy, inadequate clothing).[45] Boyarin suggests that Paul's view of the body/spirit dualism that is unlike other dualisms in that it does not reject bodily natures. Rather, Paul's dualism understands spirit as of a higher order than flesh. Boyarin sees Paul's privileging of celibacy over marriage as a physical manifestation of his privileging of spirit over flesh throughout his writing.[46]

Paul also lives in the Roman Empire that privileges Greek philosophy and culture. The Corinthian church to which Paul writes is letter is a Hellenistic, Greek-speaking community in the busy port city of Corinth. Greek architecture, language, and ideas pervaded Paul's first-century world. This is in part due to the influence of Alexander the Great and his empire, which established dominance in the Middle East from Egypt to India three centuries before Christ. Alexander dominated on the battlefield and amassed lands belonging to other ancient empires, those of Egypt and Persia. Wherever Alexander went in battle, he brought with him engineers, surveyors, and scholars of history, philosophy, and science. He and his political descendants founded numerous Greek-speaking cities across the region, cities that became part of the region's trade routes. Greek language, history, art, and other aspects of culture grew to be the routine backdrop of everyday life by Jesus' day.[47] Greek was so important a language that one of Alexander's political successors, King Ptolemy II Philadelphus, ordered a translation of the Hebrew scriptures into Greek; indeed, by the second century before Christ, there is much evidence that more Jews spoke Greek than the Hebrew of their ancestors. Most of the earliest copies of the New Testament Gospels and letters have come down to us in Greek, as well.

The Hellenism of Paul's day meant that society was pluralistic, with many different kinds of worship sites. Archaeology of Corinth has uncovered both a Jewish synagogue and shrines to pagan gods. Greek philosophers like Plato and Aristotle were well-regarded in Hellenistic culture, including in Jewish communities. At the same time, Greek influence sometimes came head to head with Jewish and Christian practice. In Paul's letter, the community is clearly grappling with questions about the encroachment of Greek-speaking culture, including eating food offered to the gods. At the same time, the Corinthian Christian community also knows itself to be part of a broader Jewish tradition. For example, in 1 Corinthians 10:1–4, Paul writes about "our ancestors" who passed through the Red Sea and were baptized under Moses.

Paul's context is also that of a Roman citizen in the Roman Empire, and specifically as a citizen during the reign of Augustus Caesar. Augustus is well known among Christians for being the emperor during the time of Christ. In relation to Paul's letter, however, we also need to understand Rome's impact on marriage laws for the empire. Caesar Augustus came to power in a time of upheaval for Rome—a time of civil war. At the conclusion of the civil wars, many prominent Roman citizens suggested that Rome's problem was a lack of morality and that civil wars would not have occurred if its citizens had been more moral. Morality, for the ancient Romans, revolved around the proper place and function of marriage and family. In an effort to restore a sense of morality (and thus end its civil wars and resulting upheaval), Augustus promulgated a set of laws that required marriage and children. For example, the Augustan laws dictated that "all male citizens between the ages of twenty-five and sixty and all female citizens between twenty and fifty were to be married. Widows were to marry within two (perhaps three) years of their husbands' death, divorcees within eighteen months."[48] Marriages were regulated by class (slave prohibited from marrying a freed person), and celibacy was prohibited. The number of children a woman had could mitigate certain legal penalties or requirements. For example, women were required to have guardians of their person and property unless they had at least three children. Former slave women could be released from guardianship if they had four children, exhibiting, again, the class differential. A celibate woman, on the other hand, would incur taxes for her childlessness. Indeed, in general the penalty for not following the law was taxation and being unable to inherit land or legacies. In addition, those couples who had no children faced penalties on inheritance.

The poet Horace penned several lines that referred to Rome's Golden Age virtues, as contrasted with the Roman society he observes in Augustus' day. He sees that a past Golden Age had loved marriage and family; hence, Caesar Augustus' marriage laws are to be revered all the more because they have the potential to restore that Golden Age. Horace's poem *Carmen Seculare* perhaps obliquely celebrates Augustan marriage laws: "O goddess, be pleased to rear our young, and to grant success to the Fathers' edicts on the yoking together of men and women and on the marriage law for raising a new crop of children, so that the unfailing cycle of ten times eleven years may bring round singing and games that are thronged with people three times by daylight and as often in the pleasant time of night."[49] Horace connects the marriage laws of the day with a vision of what the future will look like if the laws are followed: joyous singing, dancing, and parties—all due to the proper role and functioning of marriage and children. Horace suggests that Rome's Golden Age is returning due to the Augustan marriage laws, and that happiness and joy shall reign once more. In later poems, Horace develops the theme further and presents the expected Golden Age as having arrived with the leadership of Caesar Augustus, alongside family morality.[50] Art of the era also depicts motifs (swans, roses, wheat) that emphasize marriage and fertility.

The significance of these laws and their impact on the Roman population is debated. Were they for the upper and political classes, or for the whole of society? Some see the Augustan laws as affecting only a minority, the wealthy property owners of society who had much to lose because of the laws' inheritance penalties. By this view the wealthy minority was in charge of maintaining a kind of sexual purity in relation to their class. That is, a wealthy man was entirely permitted to have extramarital or homosexual relationships beneath his station, but within his class, marriage was to be sacrosanct.[51] A different argument is that these laws affected the population more generally and were wrought by Augustus and his Senate because they were afraid of falling birth rates in the Empire. An argument in favor of the latter are the widespread descriptions and depictions in this era of ordinary people, married with children, on common objects like funerary urns.[52] Prior to Augustus' era, depictions of married commoners were rare. My own thought is that even if the laws directly impacted only the upper class, the relationships between them and other classes in the course of daily life activities would make the emperor's views of marriage more generally felt.

It is therefore worth thinking about the implications for Paul and early Christians. This is especially the case when we consider the contemporary scene, and Michael Cobb's view that our contemporary North American culture privileges marriage over singleness because it aids in promotion of a totalitarian political economy. America is not Rome, yet it may be useful to think about our own culture that privileges marriage and family with a view to Rome's own particular way of privileging marriage and family.

Paul's Roman context gives a strong political sensibility to the 1 Corinthians 7 text and becomes a call to disobey the Augustan laws requiring marriage. Scholar Jouette Bassler writes that "a young woman's decision not to marry would have been decidedly countercultural and alarming. A decision to remain unmarried after divorce or the death of a spouse would have generated mixed responses. . . ."[53] Even without that political sensibility, in an era where morality itself is embedded in the idea of marriage and having children, Paul's positive allusions to celibacy and to not having children suggest a Christian counter-morality.

As we shall see in more detail below, Paul's first letter to the Corinthians suggests that Christian discipleship and life in Christ did not depend on being married, in the way that for Roman society being moral depended on being married and having children. To the contrary, Paul favors a state of life that stands in stark contrast to the Augustan marriage laws. It is precisely the unmarried and the widows whose lives take on this particular kind of political discipleship.[54]

The First Letter to the Corinthians

Neither the Jewish, Greek, nor Roman contexts in which Paul lives quite do justice for the central focus in his letter to the Corinthians, however. Paul is a Christian, a missionary for Christ, and sees himself as a disciple of Jesus. All of his writing flows from that main idea.

> For I decided to know nothing among you except Jesus Christ, and him crucified.[55]

To know Christ means to become a member of a particular kind of community—a community that parses through all the kinds of daily life questions that Paul addresses in this letter: whether to eat meat offered to idols, how husbands and wives ought to relate to each other, whether to get married, how to behave now that the time of Jesus' second coming must be near. Paul's theology is heavily vested in the idea of "church," which he refers to in almost every letter, including the first letter to the Corinthians. "Church" refers both to the small local communities to which Paul wrote, and to the gathered group of people present. Paul's consistent concern is that people work to build up their communities and seek unity in all their relationships.[56] Moreover, for Paul (as well as for other early Christians), the Christian community is no mere community but analogous to a household that fosters particular kinds of relationships.

Jesus is the means by which Paul understands God, himself, and the world. Chapter 1 is also where Paul discusses how "God chose the foolish of the world in order to bring the wise to shame..." and "the foolishness of God is wiser than humans and the weakness of God is stronger than humans...." Christ becomes our wisdom, our righteousness, our holiness, indeed, the whole reason for living and dying in the particular ways that we Christians do. To know Christ means to know God—God, the one who saves even via the "foolishness" of Paul's proclamation, as Paul writes in 1 Corinthians1:21.[57]

Paul's introductory statements in this letter clearly show that the Corinthians belong to God as members of Christ's body, and that Jesus makes them holy (1:2). The Corinthians' questions to Paul revolve around what it means to live holy lives on a daily basis. Paul's descriptions of marriage and singleness are therefore best understood in relationship to what it means to live holy lives, daily.

Part of the Corinthians' questions about what it means to live holy lives centers on the question of how to treat our bodies. While the Corinthian Christians consider themselves to be holy, and therefore spiritual people (3:1), and that living a Christian life must, therefore, look a particular way, Paul admonishes the Corinthians that life in the Spirit does not look one particular way. Each Christian has particular gifts from God, particular charisms. Some have the gift of tongues, others have the gift of preaching and prophecy, and so on (chapter 12).

Possessing spiritual gifts does not mean that one is truly living in Christ Jesus, however! Chapter 13 is the famous passage about love: though people may have the gifts of speaking in tongues or other very spiritual kinds of gifts, if they do not have love, those gifts are nothing. Then Paul goes on to describe what love is: it is patient and kind, forgiving, bearing all, believing all, and hoping all things. The discussion of love leads to further discussions in chapter 14 about what it means to be God's holy people, members of Christ's own body. Paul concludes his letter with exhortations about who Jesus is: "If Christ has not been raised" then we will not be raised, he proclaims. Belief in Jesus, his bodily resurrection, and his victory over death are central to Christian life and witness, to the life of love and living out spiritual gifts that Paul emphasized in the previous chapters.

Paul's letter to the Corinthians (as with all his letters) can be read as an entreaty for Christians to change, radically, their vision of the world. The way we know Christ is by living a life conformed to the crucified Christ, which means that our understanding of even some of the most basic relationships changes. In the letter's twelfth chapter, Paul writes extensively about how we become a new body in Christ. This fact of becoming a new body means that we cannot simply read chapter 7 as inviting the status quo about relationships. But also, the fact of the relationship between the church, Christ's body, and the church's head, Jesus, is an intimate relationship. This relationship changes how we understand ourselves; it is meant to join us most intimately to Christ.

Paul's understanding about spiritual gifts, love, and what it means to be a member of the Body of Christ are also related to a sense that the end of time is near. Christ will soon be on the way to meet his followers. This sense of the nearness of Christ's second coming has led some scholars to be dismissive of some parts of Paul's letter, since some of his advice seems to hinge on the idea that Jesus is imminently coming. Two thousand years later, Paul's eschatological, imminent-second-coming focus does not seem helpful for our reflection on this-worldly institutions like marriage and family. Indeed, Paul's eschatological focus can lead Christians to remove themselves from worldly institutions entirely. Robert Grant finds Paul's advice essentially conservative in nature: "stay as you are [married or single]."[58] "Stay as you are" because God's reign will begin soon.

Yale Biblical scholar Leander Keck suggests exactly this kind of thinking in Paul's letter: "Because this world and its institutions, structures, social status, and so forth, have no future, Paul urges that Christians not involve themselves in it more than they must. . . ."[59] Keck suggests that for Paul, "inner freedom" to follow God was more important than one's socio-economic status, especially since the time before the second coming is so short. Another commenter says strongly that marriage is not "of the proper abiding life of the Christian."[60] These scholars suggest that marriage and family might be beneficial in the here-and-now, this life—but simply aren't relevant for the future life all of us have in Christ Jesus.

However, as I shall suggest below, Paul's eschatological vision is very helpful for rightly thinking about how to live life in marriage and states of singleness in this world, here and now. Moreover, Paul's words to the Corinthians help us contemporary Christians think through the points I raised earlier: how independence, freedom, desire, and state of life come together.

Independence, Freedom, and Desire in 1 Corinthians 7

Independence

Independence in the ways I have described above—as an absence of not only romantic/sexual relationships but also nonromantic relationships—quite simply doesn't exist for Paul. Paul proclaims that people ought to be "as he is." Being as Paul is means having deep friendships. His care for his friends shows in his references to Stephanas, Fortunatus, and Achaicus (1 Corinthians 16:15–18); Titus is like Paul's brother (2 Corinthians 2:13); Timothy is "my beloved and faithful son in the Lord" (1 Corinthians 4:17).[61]

Relationships are necessary for what it means to be human. Relationships are the point of Paul's first letter to the Corinthians, especially given his emphasis on love in chapter 13 and in his description of the church as the Body of Christ, which has many members, and each of those members has particular unique gifts that Christians must acknowledge and respect out of love for each other.

Paul appears to have a strong sense of interdependence, a healthy regard for nonromantic relationships, and a strong sense that love is something we live, give, and practice, to all people. What then, does this mean for romantic relationships? Paul writes in 1 Corinthians 7:5–9:

> Do not deprive one another except perhaps by agreement for a set time, to devote yourselves to prayer, and then come together again, so that Satan may not tempt you because of your lack of self-control. 6 This I say by way of concession, not of command. 7 I wish that all were as I myself am. But each has a particular gift from God, one having one kind and another a different kind.8 To the unmarried and the widows I say that it is well for them to remain unmarried as I am. 9 But if they are not practicing self-control, they should marry. For it is better to marry than to be aflame with passion.[62]

Paul presumes that people have relationships, as in verse 9. He does not presume that those relationships must become marriage relationships nor that those relationships must become romantic or sexual, even if someone is passionate about another. Rather, he writes about how people's relationships ought to be conducted. Each person's focus ought to be on the other person and what he or she needs: "do not deprive each other except perhaps by agreement," and if people cannot practice self-control, then they ought to marry. Here, as in other passages in this letter, Paul mentions that each person has gifts. He, Paul, respects these gifts and respects the fact that other people might not be able to live as Paul does, or might not be called to the same life as Paul.

We can see in several other verses in chapter 7 that Paul's exhortation is for Christians to think about the other person in a relationship and not about oneself. In verses 12 through 14, Paul discusses the case of being married to unbelievers. Believers, he says, ought to be concerned about the other, unbelieving person's *consent* to stay in the marriage, even with a believer. "In verses 12 through 16 of chapter 7, Paul considers marriages between a Christian convert and an unbeliever. Verses 12 and 13 specifically focus on the action the Christian ought to take: "If any brother has a wife who is an unbeliever, and she is willing to go on living with him, he should not divorce her; 13and if any woman has a husband who is an unbeliever, and he is willing to go on living with her, she should not divorce her husband." Any action taken against the marriage is delegated to the unbelieving partner, *not* to the believing partner. Paul's counsel to believers, in other words, is to live with the relationships they have at present, with respect for their partners and without trying to coerce them into divorce.

Not even belief in Christ, or lack thereof, should affect how Christians respond to the other people with whom they are in relationship. It means a radical kind of love, love for another person despite the fact that you and the other live with strong disagreements about a matter of life, love that is as strong as what he names in chapter 13: "love bears all things, believes all things, hopes all things." Christians are not called to be people who act independently of their relationships, who go their own independent way when the relationship becomes a problem.

Still further, in verse 36, Paul advises: "If anyone thinks that he is not behaving properly toward his fiancée, if his passions are strong, and so it has to be, let him marry as he wishes; it is no sin. Let them marry." Again, the point is to focus on the particular relationship with the particular person, and not on an overly abstract ideal. Simply marry if the relationship as it exists currently doesn't enable a person to love God and neighbor well.[63]

Freedom and Choice

Alongside the lack of a notion of independence, Paul has a very different understanding of freedom. "I wish that all were as I myself am," indicates a kind of wistfulness on Paul's part. Freedom, here, does not relate to the kind of state one *chooses*. Indeed, Paul refers to the states of life in which we live as gifts from God and not a choice made from a person's free will (v. 7). Freedom instead derives from the relationship Paul has in Christ Jesus. He is free to follow Christ, not free to make any choice at all.

One verse that highlights Paul's different sense of choice is in verse 9, where he writes that it is better to marry than to burn. Some Christians have interpreted Paul as meaning "burn in hell" while others have interpreted Paul as meaning "burn with inner passion." Yet neither of these views is quite right.[64] For instance, Paul uses very little language about hell.[65] One of the reasons is that either of these two interpretations is nonsensical, for in either view Paul seems to suggest "if you cannot abstain from sex and do not marry, you must still abstain from sex, even if that will give you such pain that it can be compared to being aflame or burning."[66] Another reason for Molvaer's concern is that as he reads the Greek text in verse 9, he sees Paul using words that suggest he is offering two good choices for Christians: either they can marry, or they can burn. *Kreitton* is the Greek word Paul uses here to describe these two choices. What Molvaer points out is that in every other letter of Paul's, his use of the word *kreitton* always indicates comparison of two good choices, not a good choice and a bad choice. The latter kind of choice—a choice between good and bad—is, in a sense, not really a choice, because when the "choice" is that stark, we know what we should do. Choice, here, is much more difficult. It is no assent of the free will to do something that I, as an independent person, want and desire to do. Making a choice instead requires discernment: figuring out the best course of action among two good possible actions. To do that, again, requires attention to one's particular relationships.

Contemporary discussions about marriage and singleness suggest that people have choices for either state in some kind of vague, abstract way. We have the idea, as I have discussed earlier, that a person can "choose" that he or she will get married, or decide that he or she is "called" to be married—even in the absence of any particular relationship that might lead to a marriage. This view of marriage in the abstract makes for exactly the kind of conditions that regard dating and romance as a kind of meat market where people become "past their prime." Marriage as an abstract idea provides exactly the kind of conditions for people to believe in "The One" person who is a soul mate, the person who must become exactly the right choice for marriage or else the dreaded divorce will happen. Marriage in the abstract heightens anxieties about finding romantic relationships.

It is on that note that I return to the point I made earlier about Paul's context as a Roman citizen living under the restrictions of the Augustan marriage laws. In a society that mandates marriage and children, such as the Augustan world, not to be married becomes an act of witness. Being single becomes an act of political witness against the state, such that discipleship itself is political. Never-married (as well as widowed) Christianity is its own way of life that is part of the politics of both Jesus and Paul. Paul puts both marriage and remaining unmarried into a context of living for Jesus Christ. He is not anti-marriage or anti-sex as some have suggested.

Yet Paul lives in particularities, not in the abstract. In verse 8, Paul writes that it is well for unmarried and widows "to remain unmarried as I am." Paul balances that recommendation with another recommendation: consider the relationship you currently have and respond accordingly, as best fits that relationship. If that relationship involves a lack of self-control, then it is better to marry. The choices we have refer not to an individual decision disconnected from all else to determine "whether we might get married someday." Rather, the choices are to look at the particular relationships all of us have, regardless of whether those relationships are romantic or not, and consider how best to be loving in those relationships.

Paul is clearly emphasizing a need for practical consideration of our specific, lived relationships in later verses, too, especially with regard to gender. Many commenters have suggested Paul argues for marriages of mutuality, noting that throughout chapter 7 what Paul advises for men, he also advises for women.[67] Some have also argued that sexual activity in marriage can be for mutual pleasure as well as for procreation.[68] This fact, too, suggests that the focus needs to be on the particular relationship as it is lived in relation to Christ Jesus and not on abstractions related to preconceived notions about what it means to be male and female. Paul continues his theme of exhorting people to focus on the particularities of their contexts in the next several verses (18–31), discussing how Christians ought to remain in the state in which they were called. For example, he says:

> I think that, in view of the impending crisis, it is well for you to remain as you are. [27] Are you bound to a wife? Do not seek to be free. Are you free from a wife? Do not seek a wife. [28] But if you marry, you do not sin, and if a virgin marries, she does not sin. Yet those who marry will experience distress in this life, and I would spare you that.

There is no general abstract view of how Christians ought to live—precisely because time grows short. Rather there are relationships, and Christians need to foster those relationships in loving ways.

As I mentioned earlier, many Biblical scholars have noticed that Paul decisively links his counsel about remaining in the present state to the future world that he believes is coming quite soon—and many scholars have thereby dismissed some of what Paul writes. This is a time of "present distress" he writes in verse 26, in which it is "good for a person to remain as he is." "The time is short," he says in verse 29, and "the world in its present form is passing away," he proclaims in verse 31. Yet it is precisely this end-of-time urgency that should matter to us now, for we, too, need Paul's insistence on particularities for our own lives. More than that, our own time is passing away too; we, no less than Paul, have contemporary sensibilities about the passing of an age—in the quickly changing climate of our world, in our own sense that life is short.

Desire

Paul's discussion of desire, too, takes context in his insistence and single-minded focus on being a disciple of Jesus. For example, Paul's central concern with marriage relates to anxiety and having to please another person rather than the Lord. Paul writes:

> I want you to be free from anxieties. The unmarried man is anxious about the affairs of the Lord, how to please the Lord; [33]but the married man is anxious about the affairs of the world, how to please his wife, [34]and his interests are divided. And the unmarried woman and

> the virgin are anxious about the affairs of the Lord, so that they may be holy in body and spirit; but the married woman is anxious about the affairs of the world, how to please her husband. [35]I say this for your own benefit, not to put any restraint upon you, but to promote good order and unhindered devotion to the Lord.[36]

What a person needs to do, then, is follow the path that fosters single-hearted purpose of discipleship in Christ. "I wish all were as I myself am" so that desire for God isn't overtaken by other desires, especially the good and necessary desires of caring for one's family. In his view, spouse and family are distractions in the path of following God; at the same time, Paul acknowledges that passion and lack of self-control can be quite distracting too.

Scholar Dale Martin suggests that sexual desire was *the* key problem, and the remedy was marriage: "[a]nd sexual intercourse within the bounds of marriage functioned to keep desire from happening. Sex within marriage was not the expression of desire, proper or improper; rather it was the prophylaxis against desire."[69] Unlike Molvaer, Martin finds Paul's use of the word "burn" to mean burning with sexual passion, and that his use of "burn" is similar to Greek and Roman ideas that sexual passion was a "'burning' within the body, metaphorically and physically. . . ."[70] Martin complains that modern readers assume Paul had their own modern romantic ideals about marriage in mind, and so understand Paul's critique about burning with passion to be "condemning not sexual desire in general but illicit, unnatural, or excessive passions."[71] Martin thinks that in Paul's context, the idea of non-passionate sex was possible and that the apostle recommended it.

Historians of early Christian history note several ways 1 Corinthians 7 figured in debates about Christian asceticism and how to rightly order sexual desire. Ascetic lifestyles developed a great deal in the first few centuries of Christianity, and developed precisely in relation to questions about marriage and sexuality. Verse 5, for example (reserving sex in order to pray), became part of an argument about whether Christians ought to be permanently sexually abstinent because sex was not good, or whether sex is something occasionally to abstain from because it can make prayer life better. For example, fourth-century Jerome argued that Christians ought to practice permanent sexual abstinence.[72] Other early Christians found Jerome's reading far too extreme, for example, Ambrosiaster. Ambrosiaster writes: "Although marital unions are clean . . ., nevertheless one ought to abstain even from licit things in order that prayer may be directed more easily towards its effect."[73] Sex is clean, but abstaining from sex "is a sign of a person's greater zeal and desire to be heard," as David Hunter puts it.[74]

While the focus in the particular verses in chapter 7 is on romantic or sexual relationships, the advice Paul gives, especially when seen in the context of the whole book, is that Christians need constantly to think about responding to the other person in a relationship—any kind of relationship—in loving ways. This fact should help Christians reorient their focus away from romantic love and romantic relationships as the sole kind of relationship, toward a broader, better focus.

When Paul writes that time is growing short, that is an eschatological phrase, which in our contemporary context should lead to a refusal to be abstract in attempting to live a Christian life. That is, "stay as you are" in relation to the surrounding verses about relationships. "Stay as you are" also means to be attentive to the relationships you have at the moment. It means focusing, in love, on the people you are already with, rather than on abstract concepts of people not yet known. The community of believers holds primacy in this text of Paul's.

These verses suggest that for Paul, remaining unmarried involves having care about sexual relationships, especially by possessing self-control, and receiving and living with the gifts a person has from God. Many scholars agree that in the 1 Corinthians 7 passage, Paul is responding to others of his day who take a very extreme view of human sexuality, namely that no Christian ought to be married at all. In verse 7:1 above, Paul states that he will address "the matters about which you wrote: 'It is well for a man not to touch a woman,'" which suggests that the community at Corinth housed Christians who believed in total renunciation of body and sexuality. Paul, however, takes a moderate tone. In verse 28, he insists that those who marry do not sin; he repeats that point in verse 36. There, he more explicitly refers to sexual relationships and passionate desire: "If anyone thinks that he is not behaving properly toward his fiancée, if his passions are strong, and so it has to be, let him marry as he wishes; it is no sin." Marriage is no sin and is the proper way to deal with passionate desire for another human being. Celibacy, on the other hand, is to be preferred: "A wife is bound as long as her husband lives. But if the husband dies she is free to marry anyone she wishes, only in the Lord. But in my judgment she is more blessed if she remains as she is." People commit no sin in marrying, and it is no sin to experience passionate desire and sexuality.

Yet Paul implies that he himself is never-married: "I wish that all were as I myself am" (verse 7) and later, "To the unmarried and the widows I say that it is well for them to remain unmarried as I am" (verse 8). One of his chief reasons is that being married necessarily means anxiety, especially anxiety about the other person in the couple (verses 32–34). A person who remains unmarried can practice wholehearted, good devotion to God. A person who remains unmarried can wholeheartedly direct his or her desires toward God. So this becomes about love of God, but it also becomes about love of neighbor, since desire of another person isn't a foregone conclusion. Paul's discussion of desire is important in instances when being never-married means that one has unrequited love in a relationship where the other person is not interested in confirming a choice to marry. Laura Smit, author of a book on unrequited love in contemporary life, suggests that it is important to understand that love as part of a desire for God.[75] The unrequited love may not be lessened, but the desire for God may be greater.

Choosing, Better

While Paul speaks to his own time and place, his voice in these scriptures helps provide a broader view of marriage and singleness than is often afforded by contemporary conversation. Moreover, Paul's words to the Corinthians speak to our own impulses toward independence, freedom, and desire. As I have argued here, what Christians need is a better view of independence, freedom, and desire, from which we can broaden our view of relationships and love to become much more than the romantic love that has become a cultural fetish.

By broadening our views of what it means to be in relationship and what it means to love, Christians are also in a position to provide a distinctive and important witness to an American culture that overprivileges independence, freedom, and desire, and that brings these three ideals together in very troubling ways, especially for people who are unmarried. Choice, in 1 Corinthians 7, is not choice of free-will autonomy as we commonly think of choice. There are choices to make, for certain, but these are secondary to following Christ. Paul's main focus is Christ, and he therefore offers his counsel in this letter in relation to distractions. Both of the passages I have discussed and developed above suggest that the choice we need to make is the choice that makes us most free to follow Christ. The choice is *not* whether to get married or to remain unmarried: that is, the cases where Paul advocates getting married "as a concession" are cases where people have already found themselves becoming part of a couple. The idea of looking for a vague "someone" who is a soul mate or someone with whom to share a life is not a factor. Churches need to cease from providing activities that too often become matchmaking clubs, and stop making marriage, and whom to marry, the important choices. Discernment about relationships—all kinds of relationships, from friendships, to mentorships, to care of elderly and others in our midst—need to be discussed far more. Pastors and teachers need to speak much more carefully and clearly about the nature of the choices that Christians have, and especially advise against trying to choose a state of life that is not in evidence in a person's relationships.

For the Body of Christ, this chapter should be seen as an exhortation to understand singleness, including never-married singleness, as an important and essential gift to Christian life. Just the fact of seeing never-married singles as important disciples and witnesses of Christ because they are never-married is important, in part because it demystifies romantic love and enables other ways of loving each other come to the fore. Laura Smit suggests at least two visions of how romantic love relates to love of God. There is the view from the third-century BC philosopher Plato. In one of his books, the *Symposium*, one of his characters argues that having romantic love makes us complete, and that God has given us the other person in order to make us complete. This is a "soul mate" view of romantic love, still prevalent today. On the other hand, says Smit, there is a view that romantic love points toward God, and when appropriately understood leads us to seek higher and higher forms of love. Every form of love is meant to lead us toward God.

My points here about Paul's vision of directing all our relationships toward God, and placing choice in the context of those relationships, become central to understanding the rest of the chapters in this book. In each of the other flexible and temporary states of life, we shall continue to see some of the same themes developed, including the question of how to love other people well, without idolizing romantic love (but hopefully also without belittling it).

3

Desire: Uncommitted Relationships and Augustine

CHAPTER 2 FOCUSED ON being never-married. There I presumed, along with some of the never-married authors cited in the first and second chapters, that sex does not have to be either usual or frequent as a presence in a single person's life. It is entirely possible and indeed, from the perspective of Paul, advantageous not to have sexual activities form the center of a person's relationships with other people. In this chapter, by contrast, I focus on loosely based, *purposely* short-term relationships that presume both singleness and sexual activity. I name these relationships as *uncommitted* relationships. Uncommitted relationships, in my view, intentionally aim at being uncommitted, are frequently short-term, and tend to focus on sexual activity as an important aspect (though not the only aspect). That is, many people might not say they are in relationships at all, or will specifically name that they are in casual relationships.

Uncommitted relationships have a wide range: hookup culture, some forms of dating, and some forms of cohabitation. Not all dating and cohabitation connote uncommitted relationships, however. I think that a dating couple who sees the possibility of a long-term committed relationship (even if that possibility is vague or implicit) differs from a dating relationship where one or both members purposely set out deciding that their relationship will never lead toward commitment or will end after a set time (say, at the end of an academic year). In making this distinction between committed and uncommitted relationships, I am following a similar line of reasoning to that offered by Linda Waite. Waite suggests: "All cohabiting relationships are not equal; those on their way to the altar look and act like already-married couples in most ways, and those with no plans to marry look and act very differently."[1] My range of uncommitted relationships goes beyond Waite's focus on cohabitation. I include casual sexual relationships of adults beyond college age as well as perhaps some "friends with benefits" relationships (though it may be that these are more "acquaintances with benefits" relationships that, in our era of confusion about friendship, people call "friends with benefits").[2]

While I am not arguing for Christians to embrace casual uncommitted relationships as means of discipleship, Christians in casual, uncommitted sexual relationships have a witness to make to the church. That is, there are important reasons Christians have argued against premarital sex. In order for sex to be at its best, it sees fulfillment in lifelong, committed, marital relationships. More than that, Christian discipleship is, in part, about the commitments we make to other people, especially the people in our particular Christian communities. Long-term relationships (sexual or otherwise) are therefore valued. The New Testament letters to the early churches call on people to learn peace and love, to be generous to each other and kind, learning to forgive, learning to care for others, especially widows, orphans, and others who are marginalized.[3] These are not habits that we can learn in the space of a few days or weeks, but rather in the long, unconfined space of relationships where the point is to grow in Christ. Learning this is, I think, one of the points of coming together as the Body of Christ.

Even though the church does not advocate uncommitted relationships, Christians who are part of uncommitted relationships need Christian community, and Christian community needs them. I suspect there are numerous points I might discuss, but in this chapter the specific witness I emphasize is reflection on sexual desire and its importance for human and godly life.

This chapter proceeds in the following way. I begin by using a familiar trope: the idea that secular culture is to blame for our casual sexual culture and its problems. I set up a church/world distinction on purpose because that, frequently, is how casual sexual culture is discussed. Then, however, I discuss how Christians also contribute to a casual sexual culture, especially in the ways Christians have often emphasized commodification of bodies and objectification of desires in ways that are harmful. Christians have a tendency to blame secular culture for promoting uncommitted sexual relationships, and there are good reasons to lay such blame, yet I think that we Christians are also and equally to blame.

Following my discussion of the church/world distinction (that I hope to turn on its head), I turn to the Christian guide in this chapter, who is Augustine of Hippo. Augustine was a fifth-century bishop of the Church in Northern Africa and wrote a number of influential treatises, books, and letters about marriage and states of singleness. He had an immeasurable impact on Western Christian thinking about marriage, sex, and family; depending on a person's theological bent, Augustine is either cheered or jeered for some of his thinking (as we shall see later in the chapter).

Yet Augustine was also himself a person who engaged in frequent casual sexual relationships before he converted to Christianity; as it happens, sex was one of the major stumbling blocks for him as he thought of becoming a Christian. This love of sex also troubles him, for he worries that his sexual desires overtake his love for God. Augustine helps think through the church/world trope that grips contemporary thinking about casual sexual culture because he thinks in terms of earthly and heavenly realms. As we shall see, however, Augustine understands the church/world relationship in a very different way, which in turn may help contemporary Christians rethink the church/world dichotomy, casual sex, and what it means to be a single follower of Jesus Christ.

The Casual Sexual Secular Revolution

One place to begin in describing the casual sexual secular revolution is to think about the failure of marriage. If there is one constant across discussions of marriage over the past half-century, it is that in *practice* marriages are often not great relationships. While people have often idealized marriage, as I discussed in the previous chapter, there is a simultaneous view that marriage in contemporary American is often a great failure. The divorce revolution, alongside more open discussion about domestic violence, has made people intensely aware of the fact that people can be abusive, sex can be stultifying, real people can be hurt, exactly and especially in marriage.

Moreover, historians like Stephanie Coontz have shown that marriage as we like to imagine it today (as a love relationship) has not existed in that form for all of time, including all of Christian time. There have been arranged marriages, marriages of convenience, marriages that serve economic and political purposes, which show marriage not as a love relationship but as a relationship of expediency and of making sure that women and children, as weaker members of society in previous ages, received care.[4] By contrast, many women don't need marriage relationships for economic security in the ways that they once did.[5] People can and do successfully raise children without marriage. All of these points about marriage lead people to ask: Does marriage really matter in the grand scheme of things? Some answer with a resounding no, including the variety of journalists and media stars that have been participating in a concerted "no marriage" movement.[6]

Yet, turning away from marriage has not meant turning away from sex; to be an adult is to be a sexual being, married or not. While the common cultural narrative has been that the sexual revolution and the feminist revolution of the 1960s led to the twin occurrences of demand for no-fault divorce alongside free sex, historians tell a more complicated story. One part of the story is that there have been numerous "sexual revolutions"—numerous times in which peoples' attitudes toward sex have changed rapidly.[7] The emotionally charged aftermath of the World Wars, which led to rethinking about standards of family and law compared to nineteenth century ideals, the development of contraceptive technologies in the late nineteenth and twentieth centuries, and a cultural view toward recognizing heterosexuality and homosexuality as types of sexuality are all examples of events and things that shifted (however subtly) people's sexual behaviors. For example, psychoanalyst Sigmund Freud and his followers have argued that humans have sexual desires that need to be fulfilled in order for us to be healthy. Moreover, whether and how one's sexual desires are fulfilled from very young ages impacts a person's adult development in Freud's view.[8]

Historian Hera Cook narrates the sum total of these several changes:

> These changes have made sexual acts less important in people's lives. They may well engage in more sexual activity more often, or with more partners, than was the case fifty or even thirty years ago. Nevertheless, it has become less important. When having sexual intercourse with a person of the opposite sex was tantamount to choosing them as a lifetime partner the act had immense emotional, economic, and symbolic weight attached to it. Lifelong monogamous marriage is now only one option among several.[9]

Cook's conclusions about marriage suggest that sex has simply become a tool that can be used in a variety of ways, depending on the kind of relationship a person inhabits.

Dr. Zhana Vrangalova, an instructor and researcher at New York University, thinks that casual sexual relationships are no big deal, and haven't been for some time. She is the instigator of a blog called the "Casual Sex Project," which invites people to share personal stories about one-night stands, friends with benefits, sex with exes, and more. She has several reasons for creating the blog site: one is that she finds studies about casual sex to be almost solely focused on college student experiences; another is that she believes much research is outdated, emphasizing the regrets people have about their sexual encounters when in fact Vrangalova sees that "pleasure offsets regret" for many people.[10]

So for many people in contemporary life, yes, sex can and should still be part of a range of relationships, though those relationships no longer need to be married relationships or even committed relationships. The presumption in mainstream news and online media is to assume that all people are having sex, regardless of relationship status; advice columnists often assume that casual sexual relationships are not only okay, but boons for people's health; magazines extol the latest apps for finding casual sexual relationships.[11] Exactly how many people practice casual sexual relationships is unclear. Reliant and relevant sociological data is hard to come by, especially for age groups beyond college. For example, data about college student numbers ranges between 14 percent and 67 percent for the numbers of students reporting casual sexual encounters, which doesn't suggest much for drawing conclusions. Several studies suggest that there has been a gradual increase in casual sexual encounters over time. For example, sociologists have found a steady decrease in the numbers of newly married people reporting that they are virgins on their wedding nights, from 75 percent in 1900 to 30 percent in the 1970s to 5 percent in 2006.[12] Another study compared 18- to 25-year-olds between 1988–1996 with the 18- to 25-year-old cohort in 2004–2012. Researchers found an increase in casual sexual relationships in the 2000s cohort—10 to 15 percent more people report casual sexual encounters with a date or acquaintance than in the 1990s cohort.[13]

There is also not much detailed information about what these casual sexual encounters look like, especially beyond college age, though it is highly likely that many casual sexual relationships feature friends or acquaintances. A Canadian study specifically recruited single adults ages 18 to 30 who had been sexually active within the preceding year, and found that 29 percent of those sexual encounters were one-time encounters. Of those one-time encounters, 25 percent were with total strangers.[14] Other types of casual encounters included sex with ex-romantic partners (24 percent) with whom people were often meeting solely to have sex; acquaintance sex (39 percent); friend sex (30 percent); and sex with a "partner that you may love, but without dating or forming a couple" (22 percent).[15] That there is a shift toward viewing sexual relationships as distinct from marriage, however, is constant in the data.

The presence of uncommitted casual sexual relationships represent American cultural attempts over the past several decades to create a view of singleness that is desirable, rather than prudish, sad, and lonely—a view especially needed when marriages so often appear as detrimental to human happiness. In creating space for casual sexual relationships, people have been able to name singleness as sexy, desirable, and perfect for fast-paced, contemporary American life. Television shows and movies like "Sex and the City," "Girls," and "How I Met Your Mother" have tended to glorify casual sexual relationships, highlighting excitement and self-revelation as some of the themes of a single life that can contain and enjoy casual sex.

Casual sex is supposed to represent the epitome not only of the liberated woman but of the liberated single person. Casual sex supports the commonsense adage that "one person's sexual behavior is not anyone else's concern."[16] In a casual sexual culture, we are all having sex for one in seeking to have our own particular sexual desires met. Our own sexual fulfillment is the main point, even when there are two people (or more) involved. Casual sex is simply the result of living in an American culture that prides itself on individualism. Sex is supposed to be a way to *be* a fully autonomous single person, but more than that, a way to celebrate a *truly* single life. As Lauren Winner notes, married sex gets described as boring and routine, so that "great sex is much harder to come by in the comfortable bedrooms of ordinary married Americans" than it is in the bars and at parties.[17] In the collective imagination about casual sex, the relentless emphasis on marriage as the one way to live a good life takes a back seat to the example of the sexually liberated single person.

Sociologists use the term *sociosexuality* to refer to casual sexual relationships, defining sociosexuality along a spectrum of acceptability for casual sex. Those who equate love and sex are named "restricted," while those who accept casual sex are named as "unrestricted."[18] Predictably, in studies of casual sex, those who accept casual sex find it gratifying, while those who see sex and love as intertwined find themselves bereft after casual sexual encounters. To use terms like *restricted* and "*unrestricted* seems highly biased toward casual sexual relationships: to freedom-loving, independent Americans, restrictions—especially restrictions on a biological fact of human existence that contributes to health—is negative.

For all the emphasis on the freedom and excitement of casual sex, as a society we also know that this view has its negative side. Women find themselves treated as objects in the service of male sexual desire—desire that, after all, is healthy and needs to be assuaged. Men, by similar token, can find themselves pressured to view women as objects and see sex as a necessary activity even when they feel otherwise. (Sex must be important enough to gratify individual sexual desires, but not so important that someone begins a relationship on that basis!)

For example, hookup culture has been one of the most-studied aspects of casual sexual culture, primarily among college students. Hookup sex is supposed to be detached, a way to decouple physical needs from emotional needs. It sounds easy, perhaps even good. Some scholars, such as Hanna Rosin, have gone so far as to say that contemporary feminism depends on hookup culture and casual sex, because hookup culture generates the kind of empowerment that feminism has typically extolled for women. Rosin suggests, in fact, that women are frequently responsible for cultivating hookup cultures on their campuses, in ways similar to how the popular HBO show *Sex and the City* cultivated the sense that women could manage sex, use it for their own means, and develop their own power.[19] Hookup culture enables putting off longer-term relationships so that women can focus their attention on careers and other empowering activities. Women have their physical needs met while not having to entangle themselves with messy emotional relationships that take a toll on women's abilities to pursue careers. In effect, hookups enable women to function like men in American culture.

By contrast, scholar Donna Freitas finds that the reality is quite the opposite. In order to think about sex as solely a bodily urge that doesn't relate to emotional aspects of human relationships, the college students Freitas studies frequently rely on alcohol use in order to medicate themselves against the jarring reality of a supposedly casual sexual relationship.[20] There is a connection between social media use and intimacy, too. A culture that seeks quick answers through texting finds telephone calls time-consuming because they involve speaking with real live people. In a technocratic culture, perhaps hookups become a kind of texting equivalent of sex. Rather than having to deal with real bodies in ways that engage others as human beings, we deal with real bodies in as virtual a way as possible. Donna Freitas is concerned with Rosin's thesis because she isn't sure that the women she studies find hookup culture empowering in the ways Rosin suggests. In Freitas' view, hookup culture presents no other options than to be involved in relationships that are "emotionally empty," and therefore prohibits the kind of free choice about sex that we believe we have. While Freitas knows it is true that people have hooked up in past decades, centuries, and millennia, she also suggests that today's hookup culture, especially as represented in college life, is distinctive. "College has gone from being a place where hookups happened to a place where hookup culture dominates student attitudes about all forms of intimacy"—which is exactly why hookup culture is disempowering and fails to offer choices.[21] The only form of physical contact that matters for college students subsumed by casual sexual culture, in Freitas' view, is casual sex. Other forms of physical touch—like hugs, kisses, handshakes, back rubs—are placed into the logic of casual sexual activity to the point that even a hug *must* be imbued with sexual overtones.

In a chapter on sex and emotional health, Mark Regnerus writes about a woman named Elizabeth: "She enjoys living in Boston, likes clubbing with her friends and meeting guys, and is flirtatious and fairly permissive in her sexual attitudes. There's just one complication—she doesn't like hooking up. She wants something deeper...."[22] Men, too, find casual sex to be stultifying. "The idea fostered in American culture that young men are hypersexual is largely false, and therefore a destructive stereotype to maintain. It not only perpetuates hookup culture on campus but also stunts the ability of young men to grow emotionally."[23] Cultural presumptions form and shape desires for a particular kind of sex—sexual activity that is devoid (apparently) of relationship and that forms and shapes both men and women to think that most people are satisfied with disconnected sexual encounters.

Hooking-up activities do not have the kind of meaning associated with them that might act against objectifying sex. Indeed, part of the point of these relationships seems to be exactly to rid sexual relationships of the heightened sense of meaning associated with marriage, so that sex can be more (apparently) freely enjoyed. As researcher Donna Freitas notes in her book on hooking up:

> Relationships restrict freedom—they require more care, upkeep, and time than anyone can afford to give...They add pressure to the already heavily pressured, overscheduled lives of today's students, who, according to this ethos, should be focusing on their classes, their job prospects, and the opportunity to party as wildly as they can manage. Hookups allow students to get sex onto the college CV without adding any additional burdens...[24]

Freitas notes that younger generations learn to treat sex in an offhand manner, with a casualness that is bolstered by an educational system that focuses almost solely on the negative aspects of sex. Rather than students learning about good sex, and developing an expectation that good sex should be joyful, they instead learn about sexually transmitted diseases, how to know when someone is consenting to have sex, and birth control. If we truly wanted sex to become less casual, wouldn't our focus instead be on what makes for really terrific sex?

Hookup culture uncovers other serious concerns, for example, the sexualization of very young girls' bodies simply in the clothing options that are available at stores. Author Peggy Orenstein writes about the "ongoing confusion between desirability and desire" that young girls learn in relation to how they present their bodies. Orenstein suggests that "I might give the phenomenon a pass if it turned out that, once they were older, little girls who play-acted at sexy were more comfortable in their skins or more confident in their sexual relationships, if they asked more of their partners or enjoyed greater pleasure. But evidence is to the contrary."[25] Rather than learning what it means to have a healthy sexuality, young girls are instead learning how to fulfill someone else's desires at their own expense—even when they are not yet sexually active.

Sex trafficking victims might also be counted as casualties in the casual sexual revolutionary war, as unwilling participants in casual sexual encounters. Money exchanges hands to ensure that sexual encounters remain safely disconnected from emotional attachments. Recent popular news stories have covered the horrific examples of sex trafficking in ordinary looking American homes,[26] along major trucking routes (and truckers' fights to stop trafficking),[27] and in popular websites like backpage.com.[28] CNN has named human sex trafficking as the "new American slavery,"[29] a hidden means of forced prostitution that sometimes goes hand in hand with drug use to enforce subservient relationships.

Pornography use is sometimes also seen as a part of casual sexual culture. Donna Freitas observes that "[p]orn is no longer something to hide. What's more, it's a hobby women have lately been socialized to take up with glee."[30] Pamela Paul has described the ease with which Internet use enables pornography and, moreover, supports objectification of women's bodies so that they become no more than tools for male sexual pleasure.[31] Furthermore, at least one recent study of college-aged students who participate in campus hookup culture demonstrated an association between frequent pornography use, alcohol use, and a "penetrative" hookup for men, though there is a lower association for women.[32] Freitas suggests that campus hookup culture replicates pornographic culture in such events as themed parties (CEO and Ho, Professor and Schoolgirls, Millionaires and Maids) in ways that promote women as lowly objects of men's desire and power. What is more, at "theme parties, the pressures to make oneself sexually available, to have a quick, no-strings-attached encounter—or at the very least to collect gossip about who is doing what with whom—are explicitly and visually set up as if on stage. . . ."[33]

Still another aspect of the negative side of hookup culture is the way we overlook casual sex's power structures and even our ability to resist practices we find troubling.[34] Philosopher Rebecca Whisnant describes the kind of power play that comes in trying to critique sexual practices such as pornography. In an interview about her co-edited book, *Not For Sale: Resisting Pornography and Prostitution*, Whisnant observes,

> there's something so obvious that it shouldn't need saying, but does . . . and that is that many women, including feminists, avoid the feminist critique of pornography and prostitution in order to avoid censure and backlash from the men in their lives. What are the absolute number one things you don't want to have men call you or perceive you as? Prude, uptight bitch,

> feminazi—right? Now, what's the absolute number one surefire way to get seen in exactly these ways? Object to pornography and prostitution, in particular to your male partner's attachment to one or both.[35]

Whisnant's concern highlights how certain concerns about some sexual practices typically get swept aside in favor of the dominant sexual culture. The main social rules regarding sex can be summed up in two sentences. One: sex is a good activity that can and should be pursued, according to an individual's desires. Two: the primary limit to the first rule is that sex cannot abuse another person's dignity and rationality. Hence, pedophilia can be condemned, even though people with pedophilic predilections appear to be wired to desire sex with children. As one commenter on our contemporary views of sex and sexuality observes, psychiatry and psychology often see "sexuality as an unqualified positive."[36]

Even if we were to put all the concerns about sex and sexuality aside, however, the focus on casual sex doesn't always seem to work in the ways proponents hope. A supposedly more positive view of singleness backfires in ways that are harmful for good thinking and practice of single states of life. As one example, a show like "Sex and the City" tries to highlight a positive, non-lonely, powerful view of singleness throughout its seasons, with its four single, sexually active women who inhabit powerful jobs and are thoughtful and intelligent. Ironically, "Sex and the City" also pays obeisance to the romantic ending that is familiar in so many stories about singleness: someday one of these casual sexual relationships will lead to marriage and eternal bliss, and end the singleness that is so apparently stultifying. So Carrie gets married to Big, and even unattached Samantha ends the television series in monogamous relationship.

The supposed goodness of excitement and casualness that this series (among others) celebrated gets neatly packaged back into a state of committed, married, coupledom. It is as though a vision for what it means to be human simply can't withstand the thought that being human can very well mean being single—and that being single can be positive. Marriage becomes a cure for what ails us because we can't conceive of what life looks like otherwise, especially given that people have physical desires and needs.

How Christians Contribute to the Casual Sexual Revolution

Thus far, the narrative as I have described it fits numerous Christian ideas about secular culture and sex: the feminist and divorce revolutions, combined with non-theological views of human desires and bodies, has contributed to a culture that glorifies unattached sex to the detriment of people's humanity. Christian scholars writing about the rise of casual sex have raised an important question: where sex becomes detached, a mere tool in service of fulfilling someone's biological needs, don't sexual partners also run the risk of becoming tools in the service of fulfilling another person's selfish desires or sexual fantasies? In the controversial and explosive Catholic document that teaches against the use of artificial birth control, for example, Pope Paul VI names birth control as supporting a view of sex as a mere tool. This leads to his alarm that

> a man who grows accustomed to the use of contraceptive methods may forget the reverence due to a woman, and, disregarding her physical and emotional equilibrium, reduce her to being a mere instrument for the satisfaction of his own desires, no longer considering her as his partner whom he should surround with care and affection.[37]

That is, in his view women become objects for men's pleasure, as it is his view that contraception use precisely enables seeking sex without seeking a marriage bond that enables both physical and emotional intimacy.

Yet not all the blame should be laid on "secular" culture's doorstep. Lest we think that such a move is largely propelled by a secular culture that thrives on pornography even as Christians decry pornography (but secretly use it), Christian thinkers have articulated how Christians themselves contribute to and perhaps even exacerbate easy sex and commodification of bodies, precisely through the ways they speak about marriage and sex. Christian teachings on premarital sex lead to a charge that Christians cultivate unrealistic expectations about sex and sexuality, and that Christianity is outdated and needs to adapt to the changing times. Yet, the closer we look at prevailing Christian attitudes toward sex the more it becomes apparent to me that contemporary Christian thinking is merely the flip side of the secular coin—the coin being the ways in which contemporary sexual attitudes enable objectification of people's (especially women's) bodies in the service of soothing sexual desires.

For example, Beth Felker Jones, who shares my suspicion that contemporary Christian thinking on sex is unhelpful, argues that Christians' emphasis on abstinence and sin serves as a means of commodification, that is, of making especially girls' bodies objects to be used to fulfill men's sexual desires. Felker Jones writes about an evangelical understanding of sex and marriage, which she calls the "Purity Paradigm." Purity, especially in many evangelical Protestant understandings and some Catholic understandings as well, requires that girls particularly remain "untouched," yet this leads to very troubling views of girls' bodies.

As an example, Felker Jones writes about Elizabeth Smart, the young woman who was abducted when she was 14 years old, and whose kidnapper called her his second wife and repeatedly raped her. Smart had learned particular teachings about purity and sexual virginity that led her to compare her body to a crystal vase that had been smashed. Smart wondered if anyone would any longer *want* that smashed crystal vase, and thought if that was the case, perhaps it was better after all to remain with her abductor. Felker Jones notes that this is "another tragedy on top of Smart's abduction and the violence committed against her," for "[p]eople are not crystal vases."[38] The crystal vase analogy makes it seem that Smart's body is merely an object for desire, but once ruined, is no longer capable of inducing desire among the men who might have otherwise wanted her. This analogy and others like it work within a particularly Christian understanding of sex and sexuality to promote the objectification of bodies as well as relationships. Women become commodities and men become consumers in a very individualistic way of living out the apparent freedom of sex and sexuality.

Felker Jones identifies further what the "purity paradigm" entails—a set of rules that people indirectly imbibe in many Christian churches. The rules run something like this:

1. I can expect to get married as my reward for following the rules.
2. I need to grit my teeth and work hard to avoid sexual intercourse before my wedding night (to preserve the value of the merchandise).
3. This whole thing is probably more important for girls than for boys.
4. Possessing my physical virginity makes me pure.[39]

Not only does a sexual purity paradigm support the kind of Christian marriage fetishization I discussed in Chapter 2 (since the paradigm implies that marriage must be the only solution to my sexual desires, which therefore suggests that the single life is odd and not anything to be embraced), it also suggests that states of life are mostly human endeavors that have no need of God's grace.

We might couple the way a purity paradigm helps especially women's bodies become commodified in Christian lingo together with the ways Christians frequently write about celibacy and *not* having sex. For example, prominent evangelical Christian Tim LaHaye writes that celibacy is "an idealistic and unnatural standard . . .'[40] which means marriage is the only option. Saying that a life of no sex is "unnatural" runs too easily parallel to the secular view that sex is necessary and healthy. To make sex such an imperative is to also suggest that people need to get sex by whatever means possible, regardless of which people and relationships might be damaged in the process.

That is why Christian sociologist Mark Regnerus's discussion of pornography and marriage is troubling. Regnerus finds that women, especially, are choosing not to get married to men who use pornography because they rightly see that pornification as objectifying their bodies, making the women feel like objects of lust and desire akin to the bland, two-dimensional porn queens on the screens and pages. Yet Regnerus cautions:

> The bottom line is that porn is cheap sex—meaning that it mimics real sex at no cost and no effort, and that many men will track in that direction unless prevented from doing so. And when sex becomes cheap, or alternatives are substituted (as in porn), women get put into a bind. They want to be in a relationship with men, but the men suddenly have more sexual options. Hence (many) women feel compelled to negotiate over things, like porn, that they would never have imagined in the past. But the gritty reality remains—the Church will have to learn how to navigate this and press forward with grace and truth. Men and women have to forge relationships—marriage—with each other recognizing human weakness and fostering each other's sanctification.[41]

Regnerus' controversial argument is that women ought to marry pornified men anyway, because otherwise the double bind only gets tighter for women. Porn is readily available; if pornified men are off limits, there are fewer and fewer "virtuous" men to marry, which only exacerbates men's uses of pornography, since they will want someone, or something, to fill in for those desires. Thus instead, women ought to go ahead and marry men whose sexual lives objectify women, in the hope that the two together might be able to help each other toward sexual lives filled with grace, peace, friendship and love rather than objectification.

Regnerus' and LaHaye's views are important here because these two well-known Christians expose the underbelly of default Christian thinking about sex, even as they are also stating problematic views. Their focus is that having sex is about one person (typically the man in the relationship) and one person's desires alone. Sex assuages the desires of one, without careful attention to the desires of the other person in the couple. Thus, if two people's sexual desires are going to come into play, the chief project of that relationship will be ensuring that the members of the couple help each other get what they want in terms of sex and sexuality. It sounds great: a relationship gets developed, people's needs are met, and the aim is a mutually beneficial, and blessed, sexual relationship.

Yet, all that has happened is that the word *Christian* has been added to the sexual relationship, so the pornified, objectifying culture simply gets stamped with a token of Christian approval. As we saw above with Regnerus, the token of Christian approval is marriage. Moreover, such approval really does seem to be token for many evangelicals. Robert Wuthnow, for example, demonstrates a large gap between evangelical sexual practice and thinking about that practice: 69 percent of nonmarried evangelical Christians say they have had a sexual partner within the past year.[42]

For Christians who consider themselves more progressive, however, the stamp of approval is sometimes simply to suggest that sex should be free, open to premarital couples, and consensual, and, ideally, a response to love.[43] Duncan Dormor writes,

> The Church now accepts, promotes and, broadly speaking, shares with the surrounding culture an understanding of sexuality which derives its meaning primarily from the context of interpersonal love rather than from its potential link to procreation. Perhaps inevitably, a society with such an understanding of sexuality is much less likely to be prescriptive about its boundaries. . . .[44]

In Dormor's view, the distinction between Christian sexuality and that of the surrounding culture is vanishingly small. We might add to Dormor's comments that in an age of 24/7 online sexual activity, sexual permissibility is even more an option. Christians routinely fail at curbing their own sexual desires, even Christians who tout prohibitions against premarital sex. The Roman Catholic sexual abuse scandals, the furor over theologian John Howard Yoder's sexual assaults, and the numerous reports of clergy sexual misconduct plainly demonstrate that inability.[45] Why then bother with a premarital sex prohibition? Everyone desires sex and Christians are misusing those desires.

Beth Felker Jones suggests that in the face of a Christian tradition that on one hand overly objectifies sex and marriage, and on the other hand overly dismisses it, Christians have sometimes given up discussing sex at all, to the point that sex seems unreal. Felker Jones attempts to expose the problem by using the word *food* in place of common statements Christians make about sex: "'It doesn't matter what you eat or don't eat.' 'Eating has nothing to do with your health. . . .' 'Food is a private matter.'"[46] Yet food does matter, and so does sex.

What I've tried to show so far, then, is that regardless of whether we are approaching uncommitted sexual relationships with an eye toward contemporary Christian teaching or with an eye toward a secular social view of sexual relationships, these views often leave contemporary sexual life and assumptions unquestioned. Questions raised about prostitution, pornography, and hookup culture frequently get described only within the context of those populations, without recognizing the ways that general views of secular sexual culture both help develop and draw from prostitution, pornography, and hookup culture. Christians react to secular sexual culture especially by trying to batten down the hatches, trying to prevent incursions of sexual desire until the proper moment, as though no sexual desire exists. What would it look like, instead, to consider a different narrative of sexual desire, a narrative that sees desire as capable of conversion and, moreover, capable of having a place in Christian life?

Augustine: "My One Delight Was to Love and Be Loved"

This chapter's guide, Augustine, enables us to consider desire, casual sexual relationships, and life in God, anew. Augustine was a fifth-century bishop of the church at Hippo in Northern Africa. Though he lived a millennium and a half ago, his life and spiritual struggles mirror some of the key questions and concerns of our own day—perhaps most especially his struggles with desire, sex, and love. Augustine's discussions of sexuality mirror our present predicaments in some important ways, including that Augustine had wide-ranging debates with purity paradigm proponents of his own day (the Manichee sect, of which he was a member for a decade), as well as confronted his own detaching of sexual desire from relationships that I discussed above. In what follows, I offer a biographical sketch, followed by some articulations of Augustine's theology of desire as he navigates his own versions of sexual detachment and the purity paradigm.

Augustine was prolific; many of his writings, covering a vast range of topics, are available to us via numerous translations. My brief discussion here will focus on his spiritual autobiographical *Confessions* as well the treatise that he wrote on marriage, "The Excellence of Marriage." A few other works of his will be referenced, including "On the Trinity" and his treatise "Concupiscence," which is about forming and ordering desire. It is well worth noting that much more could be said about this theologian who has been so influential on a number of theological debates in Christianity. My discussion provides only a beginning foray into what could be a much larger conversation.

Augustine's best known book, *The Confessions*, may be Western Christianity's first spiritual memoir, and it is from this book that we have many biographical details. Augustine writes this book in his early 40s, reflecting on his infancy, childhood, youth and young adulthood (and beyond). He does so partly to "confess" his own sins, and partly to confess how wonderful God is, so that the word *confession* takes on a range of meanings. Detailing remembrances of his sexual activity is not his main concern, but sex is clearly on his mind, and so is a connection between his sexual life and earthly loves, and his love of God.

Some of what we know of his life comes from this work: he is born in Thagaste in Northern Africa to a pagan father and a Christian mother. As a young student, he reads Cicero's *Hortensius*, a book that prompts him toward a lifelong journey in seeking wisdom. When he reads scripture, by contrast, his youthful self finds the words to be ugly and unrhetorical compared to Cicero's fluid elegance. Augustine leaves Christianity behind but seeks after wisdom wherever he thinks he can find it. Eventually he moves to Carthage, where he becomes fascinated with the Manichees, a sect that promoted spiritual holiness over and against the material world. Matter and physicality (and sex) are evil; spirit and asceticism are good. The Manichees represent part of Augustine's seeking of wisdom; he stayed with the Manichees for 10 years but eventually left in disgust as he realized that the leader of the sect was not interested in asking deep questions nor in having his worldview questioned. Eventually Augustine travels to Rome, and then Milan, taking posts as a professor of rhetoric. While at these posts, he studies Platonism, another direction he takes in the pursuit of wisdom. He also meets the bishop Ambrose there, a man who impresses Augustine with his ability to read silently, his rhetorical skill in preaching sermons, and his knowledge and understanding. In 387, Augustine is baptized a Christian. Eventually he becomes bishop of the church; his skill at rhetoric and argument are given in service to the church.

At Carthage, Augustine also takes up with a particular woman with whom he has a son, Adeodatus, and with whom he also has a 13-year relationship. In some important ways, this relationship does not fit with my definition of "uncommitted casual sexual relationships," especially in relation to its longevity. The woman, who is unnamed, is Augustine's partner throughout his moves from Carthage to Rome and Milan. As some scholars suggest, she would have had certain legal rights under Roman law, for she functions much as a wife would.[47] That said, there are some potential similarities to my definition of casual sexual relationships. Augustine would also have known that she would never be a marriage partner because of their class differences, so in choosing this relationship he is choosing a relationship that may mirror marriage but will not lead to lifelong vows. In addition, once Augustine's mother Monica definitively pronounces whom Augustine will marry, she sends Augustine's longtime mistress back to Namibia. The girl Augustine is to marry is not of marriageable age, however. What does Augustine do but find another mistress? He is in the relationship for fulfilling his own sexual desire, and not chiefly out of regard for the women in these relationships.

In reflecting on similar kinds of relationships in his later treatise, "The Excellence of Marriage," Augustine states: "If a man makes use of a woman for a time, until he finds someone else more suited to his wealth and social standing to take as a partner, that state of mind makes him an adulterer, not with regard to the woman he is on the lookout for but with regard to the one he is sleeping with without being married to her."[48] Augustine also describes a sex-only relationship: a couple "giving into their desires by sleeping together, and not for the purpose of having children...it is not absurd perhaps to call this a marriage, provided they maintain the arrangement until the death of one or the other of them...."[49] While he characterizes this kind of relationship as lesser than marriages that feature sex only for having children, he admits that sex need not solely be for children, and marriage can be for expressing sexual desire—provided, that is, the couple are committed to each other for life. Augustine does not believe his own relationships approximated that kind of commitment.

A Theology of Desire: Against Sexual Detachments

So then, if he believes sex is best when the relationship features commitment, where is the person to go who has no such committed relationship? Part of Augustine's answer is to make a full embrace of God by inclining even sexual desire toward God. A person's primary (and very attached) relationship must be with God, yet, as we shall see, his wrestling with casual sexual relationships has in part to do with his chagrin at being unable to "commit" to God.

Augustine is famous for several lines in *The Confessions*, including these: "Our hearts are restless until they rest in you, O Lord," and "Lord, make me chaste, but not yet." While his restlessness is not only about sex, his sexual practices represent one of the forms of restlessness he experiences throughout his conversion. He recognizes that his desire to have sex must be related to love: "What was it that delighted me? Only loving and being loved."[50] Hence he sought conversations about sex as a young boy, and later sought sexual relationships. Love is a necessary part of being human, yet love for him was equated with sex and lust, so much so that he becomes "abased by my pride and wearied by my restlessness."[51] Augustine's sex life does not lessen any of his desire for love, but instead sex becomes an insistent presence in his life, one that begins to make him feel imprisoned. He feels the desires, but the enjoyment of them becomes weighed down with a feeling of also being trapped by those desires.

It is his older self's reflections that more fully understand that his desires have become a weight because they do not lead him where he wants to be, which is in God. Augustine's youthful self does not see that the unmarried beauty of sex is "fleeting," nor does he yet understand that putting boundaries around sexual relationships might be beneficial. In young Augustine's view, sex should be free of constraints, including the constraint of marriage. After all, sex doesn't really matter; Augustine learns this from his family, who do not tame his sexual desires by finding him a wife but instead "their only concern was that I should learn to excel in rhetoric and persuasive speech."[52] As Augustine pursues his love of wisdom, however, he begins to find that sexual desire holds him back.

What Augustine knows, deeply, is that his sexual habits obscured God for him, and therefore obscure his ability to seek God's will over his own. Augustine's search to fulfill his sexual desires becomes a habit: "The law of sin is the brute force of habit."[53] He notices that despite his desire for a relationship with God, he cannot easily shake off his sexual relationships, which he believes are hindering him from God. His intellectual reflection had already come to a place of accepting that sexual activity could not be part of his life as a Christian, yet his bodily habits prevented him from taking decisive steps. He likens his experience to a person being deep in sleep: "I was thus weighed down by the pleasant burden of the world in the way one commonly is by sleep, and the thoughts with which I attempted to meditate upon you were like efforts of people who are trying to wake up, but are overpowered and immersed once more in slumberous deeps."[54] Sex is agreeable and pleasurable, just as sinking back into the delicious sleep and dreams of the early morning when a person wakes can be agreeable and pleasurable.

Thus, the closer he gets to the moment when he converts, the closer he comes to dealing with questions about sex and bodiliness, questions he has wanted to hold at arm's length. He finds himself at a crisis point, wanting to follow God but seeing that he is bound by two wills, "the old and the new, the one carnal, the other spiritual—and in their struggle tore my soul apart."[55] Augustine's view of what is carnal is not solely about sex, but his sexual life is a significant part of the conflict that takes him away from the all-encompassing love of God. For example, in *The Confessions* his wrestling is partly with his sexual desire, partly with his desire for worldly fame.[56] At one point, he evokes an image of being imprisoned by "chains" that are of his own making, part of which is his sexual lust.[57] His will conflicts with God's will, and therefore his wisdom and spiritual life cannot develop further. He is grateful that God removes both chains, eventually, for he realizes he cannot seek his life in God without also being able to devote his whole will to God.

Though Augustine sees sexual lust as the means by which he is detached from God, he is not condemning all sex. For example, while Augustine sees his own "chains" as his lust, he narrates another convert's "chains" as money, job, and status. The earlier Christian convert Victorinus. a professor of rhetoric, would have been unable to convert to Christianity, since under the emperor Julian (who ruled about 20 years before Augustine's conversion, from 361 to 363), Christians were barred from teaching as professors of rhetoric. Victorinus had to opt out of his means of livelihood rather than reject God. That said, in Augustine's view, Victorinus' chains (losing job, status, and money) are easier to deal with than his own situation, because Victorinus' chains are external, while Augustine's are of his own making and internal and therefore much more difficult to escape. Augustine's internal problem is the matter of letting God's will take over his desires, and not only sexual desires.

There is another crucial aspect of Augustine's worries about detached sex: not only is seeking a good relationship with God impossible when one's sexual desires are misplaced, seeking a good relationship with other humans is, too. Augustine describes both the misuse and the proper use of sex in marriage in terms of human relationships. In his treatise written against the Manichees (who saw evil as material, and bodies as part of evil matter), Augustine protests:

> But you are taught by your doctrine of devils to regard your parents as your enemies, because their union brought you into the bonds of flesh, and laid impure fetters even on your god. The doctrine that the production of children is an evil, directly opposes the next precept, "You shall not commit adultery;" for those who believe this doctrine, in order that their wives may not conceive, are led to commit adultery even in marriage.... Your doctrine turns marriage into an adulterous connection, and the bed-chamber into a brothel.[58]

Sex, when it is separated from human relationships, disrupts parent/child relationships as well as men's and women's relationships with each other. More than that, it prevents people from being able to turn to each other and attempt to see each other as part of God's own life. As he writes later, "the sacrament of monogamous marriage in our time is a symbol that in the future we shall all be united and subject to God in the one heavenly city."[59] Sex life can either aid or detract from that symbol, depending on how couples treat each other.

A Theology of Desire: Against Purity Paradigms

It likely seems funny to some readers to view Augustine as arguing against a contemporary purity paradigm, for he had very particular views of when sexual activity could be pursued to its best ends. Sex done rightly is for procreation, in his view, and is definitely part of being married. Yet I argue that Augustine's view is more robust and developed than either the simplistic description I just offered or the contemporary view of a purity paradigm.

To understand my central claim, it is necessary to have a sense of the Manichees, the sect I have identified as establishing a kind of purity paradigm in Augustine's own day. Much of Augustine's writing about marriage and sexuality is directed against the Manichees, a sect he describes in some detail in his *Confessions*, though he also addresses them in numerous other places. Manicheism was developed via the teachings of Mani, a third-century Persian prophet. Mani taught a dualistic view of the world: a principle of good showed congenial characteristics and existed in light, and a principle of evil existed in a material and dark realm and exhibited characteristics of evil. Manicheans' answer to the question of why evil exists was to say that darkness had touched the light; there was a primordial human who existed in the light, but evil forces created material human beings (Adam and Eve), who were part of evil. This distinction between good and evil, spirit and matter, sets up a cosmic war in which humans and all creation takes part. Human beings can, in Mani's view, participate in separating light from darkness, most especially the Elect Manichees. The Elect were ascetics, eschewing meat and marriage, avoiding sexual intercourse as well as other sins like murder, lying, and stealing, and also praying and fasting frequently. The Elect even had other members of the sect prepare their food, so as to avoid the possibility of killing anything. The emphasis was on remaining as separate as possible from the material world, and from evil.[60]

By contrast, Augustine maintains strongly that marriage is good, that sexual activity can be good, and that the material world is one that is imbued with God's grace. He states this even while he is also clear that, for him, the answer to the question of evil's presence in the world is that we humans commit evil actions from our own free will. Because we sin often, his treatise "The Excellence of Marriage" is filled with his attempts to narrate an order of good actions. At its most basic, Augustine asserts that virginity is best, marriage is second best, but both are goods.[61] Augustine here believes he provides a basic description of what Paul seems to suggest in 1 Corinthians.[62] If a couple is sexually active, that is properly done within marriage and for the purpose of having children.

Yet Augustine goes beyond these basic statements to consider more complicated questions. In his treatise, he loops out from his central points (marriage is second best and marital sex is for procreation) to consider other kinds of sexual relationships. For example, the woman who commits adultery yet "is faithful to the adulterer" is "certainly blameworthy; but if she is not even faithful to the adulterer, she is worse."[63] Adultery is not categorically all the same sin, and it is certainly not a means by which all possibility of life in God is lost. Faithfulness on the part of the woman enables her to seek God in some partial way.

Unlike the idea that broken virginity can never be recovered or repaired as cited above, Augustine has a robust view of both sin and its forgiveness. In the passage just cited above, Augustine suggests, "If then she repents of her shameful conduct, and terminates the adulterous agreement and arrangement and returns to conjugal chastity, I should be surprised if even the adulterer thinks she is unfaithful."[64] In other words, we humans can wobble back and forth, from more virtuous living to less so, but always the possibility of forgiveness and full restoration is there.

Similarly, being presumably sexually "virtuous" does not give a person freedom to exult in their apparent sin-free life, but rather requires them always to be conscious of following God's will alone. In one treatise, "Continence" (especially sexual self-control), he writes: "Those who practice some self-control, or even have marvelous control over the passions of mind and body, cannot all be said to have that continence whose value and honor we are discussing."[65] Even self-control must be rightly directed toward God. Again, this stands in contrast with a purity paradigm that sees self-control as the point and purpose of good discipleship.

By the same token, virginity is not categorically all the same virtuous life. It is possible for a virgin to be sinning more than a married woman: "not only should an obedient woman be more highly regarded than a disobedient one, but a more obedient married woman should be more highly regarded than a disobedient one."[66] He notices, also, that "what [Paul] allows as excusable is sexual intercourse that occurs because of a lack of self-control, not solely for the purpose of having children at all. Marriage does not make this happen, but it wins forgiveness for it."[67]

Augustine is quite realistic about peoples' desires for sex, to the point that he can narrate many possible ways people might fail at doing good with their sexual desires even when they are presumably doing the "right" thing. That doesn't mean he thinks practicing adultery will lead directly to friendship with God (far from it), but he knows that people might thereby find their way closer toward God anyway, and especially by God's grace. Augustine knows this fact from his own conversion as well as his work as a pastor and bishop: God is present in the midst of one's sexual desires. He concludes his treatise "Continence" by saying, "Whether we are fighting fiercely to avoid being conquered, or on occasions are even victorious with unexpected and unhoped for ease, let us give glory to him who gives us continence." God is always first, last, and the summation of Christian life.

Sexual desire is not, finally, the chief problem when it comes to seeking a relationship with God. Rather, failure to seek God's will is the chief problem. Sexual desire might be one point where failure shows, but sexual desire does not exhaust all possible failures. Obedience is, for Augustine, the more important virtue than chastity, because obedience allows for us to seek God's will: "there can be obedience to the commandments without virginity... On the other hand, virginity is possible without obedience" because a person can "show contempt for the commandments."[68] Seeking God's will ought to overtake all, and eventually will help us all—in spite of ourselves—rightly place sexual desires.

If one rightly understands sex and desire in relation to God, and receives grace from God, human relationships also become restored: "marriage and sleeping together, are necessary for friendship. The latter also contribute to the continuation of the human race, in which loving relationships are of great benefit."[69] On this point, it is important to see that Augustine's view stands in contrast to a purity paradigm that sees sex saved for marriage to the point that marriage seems to be *only* for sexual activity. While Augustine certainly emphasizes procreation as a key point of getting married and engaging in sexual activity, it is not his sole focus. Augustine's considerations of sexual desire are about *both* love of God and love of neighbor, and about rightly understanding connections between sex, love, and God.

Here I want to pause a bit from my focus on Augustine to acknowledge the work some contemporary theologians have done to describe the relationship between sexual desire and God. For example, John Paul II incorporates the idea in his *Theology of the Body*, where he describes "nuptial love" in relation to love of God and sexual desire.[70] Our sexual love, in his view, is part of what it means to be human and what it means to seek after God.

Theologian Sarah Coakley more particularly examines Augustine in her work, as she develops the importance of sexual desire for understanding God, gender questions, and sexual desire, in her recent book on the Trinity, writing: "Instead of 'God' language 'really' being about sex, sex is really about

God—the potent reminder woven into our earthly existence of the divine 'unity, alliance,' and 'commingling' that we seek."[71] If Coakley is correct, Augustine's Trinitarian language indicates something of the importance of sexual desire and how it relates to Christian life. In Coakley's reading of Augustine's *City of God*, Augustine seeks control rather than chaos, and the mysteriousness of God. Augustine's narrative of Genesis is that before the fall of humanity, people had control over their sexual desire; the fall, however, represents a loss of control, especially over genitalia.[72] In *De Trinitate*, Augustine understands that the mind is analogous to God in some mysterious way—"the mind is the image of the Trinitarian God in us..."[73] When Coakley brings together the theme of control over sexual desire with the idea of the mind as the seat of the image of God, she sees that humans therefore hope for the control—the light from darkness and order from chaos—that is properly God's.

For Coakley, loss of control (which she sees in her other interlocutor, Gregory of Nyssa, fourth-century Eastern theologian and saint) is more appropriately representative of the "ecstasy" of the Holy Spirit (and of the Trinity) than is Augustine's predilection for control. Nonetheless, she also finds, in Book 15 of *De Trinitate*, evidence of Augustine's own loss of control, in which he realizes that all his analogies about God as the mysterious Trinity do not hold. Coakley thus sums up: Gregory's and Augustine's "views on sexual relationships were in important senses *part and parcel* of their Trinitarian constructions, analogically speaking. Both these alternatives witnessed to a certain lack of symbolic adjustment between sexual desire and the desire for God; and yet both writers' systems...culminated in ecstatic moments too...."[74] The difficulty is the "disjunction between human and divine loves"[75]—the inexorable and unsolvable sense that we are not God, yet we desire God, yet we cannot get to the point of ever achieving God, especially not through our own activity.

I think Coakley is right to point out connections between God and sexual desire, but I do not think she quite has a good reading of Augustine, God, and sexual desire. For Coakley, God is manifested most in contemplative ecstasy, in which the logic of order seems to control God too much (such that Augustine's focus on control, as she sees it, does not fully show the movement of the Holy Spirit.) On my reading, however, I think Augustine's narrative about order from chaos is a direct result of his contemplative letting go of his own will. God's desire overtakes his own, such that God's order rules the day. His ecstasy at his conversion shines through, for example: "With the arrows of your charity you had pierced our hearts, and we bore your words within us like a sword penetrating us to the core."[76] He is utterly amazed at God's gracious presence in his life.

For example, God's movement in Augustine (God's grace) could not take root without Augustine's prior loss of control, especially his desire to lose control over his own will. God's order, moreover, is not like a human sense of order. While fulfilling sexual desire can also lead to a loss of control—especially rational control (for example, Augustine's concern over wet dreams and the fact that he is unable to fully control his body)—even that sexual loss of control is, for Augustine, an avenue toward God's grace. Augustine exults "with intrepidation in what your gift has achieved in me, while deploring my unfinished state, my hope is that you will bring your merciful dealings in me to perfection, until I attain that utter peace..."[77]

Put differently: Augustine is trying to narrate God's gracious action in our lives, because he himself has encountered God in a radical way that is unlike what he experiences in so much of human activity and emotion. His encounter with God is, I believe, not unlike Coakley's narrative of contemplative ecstasy. The City of God is ordered with the love and light of God; if we were to measure up to the City of God, we would find ourselves able to live our married and single lives as Augustine suggests, without any problem whatsoever. Yet we cannot. As he contemplates in the *City of God*: "we shall one day be made to participate, according to our slender capacity, in His peace, both in ourselves, and with our neighbor, and with God our chief good...."[78] Any order we find, therefore, is a means of encountering God and should be celebrated, even as we recognize that our own sense of order is not God's, and will be converted, too.

Desiring, Better

I concluded the first section by claiming that neither secular views of uncommitted relationships nor some prevalent Christian views about sex and desire enable asking, "Why sexual desire in the first place? In Augustine's view, it is quite simply obvious that fulfilling desires for physical relationships leads to the fostering of society, both because society grows via the children that are the inevitable result of some sexual activity, but also because physical expressions (whether sexual expressions or other forms of physical contact) can themselves help foster relationships. What we have to learn from people who have short-term casual sexual relationships is that being human means we need and crave physical intimacy and love and affection. Yet these are precisely the things that we are supposed be able to let go of in hookup culture, in favor of seeing the sex simply as a rational way to fulfill a physical need. Other forms of physical intimacy (kisses, hugs, handshakes, and other forms of touch) as well as emotional intimacy are almost entirely overlooked; this has done much harm to healthy understandings of what it means to be human, what it means to be single, and what it means to have a healthy sexual relationship.

Augustine's life also exposes how sexuality is so often narrated as a matter of an individual's preferences, rather than in terms of the relationship that exists between two people and—precisely because sex involves a relationship—also influences and shapes society. In other words, for all that marriage has become an empty notion in twenty-first century culture, the nonmarried states of life that involve sexual relationships ask us to reflect on what relationship means, and why we seek relationships. For Christians, I think we find that the point of lifelong vows is not, ultimately, about seeking economic security nor about securing perfect relationships in which no one is objectified—but always about love of God and neighbor.

Augustine's views of desire help us to think more carefully about our sexual practices. If the question is a general one: "Do *I* want to have sex?" the answer is probably going to be, for the vast majority of Americans, "Yes, definitely." This question is similar to the faulty question encountered in Chapter 2, however: "Do *I* want to get married?" This is sex and marriage in the abstract, which so hones and cultivates individuals' desires for marriage and sex that the answer will always be yes, of course I *want* that.

Christians, however, are about the particularities of the present relationships we have, as I suggested in my reading of Paul. We are asked what it means to respond to God, most particularly, and then to consider the needs and wants of other people in our lives. In his book *The Four Loves*, CS Lewis puts it this way: when a man states that he wants a woman, "a woman is just what he does not want. He wants a pleasure for which a woman happens to be the necessary piece of apparatus."[79] The woman, especially her body, merely becomes a tool, an object in service of the gratification of another person's desires. Thus: "sexual desire, without Eros, wants it, the thing in itself" that is the sexual act.[80] Pope Benedict XVI describes problems with *Eros* love in a similar vein when he writes, "*Eros*, reduced to pure 'sex,' has become a commodity, a mere 'thing' to be bought and sold, or rather, man himself becomes a commodity." It is difficult to look at a pornified hookup culture and not see that humans, especially women, have become commodities.

Still, as I noted in the first section, such a commodified culture happens in part because Christians themselves have perpetuated unhelpful views of sex. Sex is a commodity, too, in a conservative purity paradigm; sex becomes insignificant and nonchalant in a liberal theological stance. What Augustine teaches us is that sex is very significant, so significant that it can become unselfish, so that our own desires become surrendered to God.

It should be said that marital sex can objectify just as casual sex does. One potential way marriage could objectify people is in treating a couple as means toward an end, such as when people get married for family connections or to develop wealth. Christian tradition has recognized problems with marriage in this way. For a long time, Christian marriage has required consent of both members of the couple, even in times and places where arranged marriages were normative (for example, where parents might create a new family alliance if their children marry). To enter into marriage without freely consenting was deemed not to be part of the Christian character of marriage, the awesome sense that, as Paul has it in the letter to the Ephesians, marriage is like the relationship between Christ the Bridegroom and his Church, the bride. In more recent decades, Christians have further identified such actions as marital rape, and physical, sexual, or emotional abuse as actions that do not fit the community's best descriptions of what marriage means.[81]

Another way that married sex could objectify is in treating the couple, and the marriage, as a means toward the end of producing children. Some theologians in Christian tradition have suggested that married sex is best when it exclusively focuses on procreation. This seems to make women especially merely into vessels for childbearing, and thus objectifies women's bodies as useful only to the extent children are forthcoming. Such a view, combined with predominant ideas about women as irrational human beings not quite on par with men could, at times, make it seem that women, bodily creatures that they were, couldn't quite experience paradise and life with God in the same way as men could. Christian traditions have been guilty of this kind of objectification and have objectified women often in relation to marriage.

Therefore, while casual sex is troubling for a variety of reasons as I mentioned in the first two sections, casual sexual relationships cannot be held distinct from marriage as though one is wholly bad and the other is wholly good. Just as Augustine articulated nuances about sin and virtue with respect to adultery or living a life of holy virginity, and especially put sexual life in context of Christian living on the whole, so contemporary Christians might think more carefully about what it means to make attempts to lean toward God, even if (and really, *when*) a person is pursuing desires that aren't wholly God, because we shall all fail, even as we shall all also bear the image of God.

Pope Francis' recent suggestion of gradualness may prove a way forward, at least in terms of reorienting Christian thinking. In his 2016 apostolic exhortation on the family, the pope writes:

> Saint John Paul II proposed the so-called "law of gradualness" in the knowledge that the human being "knows, loves and accomplishes

> moral good by different stages of growth". This is not a "gradualness of law" but rather a gradualness in the prudential exercise of free acts on the part of subjects who are not in a position to understand, appreciate, or fully carry out the objective demands of the law.[82]

The way must be open for conversion from those involved in casual sexual relationships, but also conversion on the part of all Christians, for we all share in degrees of living and growing toward God. The pope writes of marriage, for example: "Gradually, 'with the grace of the Holy Spirit, [the spouses] grow in holiness through married life, also by sharing in the mystery of Christ's cross, which transforms difficulties and sufferings into an offering of love' ".[83] The gradualness is different in some respects but is still a conversion, a way of transforming human understanding of difficulty and suffering toward love. Again, this does not mean we need accept adultery (just as Augustine does not) or hookup culture, nor that we refrain from articulating arguments about what makes for God-driven sex. It does mean, however, that we do not promulgate a purity paradigm that prevents us from seeing possibilities for desire; it also means that we do not promote sexual activity as of little significance, but instead aim always to see sexual desire as part of yearning for God.

4

Perfection: Committed Relationships and John Wesley

THIS CHAPTER FOCUSES on seriously committed relationships, relationships that are aimed toward discerning whether to take marriage vows. These relationships include some of the more popularly understood committed relationships, including some forms of dating, serious cohabitation, and engagements. As I mentioned in Chapter 3, some dating and cohabiting relationships may fall more under uncommitted relationships discussed in that chapter, and some may fall more in line with the present chapter. Some readers may find it odd that "engagement" has a place in this book on singles; others may wonder why some forms of dating and cohabitation are included in a chapter on engagements.

It may seem odd, too, to discuss engagements in an age where people increasingly either postpone getting married or don't bother to be married at all, even if they are involved in a committed relationship of some kind. There are numerous reasons for an overall decrease in marriage rates, some theological and some not—but the decrease in marriage should not fool people into thinking that there is a corresponding decrease in committed relationships as such. For example, some people have remained unmarried in protest of social norms about marriage; in recent years that has particularly meant straight people protesting in favor of marriage equality for gays and lesbians. Others protest what they see as too much governmental, bureaucratic involvement in personal relationships.[1] Still others postpone getting married because they cannot afford a wedding, but want eventually to have that kind of communal recognition of their already-existing serious relationship. Given that weddings continue to be a growing industry ($55 billion in the United States in 2015)[2] and that the average cost of a wedding in the United States is $32,641 in 2015,[3] it makes some sense that people believe they cannot afford to marry due to wedding costs. Pope Francis even decries expensive weddings as putting people off of marriage in his recent letter on marriage and family.[4]

I have one key reason for putting engagements and other committed unmarried relationships in this book and bringing them together in this chapter. A significant part of what sets apart engagements, dating, and serious cohabitation is that they are not married relationships, but the people involved in these kinds of relationships are dealing with weighty questions about what marriage and family mean for them and for society (even if sometimes in protest to social norms about marriage). Just as with other states of singleness, part of what defines these relationships is that they are not married relationships, and therefore may help Christians think more carefully about states of life and what it means to be a disciple of Christ. That is, in contrast to the uncommitted relationships I discussed in the previous chapter, what ties together dating, serious cohabitation, and engagements are the ways that they ask similar questions of marriage relationships, or at least of the concept of lifetime commitments that are so much a part of our social understanding of marriage. People in all three kinds of relationships are likely to ask, "Is this someone I might spend a lifetime with?" The focus on a long-term commitment (even if no such commitment in fact exists for a particular relationship at the end of the day) stands in contrast to the kinds of relationships I discussed in the previous chapter, where I showed that uncommitted, unmarried relationships are concerned less about marriage and commitments (though that may be on the horizon for some) and more concerned simply about desire for human contact and relationship as such.

Our guide for this chapter on committed unmarried relationships—engagements, betrothals, and even dating and some forms of cohabitation—is the eighteenth-century preacher John Wesley. John Wesley is known as the cofounder of the Methodist societies, together with his brother, the great hymnwriter Charles Wesley (author of "Hark, the Herald Angels Sing"). Wesley's theology and movement influenced the development of several other Christian groups in the late eighteenth and nineteenth centuries, including Wesleyan churches, the Nazarenes, Holiness movements, some forms of Pentecostal traditions, and the Salvation Army.

John Wesley also strongly considered engagements several times before becoming married. Yet he wrote a couple of strongly worded treatises on the benefits of single life for Christians. By most accounts, Wesley's several engagements caused consternation among his family and friends who felt that the preacher should not become married or entangled in romantic relationships. They worried that romantic relationships might interfere with Wesley's single-hearted devotion to God, on the one hand, and on the other hand might not enable him to be quite the husband that society expected in married couples. Wesley himself wrestled with what it meant to be a Christian disciple and how marriage might or might not fit into a life of discipleship such as he envisioned. As we shall see below in more detail, Wesley's own example as an engaged and then married man is decidedly complex and also helpful for my discussion of engagements and other committed unmarried relationships.

Wesley's importance in this chapter also relates to a signature point in his theology: the idea of Christian perfection. Christian perfection in Wesley's terms is not the same as a typical use of the word *perfection*. Wesley's view of "perfect" does not mean that people make no mistakes, but it does mean they have a particular way of life that witnesses to Christ.

Wesley's view of Christian perfection provides a contrast to the ways perfection operates in contemporary relationships like engagements. Dating and engagements are fraught with anxiety about the state of marriage today, for no one wants their relationships to end in the messiness, pain, and trauma of divorce. Most committed unmarried relationships therefore emphasize practices aimed at preventing divorce. Yet these well-meaning practices against divorce also serve to idealize, and even idolize, marriage to such a degree that perhaps those very practices backfire. Rather than saving marriage from divorce, perhaps it is the case that our heightened anxieties about premarital relationships create an atmosphere that fosters the possibility of divorce. I use Wesley, then, to help reset our thinking about perfection with the aim of recovering premarital (and marital) relationships from over-idealization.

In what follows, I first discuss three main ways that people inhabit committed unmarried relationships: dating, engagements, and serious cohabitation. I show how contemporary Christian thought and practice about these relationships aims at a problematic ideal about marriage that backfires. To be clear: holding forth particular ideals about what Christian marriage means is good, especially if and when those ideals help us follow Christ better and enable us to love God and neighbor more. Yet ideals can also lead away from Christ, as I think is the case in much discussion of dating, cohabitation, and engagements.

After I show how marriage ideals function in relation to dating, cohabitation, and engagements, I turn to John Wesley's example, first by discussing his theology of Christian perfection and then by describing his several engagements. I conclude by drawing Wesley into conversation with twenty-first century concerns about engagements and make practical suggestions for how Christians might rethink how they do committed premarital relationships.

Committed, Unmarried Relationships in the Twenty-First Century

The Great Dating Debate...and Other Ways I Met Your Mother

Making a lifelong commitment to someone is important, a key question in deciding to date and ultimately to become engaged. Yet, so often, questions about lifelong commitments are accompanied by fear: fear that a relationship will end in divorce, fear that one will end up unmarried and alone, fear that family or friends won't understand if a person doesn't tie the knot. Yet what I will suggest in this section on dating is that these fears backfire, leaving people unable to develop good Christian relationships (romantic or not). These fears also create a perpetuating cycle: our dating fears heighten anxieties about divorce, which perpetuates idolization of marriage—which then heightens anxieties about dating and finding The One.

The central anxiety about dating is the question of whether romantic relationships are holy enough for Christian discipleship. Evangelical Christians especially have been at the forefront of writing about dating and engagement practices among Western Christians. They worry that some of the standard cultural practices that exist in pre-marriage relationships (for example, serial dating and casual sex) are impure and lead us away from God. Further, these practices actually prepare people to "practice" for their eventual divorces. That is, activities like serial dating teach us to be less than serious about our relationships, even when we are aiming at a committed relationship. Many authors have written self-help books and spiritual guides in an attempt to provide alternative ideas about finding romantic relationships.

The great dating debate began with Joshua Harris' book *I Kissed Dating Goodbye*. (It is significant, though, that Harris has recently been questioning the wisdom of his book.)[5] Harris describes several reasons why he quits dating and advocates for a patriarchal form of courtship. His concern with dating is that it is self-centered rather than God-centered. Not coincidentally, in that book he also sees self-centeredness as a key reason for divorce. Harris writes: "We see so much divorce and betrayal in our society today. Take a quick count—how many of your friends come from broken homes?...It seems that dating as we have come to know it doesn't really prepare us for marriage; instead it can be a training ground for divorce."[6] He knows from his own experience that dating involves making promises that don't get kept, and that many of his dating relationships objectify women and make him see them only as "potential girlfriends" rather than as "sisters in Christ."[7] For Harris, that meant he stopped worrying about whether and when he would get married but instead let God lead in his life. "I uncovered the incredible potential of serving God as a single."[8]

Harris' view in that book holds that dating is the result of a culture that "celebrates self-centeredness and immorality" and therefore encourages and facilitates "the sinful desires of our hearts."[9] He likens putting love-seekers in dating systems with putting recovering alcoholics in bars. Just as being in a bar might be too much of a temptation for a recovering alcoholic, the "dating system" is too much of a temptation for Christians seeking to align their sexual lives with God's love. Harris goes on to name several problems with dating: that people who date focus overly much on romance and physical feelings, mistaking them for love; that dating isolates couples from community; and that dating doesn't truly provide a good environment for seeing another person's character.[10]

Harris instead advocates for the following timeline for relationships: casual friendship, deeper friendship, courtship, which he defines as "purposeful intimacy with integrity," and engagement.[11] The friendship stages do not involve dates or expression of romantic feelings but are instead stages involving group activities that still enable people to learn more about each other. The courtship stage, in his view, ought not be entered into unless a person has studied scriptures regarding marriage, feels ready for the deep kind of commitment that marriage involves, has approval from parents, and has the peace of God about being married. Harris' view of courtship is also highly focused on patriarchal leadership: men should seek permission from women's parents to move toward courtship.

Harris' approach idealizes and perhaps idolizes marriage because of his fears about divorce and sex. Authors Donna Freitas and Jason King write in their book, *Save the Date*:

> though anti-dating advocates are willing to talk about dating [as opposed to many Christians who avoid the topic], authors like Harris root their discussions in fear. This perpetuates an association of dating with the negative things like exploitation and promiscuity. Dating is then defined as the cause of pain and hurt to others and is reduced to sex.[12]

Freitas and King worry about approaches to meeting romantic partners that presume to remove pain and suffering, for love does not guarantee a pain-free life, especially for Christians. We worship a savior whose expression of love shows most radically on the cross. Yet Harris takes a key component of marriage (its lifelong commitment) and presumes that this kind of commitment must be there in *all* pre-marriage relationships that might lead to marriage, because otherwise that relationship will end in divorce. Harris' view of commitment goes alongside his view of sexual purity as a sign of commitment.

Other authors advocate non-dating alternatives, in response to Harris, and their views, too, often have idealistic overtones aimed at avoiding pain. Jonathan Lindvall, for example, advocates "betrothal," which is a "covenant relationship that defines the process between singleness and marriage. The covenant is as irrevocable as marriage (no breaking up) but it does not authorize sexual union."[13] Lindvall's pre-marriage relationships are even more heightened toward commitment and sexual purity than those of Harris, with even more emphasis put on parental involvement for both members of the couple. Lindvall finds dating to be a sin because it is temporary, and he is explicit about the ways dating hurts: "I helped my youth group recognize that dating implies there will be an end to the romance. That means someone is almost certain to be hurt in the process."[14] Lindvall acknowledges those who think he is simply trying to avoid pain. He makes a distinction, however: he is not trying to avoid pain for himself, but to avoid inflicting pain on the other person in the couple. It is the fact that dating leads to pain for other people that makes it especially an immoral practice (and this is especially so in combination with the casual sexual culture surrounding dating).

Lindvall is correct in wanting to avoid inflicting pain on others; usually inflicting pain is not good. (There are exceptions, of course—removing splinters can be painful yet beneficial; telling a person a truth they do not want to hear can be painful yet beneficial.) It is not clear that the emotional pain of breakups is so detrimental or painful that it should be avoided at all costs. Many people who have gone through breakups describe having learned about themselves and how they want to carry themselves in relationships. Nor is it clear that Lindvall's alternative offers a necessarily better path. Betrothal represents greater control on the part of parents and the couple, which he hopes then leads to greater permanence in marriage. Yet despite each carefully controlled betrothal and carefully curated relationship, there would still be times and occasions when breakups would occur, leaving potentially an even greater emotional crisis than in dating, because betrothal is deemed so much more permanent than dating.

Harris' and Lindvall's "solutions" assume that the problem with dating is that people have a lack of commitment to the other person, which is heightened by a lack of sexual purity. Yet it is not clear that dating relationships, or the degree of commitment, are themselves the issue. Perhaps investing dating (and courtship and betrothal) with so serious a connection to marriage is one of the key issues. When every relationship must be tested in terms of whether it is of marriage quality, people once again become objects to be used toward marriage rather than people to be loved (as I discussed in Chapter 2). Anxiety about whether a person is "The One"—marriage material—does not let us see people's good character and qualities regardless of whether they are the person one might marry.

Finding "The One" is a commonplace term in popular culture, a term that connotes that One Person with whom you will share the rest of your life. Though dating is not as strictly delineated as courtship or betrothal, all three ways of meeting people reinforce the idea of the existence of "The One." As romantic comedies would have us believe, The One is the person to whom we can make a commitment, the person from whom we will definitely not get a divorce because that person is a soul mate. Courtship and betrothal simply push us toward "The One" sooner than dating would do.

Theologically, Christians should be troubled by a concept of "The One." God is the only Perfect One, the one who should rightly hold us in thrall. It is further not clear that God has "soul mates" in mind for Christians, especially given that Christian tradition privileges singleness. As I discussed in Chapter 1, it is not good for humans to be alone (Genesis 2:18), but not being alone does not necessitate marriage. I shall describe this point more in the discussion of John Wesley and his failed engagements.

Preparing for Engagements: Premarital Counseling

The serious pre-marriage stage also includes engagement, which is frequently written about in self-help books and pastoral care resources. As with dating and cohabitation, discussions about engagements emphasize the need to get it right, to be sure of the other person before proposing and entering into a permanent relationship.

For example, the book *Before You Get Engaged* by evangelical Christians David and Brent Gudgel: Brent is David's son, considering whether to get engaged himself, so when David Gudgel (a pastor and radio personality) decided to write a book on whether to get engaged, he invited Brent and Brent's possible fiancé, Danielle Fitch, to participate. David writes: "As a pastor who has done a lot of counseling, I've heard a husband or wife say... [t]hey regret having married the person they did. I think that feeling is preventable, and I believe the best time to prevent that from ever being said is before marriage. Even before engagement."[15] Gudgel's words sound commonsensical, especially for a Christian culture that so reveres marriage: of course we ought to be sure, so sure of something as important as marriage, that we determine that we should never regret having married the person we did for a whole entire life, and that the nonregrettable decision can be determined, absolutely, in the months and years before getting engaged.

Gudgel's words contain much advice about premarital counseling as well as the reasons for taking popular premarital counseling questionnaires like the FOCCUS (Facilitating Open Couple Communication, Understanding & Study, a marriage question inventory often administered to couples in premarital counseling). FOCCUS is used by mainline Christians, Roman Catholics, Orthodox, and nondenominational groups. It is not quite as self-assured of success as Gudgel is about his program. FOCCUS is an inventory that, according to its website, should not be used to "predict marital success or failure."[16] Rather, the FOCCUS questions are designed to help couples identify important questions and issues where they have some disagreement, or where perhaps they have not quite discussed the issue enough. Such issues include questions about interfaith or intercultural marriages, in-laws, money, and so on. By identifying such questions, couples are more prepared for marriage. This, in turn, results in more successful marriages, assert the researchers associated with FOCCUS.[17]

The questions FOCCUS asks, and the question Gudgel asks his readers to consider, are surely important ones. Gudgel suggests, for example, that people need to have grown up enough to have a strong identity that does not need to feel completed by others, who have a strong relationship with God. Gudgel counsels people to ask themselves, "Would I marry myself?" as part of their discernment. Alongside that question, Danielle Fitch, David's fiancé, discusses the importance of the Prince Charming myth instilled in very young girls and played out in romantic comedies on screens into adulthood, that the person a woman marries ought to be everything—handsome, a prince, the person who can rescue her and make her dreams come true. She aims to have women confront whether they're considering marrying an ideal that exists only in the imagination, or the real flesh and blood person who makes mistakes and won't, in fact, fix everything.[18] Fitch's point is well-taken, especially for an evangelical culture that is apt to proclaim, "You are a prize to be won!" to women who are waiting, waiting, waiting to be married because they believe that God has a plan for them that includes marriage and family.[19]

Another guide called *The Right One*, written by Jimmy Evans from Marriage Today, and Frank Martin from Focus on the Family, counsels people to "build a strong foundation for marriage."[20] The authors rightly worry that attention to wedding ceremonies has helped people overlook more important questions about getting married. A section in their book discusses the importance of communication, conflict resolution, and sexual purity, while also asking couples to talk about their potential future together in relation to kids, money, in-laws, faith, and other practical questions that can highlight tensions in relationships and show where a couple needs to talk and work through issues more. Similarly, Gudgel guides people to confront their relationships honestly—to ask questions that people who have been divorced wish they had asked at the beginning. Are they following their heart, are they listening to God, are they taking seriously the responses of friends and family to that relationship?

Gudgel provides a checklist for people considering popping the question and concludes the book with a discussion of how to make a good proposal. He observes, "Whatever you do, I hope you won't find yourself someday saying what this guy said when he wrote, 'I did very little to make it special or memorable. Oh how I wish I could relive that one.' "[21]

What these authors advise sounds helpful because they raise questions that people are often not equipped to ask when it comes to whether or not to be married. It is easy to confuse quick and easy romantic, erotic desires with a desire for a lifelong relationship—and it is indeed good to be careful and clear about what it means to have a lifelong relationship and how the relationship of marriage is distinctive from the starry-eyed romance that is far more familiar via mainstream media and our own expectations. To an extent, such questions are important.

At the same time, I suggest that the emphasis on sorting out likes, dislikes, and differences in approaches to life causes people to ignore another, more important aspect of marriage: whether or not a person can live with the idea that their spouse might change (and most likely will). Premarital counseling, at least as outlined by the authors and groups above, suggests too great a certainty that if you follow its methods and raise its questions, you'll have a marriage that endures for a lifetime. Yet any potential certainty about premarital questions and topics is mitigated by the fact that people can and do misunderstand questions, answer in the ways they think the other person wants to hear, or simply change their minds. What do we do then?

In addition, premarital advice tends to leave the contemporary state of engagement itself largely unquestioned. The above authors promote a particular way of idealizing marriage that is frequently not representative of good Christian theology and practice. For example, the authors mentioned above accept engagement on the terms that have been set within American culture generally—including a fancy proposal, without which no marriage would be complete. Reality television shows like TLC's *Perfect Proposal* insinuate that marriage proposals need to be well-planned surprises that especially fulfill a bride's dream. While television proposals are meant to be over-the-top, usually very public and orchestrated events, they are not out of the realm of how non-televised engagements look.[22]

Christians ought to be concerned with the idea of perfect proposals, and especially with the consumer culture that mandates such perfect proposals.

The perfect proposal goes together with the idea of a perfect preparation and a perfect decision made in terms of finding "The One." The perfect proposal is an emblem of the idea that we have certainty about the person we are marrying. Yet there is no straight line from the marriage proposal emblazoned on a scoreboard at a public stadium to preparedness for marriage.

The presumption is that if we only could get it all straight at the beginning of entering into an engagement, we'd never have cause to regret getting engaged or married. Our language about finding The One presumes we can find nearly-perfect people. Yet, seeing and seeking this kind of perfection misplaces a good Christian understanding of what it means to be perfect. In classic Christian theology, God alone measures up to perfection. As we saw in the section on dating, God alone is The One. Humans cannot hope to measure up, yet it is precisely in misshapen communities of mere human beings that God chooses to meet us. That is the case even in dating, cohabitation, and engagements.

Yet, where in these handbooks is God present, and is God's own self-revelation of perfection put forward as the ideal? Where, in these handbooks, is a recognition of the broader community in which God meets us? It happens far less often than I would hope. In Gudgel's book, for example, family and friends matter, a little, but are relegated to the last main chapter on discernment (Chapter 12). While God is mentioned, of course, throughout the book, and while God even gets His very own chapter (Chapter 11), the central focus is on each member of the couple discerning, largely individually, whether or not to get married. Similarly, much of Evans and Martin's book speaks about God but focuses much more on the couple and those two people's practical questions related to marriage.

In the contemporary period, leaving engagement unquestioned is also leaving unquestioned the presumption that we can achieve perfection ourselves. We can find The One on our own, the person of our dreams, the person to marry. Moreover, they and we can be perfect, and we can know that relatively early on in a relationship, before marriage happens. The irony of this presumption is that for Christians, marriage is meant to be a lifelong event. There is no reason to presume that people are perfect at the beginning of their relationships, that people won't change over time, that we won't have regrets even if we have seriously considered whether to be married, as Gudgel hopes we will.

Serious Cohabitation, Society, and Theology

Serious cohabitation is one of the kinds of relationships that worried Joshua Harris, because it seems exactly to be a relationship that involves neither purity nor longevity and so doesn't take seriously the worth of either member of the couple. Cohabitation not only seems not to take marriage seriously, but seems to advocate people coupling up without taking the so-called traditional route of marriage. Harris wasn't wrong to be worried about cohabitation's attraction: more and more people are cohabitating before marriage than ever before. Forty-eight percent of women cohabit, according to a Center for Disease Control survey of women's cohabitation practices done between 2006 and 2010, as compared to 42 percent in 2002 and 34 percent in 1995.[23] Seventy-four percent of 30-year-old women in the 2006–2010 cohort reported that they had cohabited at least once before their thirties, for a period of about 22 months on average. Cohabitation might lead to marriage after a period of cohabitation (40 percent) or simply a longer continuation of the relationship (32 percent), or the relationship ending (27 percent). White women and foreign-born Hispanic women with more education and more income were more likely to be in cohabiting relationships leading to marriage. About one in five women experiences a pregnancy in the first year of cohabitation.[24] The Center for Disease Control concludes its report by naming cohabitation as one main way—and an increasingly common way—that people prepare for marriage and experience long-term relationships and have their children. One *New York Times* article summed up some research by the National Marriage Project in this way:

> [N]early half of 20-somethings agreed with the statement, 'You would only marry someone if he or she agreed to live together with you first, so that you could find out whether you really get along.' About two-thirds said they believed that moving in together before marriage was a good way to avoid divorce.[25]

Cohabitation does often intend to test out what it might mean to be married, in part because couples want to avoid divorce and hope that living together before marriage might mitigate against possible divorce.

So there's a rise in cohabitation, and that rise is linked, for many people, to questions about marriage. Should that rise worry Christians, and if so, why? Some authors are worried because they see that cohabitation springs from an individualistic culture and thus prevents people from loving God and neighbor well. As those are Jesus' Great Commandments for Christians, that should be cause for worry if such a concern exists. One author, Jeff VanGoethem, writes: "cohabitation springs out of the individualism of American culture. And singleness reflects the true character of cohabiting couples—they typically do not have a joint bank account, they don't buy property together, they don't list one another as beneficiaries on insurance policies, and so forth."[26]

VanGoethem sees that cohabitation therefore lacks the virtues of permanence, loyalty, and ultimately concern for others that marriage represents.

For many Christian commenters, a key trait that enables selfless love is commitment, and cohabitation decidedly does not promote commitment. Mike and Harriet McManus observe: "Cohabitation is conditional. Marriage is based on permanence. These are radically different psychological premises for a relationship. True love is selfless. Cohabitation is based on selfishness: How will this relationship satisfy me?"[27] The McManuses go on to describe some of the negative impact of cohabiting: greater risk of violence, educational and economic disadvantages for children in cohabiting households, and higher risk of divorce if a couple does get married eventually.[28]

Commenters on cohabitation presume that cohabiters are unaware of the concern about marriage. Yet as it happens, cohabiters themselves are worried about some of the same problems in marriage as Christian theologians and commenters. Whether or not such testing works depends on the studies a person reads. Some recent research on cohabitation suggests that the anxiety associated with needing to test another person's fit is less about the commitment to get married and more about a fear that the marriage will crumple.[29] Measuring the effects of cohabitation is confusing, in part because there are a range of reasons why cohabitation might fail and why marriage might end in divorce. Some recent research suggests that cohabitation doesn't actually impact a marriage's eventual divorce as much as factors like the age of the members of the couple or having unplanned-for children. That is, regardless of whether a couple marries or cohabits at the age of 20, there is a greater likelihood of divorce and breakup than at another, later age.[30] Yet another study suggests that when cohabitation is used to "test" a relationship for marriage, that kind of cohabitation led to higher levels of depression and anxiety.[31]

The crucial point is that anti- and pro-cohabiters both have similar concerns about marriage and similar anxieties. Christians' own anxieties, masquerading as ideals about marriage as well as their anxieties about preventing divorce, simply reinforce messages that cohabiters already know for themselves. Cohabiters, however, see the solution to anxiety *as* cohabitation, while anti-cohabiters see the solution as promoting marriage by making cohabitation an enemy of a good marriage. These are two approaches to the same problem: anxiety.

The current ways most Christians practice dating, engagements, betrothals, courtships, or any other of an array of pre-marriage committed relationships offers no clear or helpful alternative to the primary fear about divorce. Christians simply seem to be reiterating what surrounding culture already does when it comes to premarital relationships, but in a different key (and often without sex).

Here, as with engagements and dating, theological discussion has dropped out of the picture in favor of assuming an ideal of marriage that strongly emphasizes anxiety about whether that marriage will last, since the ideal marriage is one that is permanent and lifelong. It is more theologically interesting to wonder what it would take, instead, for Christians to follow Jesus' commandment not to be anxious about anything. [32] What would it look like to practice premarital counseling in a way that was truthful about the fact that we cannot know anything, including our relationships, with certainty? What would it look like, instead, for Christians to address the more central concern that arises again and again: fear, and especially fear of failed relationships? I will return to this question at the end of the chapter. First, let us take a closer look at John Wesley, a man with much to say about Christian perfection and also a man with three failed engagements of his own.

John Wesley, Preacher

Wesley's wrestling with what it means to be a Christian is integral to his understanding and experience of preparing for and entering into Christian marriage. In this section, I first discuss Wesley's theology of Christian discipleship especially as he discusses Christian perfection.[33] Then I describe Wesley's pattern of engagements, with a focus on his own wrestling with whether becoming engaged to be married is a good action. The questions that Wesley helps us raise will also help guide us as we look at contemporary practices of being in committed unmarried relationships.

Wesley's Intense Christianity

Many have been charmed and compelled by John Wesley's particular vision of Christian life, and especially by the example that Wesley himself provided for his followers. John Wesley was the son of a clergyman and had a strong fervor for Christian life from his youth. This is perhaps partly because at the age of five, he was rescued from a rectory fire, "the brand plucked from burning" as his mother Susanna put it. During his education at Oxford, Wesley joined a group of likeminded Christians who were interested in religious discipline. Scholar Thomas Langford observes: "The members of this small, covenantal community supported, criticized, and encouraged one another in spiritual growth."[34] While at Oxford, Wesley became a clergyman, and following his studies accepted a post as a missionary in Georgia (the first time he considered becoming engaged). As a missionary, Wesley encountered Christians in the Pietist (Moravian) tradition, Christians who were convinced of their salvation; Wesley's encounter with them left him wondering if he were too focused on doing good works and on religious rigor. When Wesley returned to London, he sought out the Moravians and attended some of their meetings. In a famous passage from his journal where he writes about one such meeting, Wesley records: "... I felt my heart strangely warmed. I felt I did trust in Christ, Christ alone for my salvation; and an assurance was given me that He had taken away *my* sin, even *mine*, and saved me from the law of sin and death."[35] His "conversion"[36] led to changes in his life; in particular, Wesley started traveling the countryside, preaching wherever he could. He was joined by others, such as his brother Charles Wesley, and George Whitefield. Wherever he went, he found people convinced by his preaching and example, who were also experiencing conversions. Wesley therefore helped establish societies and classes of his followers and gave them rules of conduct. Some of these rules of conduct included attending very early morning prayer meetings, observing the Sabbath, and prohibition of card games, dancing, and leisurely pastimes.

Wesley's particular charism for Methodists is his understanding of grace. God offers us grace before we even know that grace is there (prevenient grace); God gives us the grace to establish and restore our relationships with God and each other (justifying grace); God continuously offers grace throughout our Christian lives (sanctifying grace). For Wesley, Christian life needs to be cultivated throughout a lifetime. As scholar Randy Maddox notes, "salvation appears neither unilaterally nor spontaneously in our lives; it must be progressively empowered and responsibly nurtured along the Way of Salvation."[37] That Way of Salvation is especially nurtured through what Wesley called "means of grace": things familiar to nearly every Christian such as prayer, fasting, and Eucharist or holy communion, but also things particular to the people who listened to him, who came to be called Methodist—such as small group meetings (named classes, bands, or societies) and love feasts. Through these means of grace, people developed holy lives dedicated toward love of God.

Christian Perfection

By living the Way of Salvation, Wesley believed that Christians could attain perfection in this life. Christian perfection, for him, means "loving God with all the heart, so that every evil temper is destroyed, and every thought and word and work springs from and is conducted to that end by the pure love of God and our neighbor."[38] If our lives and work and relationships enable greater love, so much the better. Wesley meant all relationships here, not only relationships centered on the kind of love encountered in marriage and family.

Wesley's view that Christians could reach perfection (through God's grace) was controversial, not only for outsiders to his movement but also for preachers within the movement. His dedication to the idea in his sermons underscores how important he found the interplay of God's grace in our lives together with living a life of holiness that made consistent use of the means of grace. In Sermon 35, Wesley preached on Paul's letter to the Philippians 3:12: "Not as though I had already attained, either were already perfect." Wesley observes that "there is scarce any expression in holy writ, which has given more offence than this." Christian perfection is possible—and that realization should galvanize us Christians toward living a life devoted to God.

For Wesley, perfection does not mean absolute perfection, the kind of perfection we might find in God. In Sermon 35, Wesley endeavored to say how Christians were, and also were not, perfect. They were not perfect in knowledge nor free of making mistakes. They may make incorrect judgments: "Hence they may believe either past or present actions which were or are evil, to be good; and such as were or are good, to be evil."[39] Christians who have Christian perfection are not free of experiencing temptations or of misinterpreting scripture. Yet, Wesley believes that Christian perfection consists in being free from outward sin. Wesley does not see sin as included in the kinds of mistakes and temptations mentioned above; sin is willful and habitual. Wesley makes his statement on Christian perfection in order to exhort his listeners: be doers of the Gospel!

That sense of urgent action comes forth in many of Wesley's sermons. For example, in his sermon "The Almost Christian" he first names characteristics of an almost Christian: an almost Christian believes in truth, in justice, in loving each other by feeding the hungry and clothing the naked, and in having a form of godliness. Wesley imagines his hearers are then asking, "Aren't these the characteristics of a Christian, full stop?" He imagines that some of his listeners cannot even claim to be almost-Christians. But Wesley continues on to emphasize that being "altogether a Christian" means love of God, and love of neighbor, with no limitations. Wesley draws from Paul's Second Letter to the Corinthians to name characteristics of love: that it does not envy, or boast, that it suffers all kinds of wrongs. In other words, the almost-Christian's love of neighbor via feeding the hungry or clothing the naked has the danger of coming from a place of self-aggrandizement, a place where they get to be the doers. But Wesley is pushing his followers to consider how they respond in love when their actions are not showcased as "good," when they get no personal benefit from their loving action. Nearly everyone sees feeding the hungry as a good thing to do, but that is only "almost" Christian behavior. What about loving one's enemies? What about the ways in which we take offense (or not)? Those less well seen or respected actions display more whether a Christian is "altogether" a Christian.

John Wesley's beliefs about God, and his theology, are therefore inherently practical. Another scholar, Thomas Langford, observes that for Wesley, "theology was not so much for the purpose of understanding life as for changing life; theology should help effect love of God and neighbor."[40] For Wesley, our whole lives are theological. We are always saying something about God in what we do, and we are especially saying something about God in the ways we live relationships.

Wesley's Engagements

What, then, might John Wesley be saying about God when it comes to being engaged and to loving neighbor in this particular way?

Wesley himself is extremely ambivalent about being engaged and getting married. Wesley's ambivalence shows clearly in his first consideration of engagement to Sophey Hopkey. On a missionary trip to America in 1736, Wesley met and fell in love with Sophey Hopkey, niece of the chief magistrate in Savannah, Georgia. In his writing, Wesley appears quite romantically taken with Hopkey, and yet at the same time hesitant about how his affections for Hopkey affect his service to God. Wesley writes: "I looked upon her, and should have said too much, had we had a moment longer. But in the instant, Mrs. Causton [Sophey's aunt] called us in. So I was once more 'snatched as a brand out of the fire.' "[41] The term 'snatched out of the fire' is significant for Wesley in comparing being saved from burning to death in the fire of his childhood home to being apparently saved from romantic entanglements. Being "snatched as a brand out of the fire" seems to imply that romantic entanglements might lead to death, or at least the death of his own ministry. He wrote many other times in his journals from the period that he thought it was better for him to live a celibate life. Even as he found himself increasingly in Sophey's presence, he continued to maintain his ideal of singleness. Sophey, however, did not. When Wesley informed her that he was dedicated to remaining single she became angry; Wesley himself continued to spend time with her and found himself wavering on whether to marry her. She forced the decision by becoming engaged to another man. Wesley was anguished by the fact that Sophey had married another, yet could not bring himself to propose.[42] He was resolute about the benefit of singleness for himself.

Wesley took his thinking about Paul's words further than Paul himself ever did, a fact that led to much consternation among his group of Methodists. After he returned to England, he wrote a 1743 manuscript for his followers called *Thoughts on Marriage and a Single Life*. Wesley "argued that every believer is given the gift of continence at the time of his or her conversion!"[43] For him, this was " 'a counsel of the Gospel' for the spiritual elite,"[44] but not a command for all. Still, "anyone who married was therefore throwing away the gift of God" that had been received via conversion.[45]

In 1748, at a regular conference of Wesley and his preachers, some preachers objected to Wesley's advice, insisting that "a Believer might marry, without suffering Loss in his Soul."[46] John Wesley seems to have developed his thoughts following that conference, and in 1764 (as a married man) wrote "Thoughts on a Single Life." In that essay, he still believes that people receive the gift of continence when they experience conversion, but "with most it does not continue long."[47] As often as possible (and even four days after deciding he himself should get married), Wesley writes: "I met the single men, and showed them on how many accounts it was good for those who had received that gift from God to remain 'single for the kingdom of heaven's sake'; unless where a particular case might be an exception to the general rule."[48] Wesley's admonitions to his followers not to get married are stronger than Paul's advice, for he approaches marriage with a much starker dichotomy between being married and remaining unmarried than Paul does.

Part of the reason for his expressed preference toward celibacy is that he believes getting married displaces communion with God. In 1746, he wrote the following poem: "I have no sharer of my heart/To rob my Saviour of a part/ And desecrate the whole; /Only betrothed to Christ am I/And wait his coming from the sky/To wed my happy soul."[49] A single person not only could devote life to God, but could be married to God in greater bliss than any human relationship could entail.

Events other than the 1748 conference influenced Wesley's thinking. In fall 1748 through the spring of 1749, Wesley entertained a second, more notorious engagement to Grace Murray, with whom he actually entered into an understanding of engagement. He writes: "St. Paul slowly and gradually awakened me out of my Mystic dream; and convinced me, 'The bed is undefiled, and no necessary Hindrance to the Highest Perfection."[50] Moreover, Wesley started to wonder whether marriage could be beneficial to God's service. Was it possible to marry someone whose own life was so full of the Gospel as well, that to marry might "exceedingly further me in the Word of the Gospel...."[51]

Wesley felt that he had found such a person in Grace Murray. Murray was his housekeeper who had nursed him to health when he fell ill in August

1748. Wesley thought she could help him in his own vocation; further, Wesley saw marriage as a way to provide himself with "a companion and nurse and a bulwark against emotional females and scandal."[52]

In the journal that also describes his romantic relationship with Grace Murray, his ambivalence still shows as he discusses how his views on celibacy developed.[53] Wesley describes how, as young as "six or seven" he considered he would never marry because he would be unable to find a woman as good as the one his father had found.[54] As a young adult, he read early Church fathers and meditated on Paul's first letter to the Corinthians, he became convinced that "Marriage was the less perfect state..."[55] because of its power to distract from service to the Lord. It was, in fact, with that sense that John Wesley might be distracted from his service to God, as well as a sense that Grace (as John's former housekeeper) was not worthy of the match, that his brother Charles prevented the marriage.

That is, the marriage to Murray was not to be. While in conversation with Wesley, Murray also had a romantic entanglement with a Methodist preacher, John Bennet, with whom she also entered into an agreement. While she initially determined to break off the agreement and marry John Wesley, Wesley's brother Charles intervened. He compelled Murray to marry John Bennet, and presented his brother with a fait accompli: Murray would not become John Wesley's wife, because she was already Bennet's wife.[56] Wesley states in his journal that he was not angry with Charles; still, he was upset by the loss of the relationship to Grace and did appear still rather angry with Charles.

The third instance of engagement was also to a woman who nursed Wesley back to health following an ankle injury: Molly Vazeille. When he finally decided to marry Molly Vazeille in 1751, he wrote, "For many years I remained single, because I believed I could be more useful in a single than in a married state. And I praise God who enabled me to do so. I now as fully believe that in my present circumstances I might be more useful in a married state."[57] Wesley stated that marriage, in fact, had not changed his sense, his fervor, nor the physical fact of his vocation: "I cannot understand how a Methodist preacher can answer it to God to preach one sermon or travel one day less in a married than in a single state. In this respect surely 'it remaineth that they who have wives be as though they had none. '"[58] Marriage is simply incorporated into the entire life of a Christian disciple.

As with his other romantic entanglements, Wesley continues to display ambivalence. Just prior to his engagement and subsequent marriage to Molly Vazeille, he preached a sermon (February 4, 1751) to some unmarried ministers in the Methodist movement, discussing the importance of this gift of singleness. On February 10, 1751, he resigned from the Holy Club at Oxford, a group of friends of Wesley's since his student days at Oxford, who had all promised to be "eunuchs" for the Kingdom of God. That same day, he slipped on the road while returning home from the club, and was taken to Molly Vazille's house to recover.[59] He praises and emphasizes celibacy, while also directing himself toward marriage.

The crucial question for Wesley was about being a Christian disciple while married. Could Christian perfection still be had? It is important that in the first letter Wesley wrote to his wife, he emphasizes the need for her to be a disciple: "Do not you forget the poor? Have you visited the prison? My dear, be not angry that I put you upon so much work. I want you to crowd all your life with the work of faith and the labour of love. How can we ever do enough for him that has done and suffered so much for us? Are not you willing to suffer also for him?"[60]

Wesley's marriage turned sour and ultimately failed, by both eighteenth century standards as well as our own standards today. Wesley did not seek divorce, but he and Molly lived apart for most of their marriage. The marriage itself was far less than perfect, though still Wesley continued to see that Christian perfection is possible in this life. Historian Kenneth Collins suggests Wesley was simply too enamored of the rigors and valor of a celibate life. Collins writes:

> Thus, his celebration of virginity, which perhaps was amplified by his reading of the early church fathers, the tension which he felt between affection for women and the love of God, and his reluctance to allow the mundane concerns of his spouse in any way to interfere with the higher work of his vocation, all suggest a seriousness and a diligence which should have been left to prosper in a celibate state.[61]

The failure of marriage came because Wesley was already "married to the Lord" and had been for some time—at least that was Wesley's spiritual discussion. Wesley also did not seem able to foster excellent relationships with women; he appears to have been too willing to be involved in his female parishioners' lives, while also being too demanding (in terms of discipleship) in his wife's life. He could not readily or easily include domestic concerns into his life, however much his wife was purported to be a generous, kind-hearted, and willing disciple, nor however much he himself had finally arrived at the end of his wrestlings to conclude that he could, indeed, get married.

In addition, Wesley attracted quite a bit of attention from both male and female followers, but perhaps especially from women. He continued to carry on correspondence with women even after he married, a fact that angered his new wife, who rightfully thought he ought to cease from furthering relationships that had a borderline romantic aspect to them. Yet as one scholar notes, "Wesley was often at his best in these relationships: guiding the souls of his correspondents, urging them on to perfection, advising the more intelligent on their reading, and producing some of the simplest and most direct of his descriptions of essential Christianity. . . ."[62]

To conclude this section, what might be said about Wesley, Christian perfection, and his engagements? Though I think there are definitely some points we do not need to learn from Wesley about being engaged (for example, let us find better and more honest ways of telling people we love them but are conflicted) there are two main points Wesley has to offer to our twenty-first century situations.

One crucial point is that Wesley consistently directs our gaze away from any particular idealized concept of marriage, because *the* ideal for Christians is God. No concept of The One, nor the perfect proposal (or dress or wedding), nor even the perfect lifelong marriage should overtake contemplation of God, the Beloved. In focusing attention on the problems of imperfection that exist, precisely because we are human we are unable to enter into the kind of Christian perfection that Wesley espouses.

This leads to the second point: Christian perfection means "loving God with all the heart, so that every evil temper is destroyed, and every thought and word and work springs from and is conducted to that end by the pure love of God and our neighbor." Wesley's conviction about this Christian perfection meant he was extremely ambivalent about marriage. Could he love God and neighbor well if he married? Could he continue on the spiritual journey toward God that he embraced each day of his life? That is a question that helps direct engagement toward God, for it leads to other practical questions: Will getting married help me love God and neighbor more? Can I learn to love my spouse as my neighbor, despite all of my imperfections (and the ones I perceive of my spouse)?

Engaging Better . . .

The implications of Wesley's theology, and the theological concerns I have raised about committed unmarried relationships, ought to change some of the ways Christians think about and practice dating and engagements. While we may have good reason to fear divorce and seek to avoid relationship failures, the kind of perfection assumed and espoused in dating and premarital relationships is theologically troubling. God is our One, and we, however much we aspire to be perfected in our love of God, are merely human. John Wesley's theology of Christian perfection enables seeking perfection in God while at the same time acknowledging human mistakes and problems. Wesley's vision is helpful for a generation that sees choosing marriage as fraught with anxieties.

Fortunately, Christian tradition has offered some less well known alternatives to some of the more popular dating and premarital counseling thoughts I described above. First, I suggest we might consider more carefully Lauren Winner's suggestion to practice countercultural dating.[63] Countercultural dating is one way of practicing dating that enables us to love God and neighbor in better ways. That's because countercultural dating is communal dating. Communal dating does not mean some version of Harris' "friendship" stages; Winner thinks people ought to go out on one-to-one romantic dates. Rather, Winner thinks that couples, married or not, ought to be spending much more time with single people, and vice versa. We should not be forming enclaves of people with like situations, for that does not help us foster love of neighbor. In the context of developing a broad range of relationships, a person's romantic relationships can be supported and affirmed—or, as the case may be, friends can critique the romantic partner who shows some alarming, potentially abusive characteristics.

In response to Harris' concern that dating doesn't help us love others because it is a hurtful form of casual relationships, Donna Freitas and Jason King suggest that on the contrary, learning to have loving relationships means being in a variety of relationships. They write: "[d]ating helps us to understand we are relational creatures and that through relationships we learn what it means to love another person in a one-on-one relationship."[64]

Second, Christians have had betrothal rituals that have more theological richness for Christian formation than the current ways Christians conduct premarital counseling and related conversations. Adrian Thatcher argues that "[t]he loss of betrothal is very much more serious than the disappearance into disuse of a pointless rite. The sense of the betrothal period as a spiritually rich and theologically educative phase of a couple's life has been lost."[65]

Thatcher raises an important argument, quite aside from the question of premarital sex. In my view, all the premarital counseling one pastor does can't quite approximate a prayer ritual that the church community prays. For example, Greek Orthodox liturgy publicly and communally observes betrothals, which typically takes place after the Sunday liturgy and is the point where the couple make vows to each other. (In Orthodox liturgies, the couple does not make vows at the celebration of the sacrament of marriage; in that rite, the liturgy emphasizes the eschatological character of marriage—the fact that the man and woman being united in marriage are analogous to the marriage between Christ and the Church). The betrothal ritual includes prayers of the community, prayers that aren't even specific to the couple.

Only after the priest has requested prayers for the particular local church community and for the bishops and clergy of the region does he then offer a prayer for the couple: "For the Servant of God (name) and the for the Servant of God (name) who now pledge themselves to one another, and for their salvation, let us pray to the Lord."[66] There follow prayers for the character of the marriage, for children, for peaceful love, for oneness of the couple, for their faith and harmony and that their lives be "blameless." Then, the prayers conclude with more general prayers for the congregation as a whole: "That we may be delivered from all tribulation, wrath, danger, and necessity...."[67] The very structure of the prayers set up a context for this couple: they are within the church, they are nestled within the community, which surrounds this couple, and the community itself is held by God.

The Orthodox rite continues with the exchange of rings in the name of the Trinity. Then the priest recalls the scriptures where pledges were made (Isaac and Rebecca), and rings were given (Daniel, Joseph, the prodigal son). The rings signify the presence of God, might and truth. Thus the couple getting engaged is brought into the great story of scripture—their pledges and their rings are part of the whole story of God, whose people have also on significant occasions made pledges and given rings.

There is a strong contrast between the kinds of perfections contemporary Christians presume in romantic relationships and the words of prayer described here. As the representative of the church, the pastor offering premarital counseling asks the questions. The church community itself often won't see the couple or be involved in the engagement process unless or until the community is present at the wedding. Sometimes this singular emphasis on the voice of the pastor speaking perfection is mitigated by older married couples' mentoring of newly engaged couples. I think this practice could be developed toward a better view of marriage, as well. Yet premarital counseling is the main way that Christian churches in the West have operated in recent decades concerning marriage. The relative lack of involvement in the engagement wasn't always the case: beginning in the medieval period, Western churches published banns to "inform the community about the impending marriage, so anyone could come forward if he or she knew of some reason (such as a prior marriage) that the wedding should not take place."[68]

By contrast, betrothal service is an offering of prayer, both from the couple and from the community. The prayer requests presume that the couple is not perfect, that the two people may be entering the marriage for reasons that are less than perfectly discerned. The emphasis is, instead, on presuming that God's activity will make the marriage what God has promised marriage is: a relationship in which we see, at least partially, the reality of God's love and unity. The betrothing couple thus enables the community to consider its own stories about perfection and imperfection.

5

Friendship: Same-Sex Attracted, Single, and Aelred of Rievaulx

I DOUBT THERE'S a more contentious state of singleness than being same-sex attracted and single. As part of that contentiousness, I will note here that I am aware of the contentiousness of labels: gay, lesbian, homosexual, same-sex attracted, LGBTQ+, transgender, intersex, asexual, and so on. For my purposes in this chapter, I will use "same-sex attracted" much of the time, though will also use gay, lesbian, bisexual, and sometimes LGBTQ as the occasion warrants. I recognize that transgender, intersex, and asexuality often bring different questions to bear with respect to singleness than questions about same-sex attraction, because attraction to people of the same sex is not often the central point. Undoubtedly there are theological questions to discuss in relation to transgender, intersex, and asexuality, but those questions are beyond the scope of this book. This book will focus on same-sex attraction because one of the key Christian debates related to singleness and marriage is stated something like this: can same-sex attracted people be involved in romantic, sexual relationships, or must they remain single and celibate?

For the purposes of this chapter, what I mean by same-sex attractedness is that a person's sexual desire for another person of the same sex is part of a person's identity. I am not referring to any particular kinds of sexual acts. In other words, I am assuming here that same-sex attraction is not a *choice* a person makes about sexuality. This goes along with the teachings that exist in many (though not all) Christian communities, including my own Roman Catholic tradition, though I also know that public teaching does not necessarily correspond with how people are treated.[1] Same-sex attraction is *a* part of a person's created being.

Gay and lesbian single Christians find themselves in a unique space. The force of recent Christian conversations about homosexuality has been undertaken in relation to marriage (or civil unions or covenant partnerships, depending on who is writing). The force of much Christian activism relating to LGBT issues has also been directed toward marriage—whether that is among progressive Christians advocating same-sex marriage or conservative Christians advocating heterosexual marriage for a "transformed" person.

Here are some of the questions and reflections Christians consider in relation to marriage and same sex-attraction.[2] Many Christian churches have affirmed that being attracted to people of the same sex is not a choice that someone can make, because sexuality is part of a person's God-given body. Yet simultaneously, some of the same churches have said that gays and lesbians cannot make a choice (at least in that particular Christian context) to be married or experience a lifelong partnership that is blessed by other Christians. This is puzzling—how can one affirm no choice on the one hand yet deny choice for a Christian-blessed married relationship that enables not only sexual activity but also lifelong fidelity, an acknowledgement of love, and more? Moreover, while many churches decry bigotry and violence against gays and lesbians, and find that sexual orientation is no choice a person makes (speaking here from my vantage point as a Roman Catholic theologian), those churches are often themselves places where such bigotry happens, including loss of church-related jobs, hateful speech. There is also the argument that Christian teachings about marriage are bigoted precisely because they deny the sacrament of marriage to a same-sex couple. There are Christians that have taken a decisive stance in favor of supporting same-sex marriage, but the tensions and questions remain.[3]

For the obvious reason that this book is about singleness and not marriage, in this chapter I am not participating in the arguments about same-sex marriage, though as I will show, some of those arguments affect how we might understand what it means to be gay and single. (Moreover, there are numerous very well-done books about same-sex marriage from a variety of perspectives, presenting several terrifically articulated arguments that provide much good thinking and insight. See a list here.[4]) For my purposes in this book, I want to emphasize that it is important to think about how being same-sex attracted and single contributes to Christian life.

My overall argument in this chapter is that being Christian, gay, lesbian, or bisexual, and single, comprises a state of life that has something important to say to other Christians about love and God and neighbor. Moreover, the presence of gay and lesbian Christians among us ought to call all of us, as the Body of Christ, to be radically better witnesses of that love. We need each other, and Christianity needs the witness of same-sex attracted, single, Christians.

There are several people serving as guides for this chapter. This is in large part because Christian tradition has not long dealt with what it means to be same-sex attracted and single, at least not in a concerted, public way. My central guide is a medieval monk, Aelred of Rievaulx (in York, England). Aelred wrote a couple of popular works in his own day that dealt with "spiritual friendship." I think it is anachronistic to name Aelred as a gay man from our twenty-first century vantage point; other scholars have felt much more freely to state that they believe Aelred was gay. For my purposes here, I am far less interested in identifying Aelred's sexuality, if that even could be done, and far more interested in exploring the impact that Aelred's writing has had on contemporary gay, lesbian, and bisexual Christians.

The other guides for this chapter come mostly from a small group of people who are trying to develop Aelred's "spiritual friendship" as a particular gift of gays and lesbians for the church.[5] Spiritual friendship speaks to us about what it means to be a disciple of Christ and enables thinking about erotic love more expansively. Some of Aelred's more contemporary commenters include Eve Tushnet, Wesley Hill, and Elizabeth Stuart. I know these are provocative choices for guides. Tushnet and Hill, among others, have made dedicated statements about being Christian and choosing to live a celibate way of life *because* of their Christian faith. As same-sex attracted people, they have taken a stand in favor of most churches' teachings about marriage as between a man and a woman, which has put them in the center of furious same-sex marriage debates.

On one hand, they stand with "traditional marriage" and with those Christians who are often tempted to trot out Hill and Tushnet (among others) as shining examples of what it means to be a good homosexual person. However, these same traditional Christians often overlook some of the points Hill and Tushnet make against traditional Christianity's bigotry and hatred of LGBTQ people. Hill's and Tushnet's stances also put them in some conflict with LGBT activists and so-called progressive Christians, who find traditional Christian stances on sexuality to be repressive. Some have even expressed dismay that Hill and Tushnet might hate themselves so much that they would speak in favor of celibacy.

Elizabeth Stuart stands somewhat in contrast to Hill and Tushnet. She makes a different argument using Aelred. She, too, speaks to spiritual friendship but does not see celibacy as a *necessary* aspect of spiritual friendship. Stuart attempts to bypass the question of same-sex attracted marriage by putting forth friendship as an alternative. Still, while Stuart does not hold to the view that same-sex attracted people must be celibate, her argument is unsatisfactory for both traditionalists and progressives in debates about same-sex marriage.

I worry that in the midst of the debating about marriage, and the central place that marriage (gay and straight) takes in public discussions, people are apt to miss the beautiful and deep discussions of love and friendship offered by Aelred and his commentators. Spiritual friendship is something that Christians can and should seek more often, and that is a gift being offered here. It is a gift, moreover, that does not depend on convincing "the other side" about the particular rightness of one's own view on sexual activity. Sex and sexuality in the context of romantic relationships—gay and straight—has become the lens through which almost all relationships are discussed and understood, and especially the main way in which erotic love is understood. Thinking about sex is intensely important, especially in an age of awareness about rape culture and human trafficking. Still, it is only one lens.

In this chapter, I first develop in more detail some of the contemporary experiences and problems related to being gay and single. Then I turn to Aelred of Rievaulx and provide an account of his understanding of spiritual friendship in relation to Christian discipleship. I conclude with thoughts from Stuart, Tushnet, and Hill, with help from still other commentators, on how Christian life looks going forward.

Same-Sex Attracted and Single

Being gay, lesbian, and single may not seem much different than being straight and single, at least when it comes to what Christians say about how to live a single life. In many Christian groups' articulations of their beliefs and practices, sexual activity is not supposed to be in the picture when a person is single because sex belongs in marriage. Therefore, all singles are supposed to be celibate, and moreover it is usually presumed that all experiences of celibacy must be more or less the same.

On the other hand, being gay and never-married (for example) is distinctive from being straight and never-married. While I do think there can be similarities in experiences of being never-married, in casual sexual relationships, in serious and committed relationships, and so forth (and I hope that some of what I say in all my chapters is truthful across sexual identity categories), I see that gay and lesbian Christians have experienced far more bigotry, shunning, and violence in their communities than straight Christians. Moreover, for same-sex attracted Christians, there is a pressure to side for or against the idea of marriage in yet an additional way compared to straight Christians. While I think that Christians can be guilty of so over-highlighting marriage as an ideal that it seems impossible for single Christians to find a place, gay Christians face even more of a question mark about marriage, as well as whether it is possible to be Christian, by virtue of sexual orientation.

One wise and articulate commenter helps show how same-sex attraction and singleness offers some different experiences than for heterosexual single Christians. Tim Otto—gay, Christian, and living in an intentional Christian community known as Church of the Sojourners in San Francisco—writes about the particular pain of being Christian and being gay. He talks about how in fourth grade, his peers had "amazing good 'gaydar.' I got called names like 'faggot,' 'homo,' 'gay,' and 'queer' all the time. I began to realize, 'Oh those words actually apply to me.' And so my peers taught me the words with which I would hate myself."[6] Otto writes of his search for what Christians think about being gay; in his search he found a book by James Dobson that proclaimed "If you can learn to channel your sexual impulses the way God intended, this part of your nature can be one of the most fascinating and wonderful aspects of your life . . . ."[7] Otto took on "channeling his sexual impulses" as a personal challenge, hoping he could find ways to choose to be attracted to girls. Other kids beat him up often as he made his way home from school. He writes, "I believed that if anyone knew I was attracted to guys, he or she would despise me. Believing I was fundamentally loathsome, I settled for what I unconsciously thought would be a substitute for love: admiration."[8] As a young adult, Otto finds himself in an adult bookstore, where he has his first gay sexual encounter. The sex makes him feel so good, yet afterward, as the stranger leaves, he finds himself bereft, even contemplating suicide, because he has not been able to overcome the sexual feelings that cause so much self-loathing.

Otto writes poignantly:

> Now, as then, I wish that somehow, rather than ending up in the arms of that anonymous man, I could have found myself in the arms of the church. I wish the church had communicated to me that it could be trusted with my deepest secret, with my sense of alienation, with my self-loathing. I wish in the church I had found myself loved.[9]

Otto's story continues. At his Christian college, where he seeks counseling help, he is referred to a group that tries to help people change their sexuality; two options are presented: celibacy, or heterosexual marriage. The reparative therapy fails, for Otto finishes the yearlong program knowing he is no different than he was. Friends of his who also go through the "reparative therapy" sessions find themselves leaving the church rather than "leaving" their orientation.

Otto's experience of growing up Christian and trying to figure out his sexuality is that of so many LGBTQ people. There are two points I wish to highlight here in light of Otto's story of being gay and Christian. First, I reiterate my starting point: same-sex attraction is so clearly not a choice in the way that we contemporary American Christians would prefer to understand choice, as something a person picks between two or more alternatives (as I discussed in Chapter two). Second, Christians clearly so vilify same-sex attracted people, not merely associating sexual activity but also attraction itself as something sinful and horrifying, something needing to be changed and torn out of one's life. Moreover, Christians offer as the only two choices either heterosexual marriage or lifelong celibacy, and provide little or no support for either of those options—with no clear examples from the faith, or witnesses to how one might try either option. The assumptions about choice, the vilification, and the lack of either communal formation or support in any direction come together in conclusions that many make: how can there be any other possibility than self-hatred? Bodies become sites of hatred rather than images of God that are to be loved. Relationships become overwrought with talk of sin. Love, especially the sexual romantic love that leads to (heterosexual) marriage and that contemporary culture tends to emphasize over all other loves, seems an impossibility for LGBTQ people.

In fact, what Otto describes is not the only position Christians have taken, though in my own reading of peoples' coming out stories and accounts of LGBTQ Christians, the general perception about Christians and LGBTQ people is to see the two as utterly distinct, opposed communities. Yet there are many faith-filled LGBTQ Christians and supporters who have wrestled seriously with Christian theological arguments and sexuality and have suggested arguments in favor of same-sex marriage. Marriage to someone that one has attraction and sexual desire for has become, for some, a possible Christian state of life, regardless of hetero- or homosexual attraction. Same-sex marriage becomes a path away from self-hatred and loathing and a means of encouraging Christian communities to be loving, rather than hateful, toward same-sex attracted people.

While I stated above that this chapter is not about same-sex marriage (and it isn't), it is important to know some of the trajectories of same-sex marriage arguments in order to see better arguments about being gay and single. It is also important to know that arguments for same-sex marriage have fallen along two main distinctive lines of thought.

One line of thought is the "liberal argument." The "liberal argument" is philosophical liberalism, or, (as Tim Otto's pastor put it) a focus on FIRE: freedom, individualism, rights, and equality.[10] If these liberal values are the highest and most important values, then, as Otto puts it, "the good of same-sex relationships is a no-brainer." If people should be free to love, if their individual experience and right to marry is to be respected, and if all people are equal, then marriage equality is a foregone conclusion. Arguments based in liberal accounts of Christianity appear in numerous works by important Christian thinkers.[11] We should additional recognize that the tenets of philosophical liberalism have given Christians much to be thankful for, especially minorities, women, and LGBTQ people whose lives have been improved because of that focus on freedom, individuality, rights, and equality.

Yet when these liberal values are set above and apart from their place in Christian tradition, much is omitted from Christian practice. Otto thinks we Christians need to recognize the difficulties with the liberal argument. He spells out what is left behind, to the detriment of Christian life and practice. For example, he argues that Christians are not free to do just anything, but are called to be free in Christ in order to love others. "Do not use your freedom as an opportunity for self-indulgence. . . ." Otto reminds us, citing Galatians 5:13. Nor are we merely individuals in Christ; we are members of the Body of Christ, such that community has a hold on our individual wants and desires. When it comes to rights, Otto suggests, "Christians ought to think carefully about rights language, because at the heart of our faith, we see Christ choosing to give up his rights." While rights language might work in a pluralistic and democratic society, it is not clear that rights language is helpful in Christian terms.[12] Christians are asked to give up rights for the sake of the Gospel. Finally, Otto notes that equality is important in Christian thought, because equality highlights "the beautiful truth that we are all equal in God's eyes."[13] Yet equality can often become a reason for not listening to others, especially when equality is combined with individuality as supremely important. In Christian thought, other people who are faith-filled, and who are witnessing the Gospel in a fruit-filled life, are people I need to listen to, and their thoughts are superior to my own.

A second line of thought regarding same-sex marriage, therefore, is what has sometimes been called a *post-liberal* way of thinking. In this post-liberal view, Christians are right to be worried about theologies that too readily make use of individual experiences or that see "self-grounded truth standing autonomously over scripture and tradition."[14] If Christ is the Gospel we proclaim, then Christian tradition and language, especially the language of the Bible, become central to theological reflection. For a theologian like Robert

Song, attention to scripture and tradition does not mean that Christian thought and practice always remains static; rather we are always called to seek out God faithfully and humbly in scripture and tradition, knowing that our own views might be wrong. Song speaks against using "rights language" in developing a theology about same-sex marriage, preferring instead to argue for same-sex relationships in other ways that stem more clearly from Christian tradition. So Song states that "talk of 'my right to sexual self-expression' is not likely to be the language of choice for those who have come to know that they have been bought with a price, and that their body is not their own."[15] Moreover, Song is concerned that rights language "too easily suggests a vision of society as constituted by self-sufficient individuals who contract to enter into social relationships only when it suits their interests, and who fail to recognize that from before the day they are born they are embedded in a network of relationships which sustain them and which in turn they are called to sustain."[16] Song then enters into the fray of debate with some thorough discussions of scripture and tradition; he takes a distinctive position in the debate, neither wholly eschewing those who read scripture and see prohibitions on same-sex relationships, nor wholly embracing those who read scripture and see same-sex relationships as requiring Christian blessing by way of marriage. Song's proposition will be discussed more, later in this chapter.

The second, post-liberal, path of arguments for same-sex marriage more squarely hits on the kinds of discussions Aelred and his contemporary commenters are having about spiritual friendship. The first path of liberal arguments might have a place especially in pluralistic, democratic discussions in contemporary society, but when it comes to conversations about what it means to be a Christian disciple and a follower of Jesus, it is the second path of arguments that resonates more deeply for many Christians interested in their spiritual life.

That said, I think that much of the work done in this second vein tends to overemphasize sex and marriage, to the detriment of considering singleness. So, in order to show the distinctions between arguments for same-sex marriage and arguments for spiritual friendship, I will here offer a brief account of some theologians whose work navigates the second path: Rowan Williams, David Matzko McCarthy, and Eugene Rogers. The key for many scholars following the second path is to see that sexual desire is inevitably linked to God. This supposition follows from what I already discussed in Chapter 3 about the nature of sexual desire as we learned from casual sexual relationships. Sexual desire relates to several crucial Christian doctrines on grace and salvation, the Trinity, who Christ is, and what makes us human.

Rowan Williams, former Archbishop of Canterbury, begins with the Christian idea of grace. Grace is God's utter gift to us humans, for we can never be God. Yet God loves us and seeks relationship with us. Williams describes grace as "a transformation that depends in large part on knowing yourself to be seen in a certain way: as significant, as wanted."[17] God wants us and God has desire for us "as if we were God."[18] We learn about this desire in our bodies; we humans who have been made in the image of God find that we desire other people. That desire for other people "is drawn to God's faithfulness and patterned in mimesis of God's enduring love," as David Matzko McCarthy suggests.[19] In other words, our bodies aim at patterning themselves after God's great and constant love for us, and that is especially true in our sexuality.

Rowan Williams asks about the significance of sex and the body by posing these questions: "How much do we want our sexual activity to communicate? How much do we want it to display a breadth of human possibility and a sense of the body's capacity to heal and enlarge the life of others?"[20] For Williams, the answer is obvious: sex ought to be able to communicate. This does not mean that sex is always good: "Distorted sexuality is the effort to bring my happiness back under my control and to refuse to let my body be recreated by another person's perception. And this is, in effect, to withdraw my body from the enterprise of human beings making sense in collaboration, in community, withdrawing my body from language, culture and politics."[21] When we allow ourselves to take risks by allowing other people to perceive our vulnerabilities and let them change us and draw us toward love rather than toward ourselves, we are also allowing for the possibility of God's grace and the possibility to be dependent on God. Sexual relationships are occasions for joy; they do not have to be justified for anything, precisely because our bodies are a way of communicating to ourselves and to others who God is.

Williams and McCarthy both argue that a lifelong, faithful, monogamous sexual relationship is the ideal way to come to understand God, ourselves, and our bodies in all their sexual glory. Christians have the task of helping each other see and respond to this desire of God's, and we do so especially in our unique practices—such as the sacrament of marriage (or in traditions where marriage is non-sacramental, the particular kinds of prayers that surround Christian marriages). McCarthy goes further to argue that our contemporary capitalist society militates against understanding our bodies, our sex lives, and our very home life well, because capitalism trains us to desire and expect the extraordinary, the "moments of self-discovery, liminal experiences, and abandon."[22] Capitalism trains us to want shiny, new things—and moreover, shows us that we can get them.

By contrast, elements of Christian traditions help us to mitigate such a high view of the married couple, surrounded by romance and imbued with too much significance in capitalist society. McCarthy advocates for an "open household," that is, a household which is surrounded by networks of other relationships that bring marriage back to earth. Neighbors and church people, among others, help support married couples. The ordinary everyday stuff of life becomes the focal point of marriage, the place where we practice daily acts of love and sex. Sex and romantic love thus lose their frenzied capitalist significance even as they gain a deeper Godly significance, which is to recognize that daily acts of love help form us toward God better.

Theologian Eugene Rogers takes up Williams' and McCarthy's thoughts by proclaiming that "Marriage and the Eucharist (as well as baptism and monastic vows) tell Christians what bodies are for before God, or what they mean, by incorporating them into the body of Christ."[23] Marriage teaches us what it means that God desires us as God's own people, including in our bodies. To bless sexual relationships like marriage, then, is to "give [a couple] a life so that they may have a certain freedom to 'take time' to mature and become as profoundly nurturing as they can."[24] Faithfulness becomes a hallmark of marriage, though Williams is quick to point out that sexual relationships that do not have this keystone of faithfulness are not *necessarily* devoid of God's grace. Yet a life of faithfulness is a Christian's aim so that we learn more, and more deeply. Marriage is the name Christians give to sexual faithful relationships, and there is no reason from Rogers', Williams', nor McCarthy's points of view to deny marriage to same-sex attracted bodies that also can learn love from sexual desire and fulfillment. People ought to learn that they are loved and loveable, and this is especially learned in marriage.

These three theologians are traditional theologians in the sense that they hold two main states of life for Christians, marriage or vowed celibacy. For them, marriage needs to be a state of lifelong monogamy and fidelity, but need not be confined to one man/one woman. In holding that both marriage and vowed celibacy are important, they are in agreement with Pope John Paul II and his work, *Theology of the Body*, which also describes human sexuality in relation to God and the importance of *both* marriage and celibacy in Christian life.[25] Sexual life is an important part of Christian discipleship and can encountered in marriage, or given to God in celibacy. The presence of celibacy in Christian life helps all people, married or celibately single, rightly order and orient their sexual desires toward God. Celibate love shows the pinnacle of how sexual desire is brought into a person's life with God.

At the same time, Williams, McCarthy, and Rogers argue that celibacy ought to be much more carefully practiced and advocated. While they see that celibacy is essential to Christian life and witness, celibacy is also excruciatingly difficult for most. As Williams says, "Finding a bodily/sexual identity though trying to expose yourself first and foremost to the desirous perception of God is difficult and precarious in a way not many of us realize, and it creates problems in dealing with the fact that sexual desiring and being desired do not simply go away in the single life."[26] Williams points to vowed celibates who have argued in favor of same-sex marriage, precisely because these vowed celibates know the cost of celibacy; just because someone is LGBTQ does not mean that person is endowed with a gift of celibacy. Celibacy is only for a few hardy souls.

Marriage, however, appears to be for the vast many, for Williams, Rogers, and McCarthy. Single gay people, whether single by choice or by circumstance, have little room to maneuver. If they don't find a person to marry, nor feel that they are one of the hardy souls called to celibacy, there is no alternative that readily emerges from these theologians' works. Williams opens the door a bit toward casual sexual relationships, for he sees that even in casual sex the body can learn about its grace and ultimately be directed toward God; still, casual sex is not the ideal. (Williams does not make mention of how it might be difficult to seek God in the midst of casual sexual relationships, nor whether it might be equally as difficult as trying to live a celibate life.)

Christopher Roberts makes an important counter-argument about these three theologians' claims. He argues for taking seriously that we are created male and female in relation to marriage and celibacy, finds that Williams, McCarthy, and Rogers, among others, are too easily dismissive of sexual difference. He charts a long history of Christian thought that sees sexual difference as distinctive of humans, as part of what makes us created in the image of God. Roberts thinks same-sex marriage *might* still be possible, but that it needs to be put much more in conversation with arguments about sexual differentiation. Roberts sees that we live in an era where sex is exploited and commercialized, to the point that both marriage and celibacy are very difficult ways of life, and that the church has ill-equipped everyone to live in the morass in which we find ourselves. Roberts argues for the importance of sexual difference, suggesting that if Christians were to take sexual difference seriously, then gay sex would not be singled out as sinful. Adultery and lust across the board would be seen as vices of a contemporary culture, against which the church provides an alternate witness. In emphasizing problems with adultery and lust, marriage remains the focus of our considerations about sexual difference and desire. Thus Roberts asks, "What new tone of voice would need to be adopted if Christians realized that everyone who has ever lusted selfishly is judged by the tradition's teleology for sexual difference, and not just the homosexually inclined?"[27]

In the end, the arguments in favor of same-sex marriage leave significant questions about *both* marriage *and* singleness untouched, especially in relation to LGBTQ concerns. The arguments presume a particular view that marriage is necessary. As I've suggested in earlier chapters, a presumption toward marriage is not a view that I think Christians ought to hold. More importantly, though, what are gay and lesbian Christians to do if they are not directly faced with marriage as a question—whether that is because they agree with the teaching that marriage is between a man and a woman, *or* because none of their relationships seem to be offering marriage as a potential vocation? Some Christians have therefore cast about looking for alternative answers in Christian tradition, and one of the key figures for an alternative is Aelred of Rievaulx. It is to his work that we now turn.

Aelred of Rievaulx on Spiritual Friendship

Aelred of Rievaulx was a well-known twelfth-century Cistercian monk in Yorkshire, England. The Cistercians were a monastic community that followed the Rule of Saint Benedict. Aelred eventually became an abbot of his monastery. In Aelred's world, that didn't just mean he held a position of authority (eventually, he came to be head of over 600 people at the monastery); it meant that he was involved in the region's politics. He negotiated relationships between his monastic order and the crown, as well as intervened in papal politics and provided mediation in a number of disputes in his day. He was therefore a noted and well-regarded leader.

Aelred's treatise on spiritual friendship is one of his most well-known works. He wrote *Spiritual Friendship* toward the end of his life and it was copied numerous times, indicating both the book's and the author's popularity. The book is written in a common philosophical/theological style, in which the author sets up a conversation between two or more people as a way of showing a discussion about a particular issue or question. In this writing's case, Aelred sets up a conversation between himself and a monk named Ivo. In the first book, Ivo comes to him seeking help in understanding what spiritual friendship is.[28] Aelred guides Ivo through reflection on spiritual friendship. Between the time of the first book and the second and third, however, much time has passed and Ivo has died; people named Walter and Gratian remind Aelred of his conversation with Ivo and ask him to further develop his thoughts on spiritual friendship.

Aelred is clear that love and friendship are intertwined. "[F]rom the word for love comes that for friend. . . ."[29] A friend is a "guardian of love," and "Though challenged, though injured, though tossed into the flames, though nailed to a cross, a friend loves always."[30] True friendship therefore never really end. Aelred names three kinds of friendships: carnal, worldly, and spiritual. Carnal friendship thinks only of mutual enjoyment of passing moments, of fleeting lustful attractions. For those in carnal friendships, friendship appears as the highest possible good; there is no room for God, and it is not a settled kind of friendship. Worldly friendship is "marked by fraud and deception"[31] and has the aim of helping each other gain more stuff. Friendships marked by greed, however, are not made for longevity or loyalty.

Spiritual friendship, in contrast, involves "likeness of life, habits, and interests, that is, by agreement in things human and divine, with good will and charity."[32] Many authors, from ancient times to the present, have seen friendship as something available only to members of the same sex. C.S. Lewis, for example, is clear in his discussion of four types of love (Acquaintance, Friendship, Erotic, and God), that friendship is that held between same-sex people, even as Lewis speaks disparagingly of gays and lesbians.[33] Yet Aelred sees that true friendship is available between women, between men, and between women and men. He offers a reading of Genesis 2:21–22 as evidence: woman is created from the side of man, so that "nature might teach that all are equal or, as it were, collateral, and that among human beings—and this is a property of friendship—there exists neither superior nor inferior."[34]

It is especially significant that Aelred uses the passage from Genesis, for Genesis 2 often is used in descriptions of marriage. Aelred uses it, however, to describe friendship, and it is friendship that forms the basis for human society. Envy—a desire for Eve's taste of the forbidden fruit—is what leads to sin creeping into relationships. Where we seek things and objects for our own private benefit, this leads to hatred and destroyed relationships. The person "who remains in friendship remains in God";[35] friendship becomes a means of attaining life with God.

Moreover, whereas Paul suggested that marriage might best be *avoided* because it generated anxieties, Aelred has no such qualms about spiritual friendship. "What kind of wisdom is it to loathe friendship in order to avoid anxiety . . . ?"[36]

It should be no surprise, then, that for Aelred friendship is necessary for living human life. People cannot do without friends. Aelred even suggests that a person without a friend is more like an animal than a human, and is truly, truly alone. "Nothing in human life is hungered for with more holiness, nothing is sought with more utility, nothing is found with more difficulty, nothing is experienced with more pleasure, and nothing is possessed with more fruitfulness."[37] Aelred expounds on friendship, suggesting that perhaps even one true friend is, for exiles, like having a whole country, and for people who are sick it is like medicine.

Yet, there is still more reason to seek friendship: "One truth surpasses all these: close to perfection is that level of friendship that consists in the love and knowledge of God. . . ."[38] Friendship is the means by which people make their pilgrimage toward God. As Aelred says, friendship "begins in Christ, advances in Christ, and is perfected in Christ."[39] Friendship always leads to and through Christ. The friends who share Christ share life together. Because spiritual friendship is about life in Christ, friends ought to be willing to give up their lives for each other.

Aelred's view of spiritual friendship involves very physical, even sexual, imagery. As many Christian commenters have done, Aelred provides a commentary on the erotic imagery of the book of the Bible known as Song of Songs (or Song of Solomon), including discussion of such imagery as: "Let him kiss me with the kiss of his mouth." On Aelred's reading, physical affection, even and perhaps especially in the life of a celibate monk, can be a sign directing people toward God. Aelred describes how physical kisses can be used for good and can be honest: kisses can be signs of reconciliation, peace, love, and unity in that kisses join people physically. Aelred also draws spiritual conclusions about kisses: a "spiritual kiss" connects people spiritually and binds people together in Christ.

Friendship is Aelred's way of discussing what Christian discipleship means. He says that friendship "can last only among the good"[40] ("hardened criminals" could not have friends). Yet it is worth noting that his view of good people does not mean perfection. Instead, he writes: "I call those good who within the limits of our moral life live sober, upright, and godly lives in this world. . . ."[41], for it is these people who can grow in perfection. In other words, friendship in Christian life requires growth and is not accomplished all at once. Therefore, Christian friendship involves loyalty to other people in the sense that there must be commitment to the other person's relationship to Christ. Each friend must be interested and actively engaged in seeking God in Christ.[42]

If Christ is the source of the friendship, that does not mean the friendship involves no troubles. True friends will call each other out on their sins: Aelred supposes that Adam would have been better off to name Eve's eating the forbidden fruit as a sin of "presumption" rather than also taking part in the sin.[43] Moreover, a spiritual friend will "choose danger over security" for the benefit of their friend, and will choose to be sad with a friend rather than be happy with one who is not a friend.[44] "A friend is medicine for life,"[45] which means that a spiritual friend is a person who can be counted on to share in joys and sorrows.

A spiritual friend is also one who has developed certain characteristics that help in fostering friendship. Aelred reads from the book of Sirach that friends should be people who don't speak badly of others, who are not arrogant (but humble enough to confess when they are wrong), who will not tell each other's secrets, and who will not act against a friend in treachery.[46] Again, potential friends do not need to be perfect: they may be people who are angry, too easily prone to tease others, too suspicious of other people—but they have learned to be virtuous. They "overcome anger by patience, check levity by respect for gravity, and banish suspicion by focusing on love...."[47] The idea is that people who are friends with each other are each so interested in cultivating lives of love in God that they are interested in helping each other become more and more loving and generous, even when the other person acts badly.

In fact, Aelred commends people who remain steadfast to their friends despite the fact that their friends might act badly toward them. True spiritual friendship is meant to be lifelong, a strong bond of love between people.

Contemporary Commenters on Aelred's Spiritual Friendship

Numerous Christians have made use of Aelred's work in their thinking about same-sex attraction and friendship. I do wish to note, however, that while Aelred's concept of spiritual friendship is clearly an intimate relationship and often exists as same-sex, I think Aelred believes that cross-sex relationships can also feature spiritual friendship. His use of Genesis 2 and Eve, as I described above, is one point I would make in favor of spiritual friendships as broadly understood.

Some scholars articulating same-sex friendship have used Aelred in small ways to help describe the possibility of sexual, committed same-sex relationships that are *not* marriage. Elizabeth Stuart and John Boswell (for example) are two such scholars, writing in the 1990s and 2000s. These earlier explorations in lesbian and gay relationships often avoided marriage as a necessary category for Christians and instead focused on other kinds of relationships that Christians have, in fact, supported in liturgy and theology over the centuries.

In Stuart's and Boswell's views, such friendships are not marriage but something distinctive, even better than marriage. As Stuart says, "Aelred was not overly concerned with the dangers of friendship leading friends into sexual relationships.... True friendship does not pair people off, creating factions, but builds community."[48] Marriage as traditionally practiced has the tendency to pair off and exclude, prohibiting community. By contrast, for Stuart friendships and sexual relationships could blur into each other, which leaves the kind of space necessary for committed lesbian relationships. Moreover, committed lesbian relationships build community in ways that a heterosexual marriage might not, in Stuart's view, because friendship in Aelred's view has more diverse meanings than marriage does (or so she thinks). Stuart thinks that the church ought "to become the principal advocate of friendship as the primary ethical basis for relationships in the Western world. . . ."[49]

John Boswell, for his part, wrote histories of Christian thought and experience that centered on gay love. The twelfth century especially was a period of flowering for gay love, even if that love was celibate. Boswell wrote about one of Aelred's contemporaries, Saint Anselm, who describes monastic love with an erotic fervor and who wrote love letters to many of his correspondents. (For example: "Brother Anselm to Dom Gilbert, brother, friend, beloved lover. . . .")[50] Yet it is Aelred who takes that love still further, in Boswell's view:

> Aelred developed a concept of Christian friendship which, in its emphasis on human affection, surpassed any earlier theological statements, and explicitly expressed in prose much of the implicit correlation between human and spiritual love long characteristic of clerical love poetry.[51]

Boswell believes that "[t]here can be little question that Aelred was gay and that his erotic attraction to men was a dominant force in his life."[52] For Boswell, Aelred's romantic attraction to other men (including to at least two monks in his monastery) shapes how he understands spiritual love. Boswell is also well known for suggesting, in his final book, *Same-Sex Unions in Pre-modern Europe*, that the church once had a spiritual friendship liturgy, a liturgy that could unite same-sex couples in eternal union. Though he is careful to say that people in the medieval period would not have understood anything like our concepts of being gay, or same-sex marriage, Boswell's work has clearly influenced and affected Christians focused on arguing for same-sex marriage in Christian contexts. That said, Boswell's argument is less about same-sex marriage than about noting places in Christian tradition where same-sex relationships are acknowledged.

Alan Bray has similarly noted points in Christian tradition that have respect for deeply held significant same-sex relationships. His work examines such instances as a tombstone found in Christ's College, Cambridge, where two men are depicted in an embrace of each other. The tombstone also features a wedding knot. Bray concludes that a relationship like this was not a marriage as such, but a spiritual friendship that has existed for many Christians including people like John Henry Newman and Ambrose St. John. Bray is among many scholars noting the significance of rituals and prayers for spiritual friendships that still are practiced in some churches to this day.[53]

Important contemporary work has been done by scholars like Robert Song (mentioned in the first section of this chapter above), who have argued somewhat similarly to Stuart that Christian marriage has, and should have, a unique character appropriate to cross-sex relationships. Song does not use Aelred in the ways that Stuart and Boswell do. That said, he does present a more contemporary case for an alternative relationship to marriage. Song is concerned to read deeply in scripture and to acknowledge the importance of Christian tradition. He sees that sexual difference matters, and that marriage (heterosexual and procreative) along with celibacy are important Christian callings.[54] However, that does not exhaust possible relationships nor deny the importance of alternative kinds of relationships. Using scripture and developing tradition further, Song puts forth the idea of covenant partnerships; these might be heterosexual or homosexual. He makes an argument for covenant partnerships by first considering the case of childless couples, whose sexual activity does not and will not result in children, even if the couple should remain "open" to children. From there, Song makes a connection to same-sex sexual partnerships especially by focusing on the fact that for Christians, there is no procreation at the end of time when God will be all in all. Song concludes tentatively with the thought that such covenant partnerships are more the picture of what marriage looks like in the radical aftermath of Jesus' resurrection than heterosexual marriage with children does; perhaps it is even the case that his third calling, covenant partnership, is the new form of marriage Christians ought to acknowledge. Procreative, heterosexual marriages might then become the minority kind of relationship.

While Aelred's writing has been used to think about same-sex committed relationships that are decisively *not* seen as marriage, Aelred has also become a key figure for gay and lesbian celibate singles. These readers emphasize that Aelred was committed to practicing celibacy and that it is in his monastic context that Aelred is writing.[55]

One of these commenters, Wesley Hill observes: "Most of us are reading it [Aelred's work] from contexts that differ markedly from that of Aelred. We live in a secular society, and one which is highly individualistic. As much as we may disavow secularism and individualism, they remain a part of our lives...."[56] Aelred's erotic, quite physical, but also nonsexual and celibate love has been a cornerstone of Christian reflection for several gay and lesbian single Christians. Aelred's view of friendship helps to re-describe human relationships away from primarily romantic sexual relationships. Spiritual friendship becomes the primary category by which a person is defined, rather than by relationships dependent on sexual activity. Wesley Hill has been accused of hating himself precisely because he is seeking ways to be single and gay.

Wesley Hill wonders why "we can't see our way clear anymore to understand friendship the way we once did,"[57] that is, as serious, sustainable, long-lived relationships. The fault, perhaps, is Sigmund Freud's, who had a "suspicion that all relationships, at base, involve eroticism—that the desire for sex is the secret truth of every relationship, so that any mutual liking or interest must be something *more* than chaste affection."[58] Hill provides several other reasons for why we collectively couldn't care less for friendship. One is idolization of marriage and family, which are seen as The Relationships par excellence. Another is a cultural penchant for freedom—that we can only be our most authentic, free, selves when we are most independent.

Hill provides a significant counterpoint to arguments by Williams, Rogers, and McCarthy, because he suggests that "the belief that sex wholly explains the depths of our most profound relationships" is a myth. The myth has led people to "feel suspicious of, uncertain about, and at times even ashamed of deep friendships."[59] A worry about this myth leads Hill toward many and varied writings on friendship, including a discussion of Aelred. Hill argues against Boswell to suggest, "Aelred promoted an intimacy between friends that wasn't simply reducible to romantic love."[60] Hill's study of spiritual friendship unearths the fact that at times and places in Christian history, deep intimate friendship with even physical contact (though not with consummated sexual relationships) has been normal. Moreover, such friendships found their ways into the pattern of political, legal, and economic life by creating bonds between families, not unlike the alliances that families desired in marriages.

Hill notes the resistance he meets from many people who disbelieve that there can be (really) any kind of love other than erotic, romantic love. Or, put differently: "if friendship is the place where celibate gay Christians will try to invest their love, won't that somehow taint or transform friendship into a form of erotic love—the very thing friendship ought not to be confused with if it is to remain friendship?"[61] Hill recognizes the difficulty and notes that it is highly likely that friendships he forms with other men will generate erotic feelings. Yet for him, the question is what to do with those feelings. Rather than dismiss them, Hill aims to face these feelings head on and note the vocation that is hidden within those feelings: "Rather than interpreting my sexuality as a license to go to bed with someone or even to form a monogamous sexual partnership with him, I can harness and guide its energies in the direction of sexually abstinent, yet intimate, friendship.... My being gay and saying no to gay sex may lead me to be more of a friend to men, not less."[62]

Hill goes even further, to offer his take on spiritual friendship as a gift for the rest of the church to accept. He calls on heterosexual people in and outside sexual relationships to take friendship far more seriously than has been done in recent years, to consider renewing an understanding of what real, deep, lifelong friendship of the kind that Aelred offers might look like these days. Hill offers friendship as a serious means of Christian witness to a world that has eyes for almost nothing except sexual desire and marriage. He further takes the church to task for not providing the kind of community that might support and sustain people, gay and straight, aiming for lives of chastity, including celibacy. He concludes with a story of forming a Christian community of several people that buys and lives in a house together. Hill's intentional Christian community, like many such communities, offers a different way forward. It is a way that does not reject marriage or vowed celibacy but that aims for new possibilities.

Eve Tushnet is one of the better-known celibate lesbian activists. Like Hill, she has been castigated in and outside LGBT communities for promoting celibacy. The reactions against Tushnet's writing suffer from the kinds of reactions people are generally prone to these days: if the headline we see as we scroll down Facebook smacks of something we think we're against (or for), we're likely to click "like" or dismiss it even without reading it.

To ignore Tushnet is to miss very important, nuanced, and perhaps even compelling arguments, however. For example, Tushnet is very aware of several complicated problems with being gay and Christian. She is not attempting to ignore those problems, nor to ignore or belittle her friends who have chosen to be in same-sex sexual relationships. She is quite clear that the church that she has joined (she converted to Catholicism in college) also shows a great deal of homophobic tendencies. She is entirely willing to loudly proclaim homophobia where she sees it existing. She is aware, too, of the controversies about the main Christian stance that those with same-sex orientations ought to remain celibate.

Tushnet's main argument is that Christians, especially same-sex attracted Christians, ought to develop the deep kinds of spiritual friendships that Aelred discusses. While many Christians worry about Christians (same-sex attracted or not) developing too deep a friendship with others of the same sex, Tushnet wants to encourage such friendships anyway. She writes: "I don't want to minimize the concern. If you're queer and faithful to traditional Christian teaching on chastity, and you fall for your friend, those feelings can be terribly painful."[63] Yet Tushnet also writes that "we all actually do have to learn to have nonsexualized relationships with those of our own sex..." because "same-sex friendship is a deep longing in our nature."[64] Same-sex attracted people have more experience than straight people in learning how to have nonsexualized relationships, in fact, since locker rooms, dorm rooms, and the like tend to be separated by sex. "[W]e become used to the experience of choosing to leash and manage sexual desire in order to maintain casual relationships and deep friendships that would be disrupted by desire."[65]

This kind of learning to manage sexual desire is something that straight people could learn from their Christian same-sex attracted brothers and sisters, in fact. It is not healthy (as I discussed in Chapter 3) for heterosexual men and women to treat each other solely as objects of romantic, sexual lust in the ways that contemporary culture promotes, because that desire threatens to overtake any other sense of who that person is. It prevents us from seeing the complexities of who all of us are as people.

Friending, Better

Friends are not a well-respected relationship, these days. Put more accurately, friends are the relationships we take advantage of, presume they'll always be there. Aelred suggests that there are characteristics we ought to look for in spiritual friends, yet I doubt that most of us take the time to consider what it takes to be a good friend beyond whether we each like the same things. Popular references to friends suggest friendship as limited in some way. For example, the co-creator of the 1990s sitcom "Friends" described the show as being "about the time in your life when your friends are your family."[66] The assumption is that this is a limited, chiefly young, time in a person's life. Yet "Friends" did highlight how much we need people in our lives who can help provide many of the things family used to do. Likewise, Facebook's concept of "friends" has frequently been derided as an insufficient and wrong-headed use of the word "friends."

To sum up: the reading that Hill and Tushnet (but even to an extent Stuart, in the way she articulates friendship as a better kind of relationship than marriage) offer is this. Friendships can become deeper, focused on Christ, and even ritualized in the kinds of prayer services that were once more common. Vowed friendship might become more of a present-day possibility that can be accompanied by the prayers, blessings, and rituals that were once more common.

The central conclusion of this chapter is a question: can we take seriously the challenge that Hill, Tushnet, and Aelred lay before us, to recover spiritual friendship as an intimate way of being with others that can lead us toward

God? As a corollary, can we take seriously the idea that being sexual might not be the sum total of everything that love has to offer, whether heterosexual or same-sex attracted? The questions get at the heart of the argument, for I am not sure how Williams, McCarthy, and Rogers, with their focus on the meaning of the sexual body as linked to God, might respond.

Given the kinds of riches of friendship that Aelred and his commentators describe, however, I think it is worth trying. As I alluded to in both Chapters 2 and 3, part of what ails American society is its hookup culture and casual commercialized pornographic sex, which objectify bodies and sex both and which leave people feeling dissatisfied with themselves and their relationships. I also mentioned the ways in which Christians themselves overly focus on sex in unfruitful ways that do not witness to the Gospel of Christ. Furthermore, potential sexual obsessions aside, I think friends are important in a global capitalist society. We ought to be more free rather than less free to give ourselves to friends, to support each other monetarily, and so forth, though law tends to privilege only kinship ties. Kinship ties by blood ought not to be the main/only way to determine inheritances or hospital and prison visitations, among others. We know this, and have known this, for a while—especially as the dearth of kinship relationships becomes more and more evident in a global capitalist world. We have become a mobile people, often living far from parents, siblings, and other family members.

Friendship is a relationship humans need, however successful we have become at pushing it to the background. Friendship is a place where love develops and grows. Moreover, it can and should be a much more heralded, strongly understood relationship. This is especially so for Christians, for whom marriage is decidedly not the final word in relationships.

Developing friendships more intently might help us understand choice in better ways, too. In Chapter 2 I discussed how choice, and lack thereof, was part of the difficulty with a never-married state of singleness. I suggested above, further, that we Christians tend to operate with a sense that a person can choose either a marriage vocation or for some Christian traditions, a religious vocation of celibacy. Yet, as I said in Chapter 2, our choice is rarely if ever for either of those vocations in the abstract. Rather, choice involves the specific flesh-and-blood person you've encountered and the relationship that might develop (or not). Understanding friendship as a potential choice for how a relationship might develop, and including in that understanding of friendship that love is necessary, helps expand how we think about relationships.

Understanding spiritual friendship might also help reorder how we think about sex and sexuality. Kathleen Norris once wrote about the fact that "Americans are remarkably tone-deaf when it comes to the expression of sexuality. The sexual formation that many of us receive is like the refrain of an old Fugs' song: 'Why do ya like boobs a lot—ya gotta like boobs a lot.'"[67] We have difficulty believing that sexual desires can be "sublimated," to use Norris' wording. "[C]elibacy, like monogamy, is not a matter of the will disdaining and conquering the desires of the flesh but a discipline requiring what many people think of as undesirable, if not impossible...."[68] Yet Norris goes on to describe when this kind of "giving up the sexual pursuit" works. "I once met a woman in a monastery guest house who had come there because she was pulling herself together after being raped, and said she needed to feel safe around men again. I've seen young monks astonish an obese and homely college student by listening to her with as much interest and respect as to her conventionally pretty roommate."[69]

Tushnet's and Hill's discussion of celibacy is patently not the same as that of monks making lifelong vows in a monastery. Yet their point—that one needs to learn to have nonsexual friendships—is crucially important for a church that is overly obsessed with sex, heterosexual and homosexual. Tushnet points toward the possibility of something different, new, possible, when it comes to sex and sexuality—that romantic relationships need not frame the basis for life, the universe, and everything. She describes how frustrating it can be if friends with families "take their single friends' support for granted, acting as if our time is less valuable than theirs...."[70] Yet, "these conflicts will probably increase as friendship becomes more important in your life, since you will have rejected our culture's answer: the answer that you should obviously sacrifice friendships for romantic relationships...."[71]

If we were to take up the challenge and pursue friendship, it would mean changes in the ways Christians live out their discipleship in the Body of Christ. In what ways can Christians—not just same-sex attracted Christians but all Christians—be a community that supports spiritual friendships? Tushnet and Hill suggest a number of small beginnings. For example, how might employers enable employees to provide care to friends and neighbors? How might married and single people both support and help each other? I think it would also mean more clearly acknowledging such friendships via prayer and liturgy, as present and potent for Christians no matter their sexual orientation. Hill, for example, calls for "the possibility of vowed spiritual siblinghood,"[72] a new way of reconceiving and developing our ties with each other and of naming relationships that come with communal support as well as responsibilities and expectations. "We need stronger bonds between brothers and sisters in Christ;"[73] we need ways to help us live more of what we say we are.

We say we are a Church, the Body of Christ, and that we are new kin for each other. In the contemporary period, we do not live out that kind of new kinship very well, or very often. There are a few examples, including some of the people discussed in this chapter. Singleness calls Christians to reach beyond their families, to seek relationships with others. The gay single Christians discussed in this chapter beckon us still further: to recover the importance of friendship for living a faithful Christian life.

6

Proclamation: Widowhood and Elizabeth Ann Seton

UP TO THIS point, I have examined single states of life that involve being unmarried before getting married. Being never-married, seeking casual relationships, being gay and single, and committed unmarried relationships each have dominant stories told about them that are unhelpful and dehumanizing when it comes to participation in Christian life. Yet in a culture that idolizes marriage, these pre-marriage states of life carry with them hope of future relationships, of bringing people together, of possibility. It should be said that these hopes are not Christian hope in God, but a secular hope in the goodness of humanity and in love and togetherness. I do not mean to disparage these hopes by saying they are secular hopes: love, togetherness, relationships should be celebrated and enjoyed, and they may give us a taste of hope in God. A danger for Christians is in enjoying these secular hopes too much – perhaps in just the ways we've seen thus far regarding the ways particular views of marriage and family take center stage, to the detriment of thinking well about Christian singleness.

This chapter, and the next, are far more about suffering and tragedy, especially regarding singleness due to loss of human relationships. Suffering and tragedy present in both widowhood (this chapter) and divorce (Chapter 7). But compounding this sense of suffering is the fact that these single states of life often go unmentioned and overlooked in churches. (For the purposes of this chapter, widowhood describes the single state of both widows and widowers who remain unmarried following their partners' deaths. "Widow" refers to women who have lost spouses, and "widower" refers to men.)

How overlooked is widowhood? Widowhood appears to be the least written-about of the single states of life in the past 30 years. It stands in stark contrast to cohabitation and divorce, which are frequent subjects of books by Christian authors. Searches for relevant books and articles show that widowhood as a subject is most often a historical subject and little discussed today; cohabitation and divorce are heavily discussed.[1] There is especially a striking contrast between the attention given to widowhood in scholarly and pastoral literature and the attention given to divorcees, sinceoth widowhood and divorce involve having once been married, and both states of life can involve significant poverty. Divorce is a sexier topic, though, because it portends the downfall of all civilization (or so it might seem); widowhood is a more certain fact of life for most married people, especially for women.

Those who have lost a spouse still describe pain, loss, and abandonment by their Christian communities. For example, Miriam Neff, widow of Bob Neff, a popular evangelical Christian radio broadcasting personality, painfully describes how widowhood means not only the loss of her husband but also the loss of Christian community:

> Loneliness and solitude are not descriptive enough of the space that becomes the cocoon of the widow. Had I been faced with these facts five years ago, I would have stated, 'It can't be so! In the community of believers, we support each other.' But I look back on my own responses to women who had become widows and realize how little I understood, how little I empathized, how seldom I walked beside them.[2]

As I have pointed out elsewhere in this book, Christians hope that their Christian communities become family—broad enough to encompass all people, and especially widows and others who are part of poor and marginalized groups. Widowhood is a state of life when that often does not happen in the contemporary era. The hurt widows and widowers encounter is all the more profound because it exists within Christian community.

In addition to isolation and loneliness, grief and loss are some key words for discussing the state of widowhood. However, in pastoral care books the grief and loss of widowhood disappear. For example, in two of the best-known pastoral care books,[3] widowhood often appears to be subsumed under discussions of grief and loss within families, without particular attention to the plight of widows and widowers.[4] Psychiatrists write about death, and so do bioethicists, with occasional references to widows from mostly secular perspectives.

Of course, there are widows and widowers who are relieved that their spouses have passed away. Abuses and annoyances, the daily grind of having to take care of another person (perhaps especially long-term in the case of degenerative diseases) give way to a sense of freedom. Their experiences may not be captured as well in this chapter. Still, the kind of isolation and loneliness Neff describes in relation to Christian community needs to considered further.

I argue in this chapter that even in the twenty-first century, there is a need for Christians to pay more attention to widows and widowers. I think Christians have forgotten to discuss widowhood and that there is a scriptural mandate to care for the widows and orphans among us. In this chapter, I aim to put widowhood much more front and center and show what this particular single state of lie has much to offer to the Christian community.

The lack of discussion of widowhood is astounding when we look at the contemporary scene against the backdrop of two thousand years' Christian witness. One of the continuous threads in scripture is surely God's commandment to care for widows. Christians have taken that call quite seriously in most times and places. Yet in our own day, care of widows is mostly relegated to therapy, pastoral care by ministers, and perhaps a church bereavement group—and I shall show, below, how these don't adequately allow Christians to follow the mandate to care for widows. In addition to not properly caring for widows, I find that contemporary Christians are not at all good at seeing widowhood as part of the cloud of witnesses. Part of this chapter's discussion is therefore to provide a short discussion of widowhood in Christian tradition.

The holy guide for this chapter is Mother Elizabeth Ann Seton, a widely regarded nineteenth-century widow who reflected a good deal on being a widow and living a full Christian life. Her writing is indelibly marked by the fact that she was widowed when she was young; death, suffering, and how those relate to God permeate her thought. As a person bridging the eighteenth and nineteenth centuries, she lived during the time when many of our modern American sensibilities about choice, autonomy, and death were being formed. As we shall see, choice and autonomy both feature significantly in death, dying, and the state of widowhood. Seton also lives in a time when widowhood was far more likely to mean utter destitution that it does in our era of Social Security; widowhood had a particular urgency that it might not have today. Seton's different situation enables us to lift up widowhood more particularly than we might do in an era when widows and widowers are more hidden. Examining her story enables us to draw comparisons to the contemporary period, in order to see what contributions widowhood might have for Christian community. Seton is therefore well placed to help us think through the contemporary complexities of widowhood, and to help Christians to reflect on the gifts that widows and widowers bring to the body of Christ.

This chapter proceeds in the following way. Following a brief discussion of the sociological status and consideration of why widows and widowers might be overlooked in contemporary America, I move to what contemporary Christians do say about widowhood when they dare to speak of it. I suggest that part of the problem comes from broadcultural ideas about death, especially what Christians name the "culture of death," but also an understanding of death as a choice. This is not only about fear of death, but about seeing death as a choice, which in turn impacts how Christians understand widowhood.

Then, I juxtapose scripture and Christian history in relation to treatment of widows and widowers, to show just how far away from scripture and tradition Christian community has moved (on the whole). Finally, I speak about Elizabeth Ann Seton and her frank discussions of both widowhood and Christian life. She shows us that one main way of understanding widowhood in Christian life is to see it as a proclamation of the Gospel.

Forgetting Widows and Widowers

Lynn Neff describes in detail all the losses that becoming a widow entails:

> [S]tudies show that widows lose 75 percent of their friendship network when they lose a spouse. Sixty percent of us experience serious health issues in that first year. One third of us meet the criteria for clinical depression in the first month after our spouse's death, and half of us remain clinically depressed a year later. Most experience financial decline. One pastor described us by saying we move from the front row of the church to the back, and then out the door. We move from serving and singing in choir to solitude and silent sobbing, and then on to find a place where we belong.[5]

We might think that these losses of friendship and financial decline impact only a small percentage of the population, and that is why there is less attention given.

In fact, widows and widowers comprise about 14 percent of the population, according to 2014 US Census Bureau data, which makes them a significant demographic group to consider, especially when we consider the size of other important demographic groups: African American population (12.3 percent), people who cohabitate (11 percent).[6]

Widows and widowers still encounter financial hardship, though they are less likely to be as destitute as in past centuries. Fifty percent of widows, and 35 percent of widowers found themselves left with incomes of less than $25,000 per year, as compared to divorced (27 percent/17 percent) and married

(13 percent /14 percent) men and women. While the majority of widows and widowers are over the age of 65, still roughly 210,000 men and women find themselves widowed at an age younger than 54. Ageism may be one of the reasons, then, for forgetting to consider widows.

A US Pew Forum Religious Landscape survey finds that a similar number of Christians (around 10 percent) are widowed, though the number varies slightly by denomination.[7] The number of widows and widowers as a percentage of Christian population by denomination is higher than the number of cohabitating adults as a percentage of Christian population, though cohabitation is far more widely discussed, as I alluded to above.

Sexism may also factor into the forgetfulness Neff mentions. Another earlier but more in-depth discussion of widowhood shows that about 1.4 million Americans are widowed, and that there is a very sharp gender gap: about a million of those widowed are women.[8] Widows and widowers also seem to experience the loss of spouse differently. In psychological studies, widows were more "likely to seek emotional support" while men were more likely to seek "solace in exercise, religion, work, poetry, or in some more destructive patterns such as alcohol."[9] Sociologists suggest that differences in grieving come, in part, from cultural norms related to gender and grief. For example, the role of "wife" may be tied more closely to a woman's central identity and role in society, while the role of "husband" may be seen as only one of many roles that shape a man's identity. If this is the case, American ideals of self-sufficiency and individualism that I've discussed in previous chapters may be in play here, with particular respect to gender. This is a point that is beyond the scope of this book, but needs more research and though. The key thought here is that as a condition that affects mostly women and that affects mostly elderly, this state of life comes outside the bounds of scholarly research that often focuses on the young and the male. Yet I think there is a still more key reason why widowhood is little discussed, and that is in how people think about death and dying.

Mourning in America, and a "Culture of Death"

One of the strongest stories about Americans and death is that we fear it, and even deny it. This fear of death has been noticed by many, to the point that activists have sought direct ways to help people engage death and bring it more into the open. For example, some activists seeking to promote our conversation about death promote death cafes, which offer a place for tea and conversation about death[10] with interested people. "The Conversation Project" also promotes conversation and awareness about death, and sends starter kits to people wishing to speak about end-of-life questions. The well-known scholar of death and dying, Elizabeth Kübler-Ross, has become an internationally-known and respected scholar, partly because of her work describe the ways we ignore death (such as determining that our children cannot handle death). We have difficulty finding words to express that someone has died, preferring instead to use euphemisms like "we lost her" or "she passed." Consequently, we have a hard time grieving, a process that Kübler-Ross spent a lifetime studying with the aim of helping those forgotten by a society that forgets death.[11]

Yet there are researchers with strong reasons for thinking that in fact, we live in a culture that glorifies rather than denies death. Death is still very present to us, but in different ways from past generations because for many people, death is a form of entertainment rather than a lived reality. Contemporary American life involves the technological and biological facts of greater longevity and the near-elimination of childhood diseases, so that deaths of children and spouses are more removed from daily life. More often, it is the "elderly" who die—people who because of their age "may well not have been widely known by the friends of those left behind," such that grief is not shared. Moreover, our American vision of family as a "relatively isolated nuclear family in which outsiders have played little if any role in child care" means that death of both spouses and children can be isolating.[12] This description certainly agrees with Neff's depiction of widowhood as isolating.

Our fear is implicated, maybe, in the dearth of cultural practices relating to death. While people are likely to still observe a practice of wearing black to funerals, black is no longer symbolic of death in the way that it once was. (It's probably more symbolic of being hip or being from New York City...). Once, we had strong practices of wearing black armbands, mourning clothes, and even half-mourning. Once, most of us had few qualms about eating picnics at cemeteries among dead relatives (some Americans do still have this practice). These practices were crucial especially for those left behind, were a way of marking grief and naming the presence of death without constantly being at the receiving end of well-meaning inquisitions about how we are doing these days and whether you needed a certain degree of latitude and particular respect. Wearing mourning clothes was a public way to name and proclaim grief; eating picnics was a way to keep memories alive. These days, both dying and grieving people are more hidden from view. Mourning clothes do not exist, making it easy to forget other people's grief. Picnics in cemeteries are macabre rather than festive—making those who would love to remember seem all the more odd and out-of-touch.

Yet I think there is more going on when it comes to death than simply our fear of it, and that "more" very much impacts how we understand widowhood. Mourning in America is only a symptom of at least two other, widespread and interrelated views about death. One of these is the "culture of death," a term increasingly discussed among Catholics but also becoming known among other Christians, especially in relation to pro-life activism. Pope John Paul II described a "culture of death" in the 1995 document *Evangelium Vitae* (The Gospel of Life), contrasting a culture of death to the culture of life that Christians must seek instead. A "culture of death" devalues all human life in favor of consumption, efficiency, greed. The pope saw that arguments in favor of abortion and euthanasia frequently mention people who are most inconvenient for a fast-paced, driven society: infants, the disabled, the elderly. Their care requires us to slow down, and at times to forego having money in order to provide for them. Arguments for abortion and euthanasia also make a case for quality of life for the young, the disabled, and the old, such that those people who do not match or measure up to quality of life as dictated by a consumeristic, fast-paced culture seem to have no quality of life at all. Fear of lack of quality of life relates to fear of death, for death means we can no longer participate in society.[13] Christians no less than others participate in a culture of death.[14]

While the pope focused his arguments on abortion and euthanasia, his discussion of a culture of death also touched on care of the environment, war, just wages, work, relationships, and poverty. A culture of death, then, is a whole way of life that is so systemic, affecting so many different and minute parts of our lives, that it is difficult for us think life might be otherwise. The pope offers the antidote: the cross of Christ is so radical that it does offer a counterculture, a culture of life, the pope suggests. Life in Jesus embraces his death on a cross, which means that neither life nor death have the same meaning for Christians as for secular society. We can take time to be with the disabled, the elderly, and children. We can give and not count the cost. We can die, and not be afraid of death. The Gospel of Life relates strongly to the traditions that have surrounded care of widows, which I describe in the next section. Widowhood becomes intertwined with the Gospel, a widow's life becomes proclamation. A culture of death denies that proclamation of the Gospel, a point that shows even more clearly when we examine Elizabeth Ann Seton's life, below.

A culture of death is bolstered by a second widespread view of death and dying, which is the idea that death is, most of the time, a choice we make. Medical doctor and Catholic ethicist Jeffrey Bishop is one physician worried about how death is named and lived in America. Technological advances in medical care now mean that respirators can breathe for us, feeding tubes can provide nutrients, dialysis machines can remove waste from our bodies. These technologies now present us with choices that previous generations would not have had: whether, and when, to "turn off" the machine and so to cause the death of the human being lying in the ICU room. In a world where turning off machines is a real choice, physician-assisted suicide and euthanasia make very clear sense because they are merely choices a person can make before they get to the ICU room. To choose when and where to die, especially when one looks at the cold, friendless, hospital bed, seems the obvious and best choice in this view. Moreover, in the guise of presenting medical information so that an individual can make an informed choice, people—unfortunately both doctors and pastors, and numerous well-meaning other people—are likely to bring up pain and suffering. Pain and suffering are evils to be avoided; the doctor has taken the Hippocratic Oath, which asks them to do no harm. The pastor knows that Jesus is supposed to bring peace. Thus, both doctor and pastor, in their own ways, are likely to influence a person's choice as they emphasize the kind of suffering and pain a patient is likely to undergo.[15]

Christians have sometimes offered palliative care as an alternative way of caring for those who are dying, a way of making death more palatable and even healing. One of the founders of the modern hospice movement, Dame Cicely Saunders, "felt that medicine had abandoned those for whom no cure was possible and did not even deal well with the physical pain of the patient."[16] Jeffrey Bishop argues that palliative care "came to mean the reversal of a disease process and became associated with the intensification of care," and care "came to mean a compassionate response to those whose bodies or psyches were in need."[17] Hospice care is an important way of addressing death in this culture. Yet Bishop's concern is that our forms of care emphasize death as a *choice*.

The assumptions we make about health care present a relatively neat and tidy way to package and control death. The patient's (and family's) main source of control is in making the choice: for cure of a disease, or for palliative care in the face of death. My own point here is not to denigrate either "cure" or "care" but to show that in our contemporary medical framework, death is seen primarily as a choice.

We might think that one possible exception to the idea of death as choice is sudden death, which is usually understood as a tragedy, not a choice. Yet even in cases of sudden death, vast amounts of writing go to suggesting how to avoid those sudden deaths, and even toward placing blame on those who might have prevented sudden deaths. In the summer of 2016 when I wrote this book, for example, an alligator tragically grabbed a toddler and killed him at a Disney resort. The parents were there, frantically grabbing for the child at the last minute, hunting down the alligator, sounding the alarm. By contrast, a mother at a Cincinnati zoo lost control of her 3-year old, who made his way into a gorilla pit. The zoo staff shot the gorilla and saved the boy. In the alligator case, blame was placed mostly on Disney for not giving enough warning about the possibility of alligators (though some blamed the parents for neglect, too); in the gorilla case, blame was placed mostly on the mother for not watching her child closely enough, while many also expressed outrage that a gorilla had to be killed. Both cases presume someone or something was to blame; tragedies can be avoided only if the proper safety precautions are in place. What we choose and control, therefore, happens before the death.[18]

Put differently, narrating that we have choices about death suggests that our ability to choose conquers death—whether those choices involve the safety procedures we put in place around dangerous, potentially sudden-death inducing activities, or the decisions made at a hospice bedside. Theologically, this move toward choice is troubling, especially since Christians proclaim that Christ conquers death: "Christ has risen from the grave. By death he conquered death, and to those in the grave he granted life."[19]

Perceiving death as a choice makes death seem both more and less than it is. In a culture of death, where death is seen as a way to take care of problems—especially the problems caused by the unborn, the disabled, and the elderly—death becomes magnified as a good option and choice. Simultaneously, choice is presented as restoring control to people who are dying. Death seems more than it is, a way to control our lives and emotions, and ultimately the world around us. At the same time, death becomes less than it is. The choices we perceive as conquering death overtake Christ as conqueror of death. Christ's Good Friday pain and suffering on the cross becomes undercut by the resurrection promises of Easter Sunday. Yet, can we understand Easter without Good Friday?[20]

What Death as Choice Means for the Widowed

Those who are actively dying have featured significantly in the books and discussions of death that I mention above. For this particular book, I am concerned with how the above narratives of death impact widows and widowers more particularly. I think that the culture of death combined with death as a choice cultivate an atmosphere where people believe they can worry far less about widows and widowers. There are multiple reasons why Lynn Neff describes feeling abandoned by her Christian family, but the presence of choice in modern deathbeds is surely one of them.

To make a choice indicates active participation and assent—so while a person might be sad at losing a spouse, there is a sense that they (or their dying loved ones) have created the situation in which they reside. Second, the idea of choice goes hand in hand with freedom. If I have made a choice, my community best supports me and my choices by not interfering with those choices. Moreover, making death out to be (largely) a choice makes death and dying seem rational. Christians are very prone to participating in rationalizing death and making it controllable.

The pat statements that grieving spouses hear at wakes and funerals indicate how we manipulate our discussions of death in order to make death out to be rational. "There's a reason everything happens." "She's in a better place." "Heaven needed him as an angel." These are pious statements Christians make in the face of death and tragedy, especially when we don't know what else to say. Yet what these statements do is simply keep up the pretense that death is explainable, rational, and therefore choice-worthy and largely nonmessy. Julia Brumbaugh observes: "These [statements] all carry the implication that some good that wouldn't otherwise be depends on this loss, often with the pious sense that God is bringing these things about, so we should be able to move through them easily."[21] Death as rationally chosen, as part of a rational culture of death, prevents grief, including and especially the long-term effects of grief.

One of the sheer difficulties with widowhood is that a spouse has lost a spouse, someone they needed in their life. Widows and widowers alike describe the confusion that sets in after a spouse has died, for now the remaining spouse is left having to fill the gaps: balance the budget, make the meals, take out the trash, do the fix-it work, get the kids to school, and the million other details that a person didn't even consider till that person is not there. While in a way all single lives must find ways to make life work, building something from a point of singleness already finds ways to make life work from that vantage point. Going from two to one, from a way of life that worked to chaos, requires building a new life up again.

It isn't just the lone spouse whose life gets rebuilt, though. Why did Lynn Neff feel abandoned by her church, and why do widows and widowers lose many of their friends when a spouse dies? Their new life doesn't fit with the people they know in the same ways as it once did. All people concerned have to make changes, but many people are resistant to making those changes and can't figure out how to make changes work in the midst of their own crazy lives. Newfound singleness is a reminder of what once was, as well as what all people will face in the future. People don't want the chaos, the messiness, and the mystery of life and death. Christians support that sensibility for the most part. A widow's grief is typically reserved for bereavement groups, for the people and places that can accommodate those changes over and against a society that expects to make quick work of grief—with mourners back at work and feeling themselves as soon after the funeral as possible.

Widowhood in Christian Tradition

Christian history provides a strong contrast to contemporary ways of treating the dying and their spouses. There are two main aspects to widowhood in Christian tradition: First is the strong command to care for widows and especially to be with them in grief (and orphans, though orphans are not specifically part of this book). Second is the way Christian communities valued widows and included them in the life of the church precisely because of their witness to Christ.

Care of Widows

Widows' care is specifically mentioned in scripture, and not only once but many times. Care for the widows and orphans is explicitly mentioned in Jewish law in the Old Testament. In Deuteronomy, scripture directly calls for care of widows, alongside other disadvantaged people such as "resident aliens":

> Every third year you shall bring out the full tithe of your produce for that year, and store it within your towns; the Levites, because they have no allotment or inheritance with you, as well as the resident aliens, the orphans, and the widows in your towns, may come and eat their fill so that the LORD your God may bless you in all the work that you undertake.[22]

Other scriptures emphasize the widow's low position in society, and proclaim that God will hear the cry of these poor.[23] Bonnie Bowman Thurston suggests one possible reason for a widow's low position: "a husband's death before old age was considered a retribution for his sins, and this retribution was apparently incurred also by the wife. Therefore, to be left a widow was a disgrace."[24] Yet God does not forget widows, nor does God want the people to forget widows:

> When you reap your harvest in your field and forget a sheaf in the field, you shall not go back to get it; it shall be left for the alien, the orphan, and the widow, so that the LORD your God may bless you in all your undertakings.[25]

Care for widows is connected to God's own blessings for those who are not widowed.

Even more of an emphasis on widows is in the book of Ruth, where a main concern is care of widows. Both Ruth and Naomi are widows seeking protection and care. By the book's end, they have found that protection. For Christians, Ruth carries the even greater significance of being an ancestor of Jesus—she who is a widowed outcast is part of the very family line of Christ.

There are many probable reasons for why God commanded care of widows in Jewish tradition. Women, particularly, were understood as being friendless and bereaved compared to widowers, because men are presumed to be able to continue care of themselves, having means for work. Women had few such resources and so, much as today, made up part of a very impoverished population. Scripture also reveals God as the one who cares for widows in their time of need. God becomes the husband and Father, in place of the husbandless and fatherless. In the book of Exodus, we find: "22 You shall not abuse any widow or orphan. 23 If you do abuse them, when they cry out to me, I will surely heed their cry; 24 my wrath will burn, and I will kill you with the sword, and your wives shall become widows and your children orphans." The text suggests just how fearful people were (and are) of becoming widowed or orphaned—and God promises a like punishment to those who refuse to care for widows.[26]

Early Christian tradition continued this strong emphasis on care for widows. In the Gospel of Mark, Jesus speaks of his religious community and its response to widows:

> Beware of the scribes, who like to go around in long robes and accept greetings in the marketplaces, 39 seats of honor in synagogues, and places of honor at banquets. 40 They devour the houses of widows and, as a pretext, recite lengthy prayers. They will receive a very severe condemnation.[27]

In the Gospel of John, Jesus assigns care to the Beloved Disciple for his mother, a widow, even as he is dying on the cross (John 19:26–27). In Acts, the early Christian community is clearly marked as a community that has the duty to care for the widows who live in their midst (Acts 6: 1–7).

Paul's first letter to Timothy suggests that there was a large community of widows present in some of the Christian churches.[28] Paul's letter includes mention of a list of widows that the church community was to care for, exhorts Christians to support widows who are relatives, and describes "real widows" in distinction to those who have family living who can support them:

> 5 The real widow, left alone, has set her hope on God and continues in
> supplications and prayers night and day; 6 but the widow who lives for
> pleasure is dead even while she lives. 7 Give these commands as well,
> so that they may be above reproach. 8 And whoever does not provide for
> relatives, and especially for family members, has denied the faith and
> is worse than an unbeliever.[29]

In the past, Christian communities have frequently referenced scriptures like these in their own care for widows.

The Widow's Reciprocal Care of the Community

It seems likely that both the early Christian church and subsequent Christian communities took matters further than simply providing food, shelter, or monetary needs for widows in their midst. Christians also seem to have developed what some scholars have called an "Order of Widows."[30] There is debate about the order's existence, and accounts of what this "order" looked like differ,[31] but an Order of Widows enabled widows in particular communities to reciprocate the care they received. In apostolic times, as theologian Cathleen Kaveny argues, "Widows made house visitations, where they comforted, fasted, and prayed with the sick and gave practical instruction to younger women."[32] The second-century writer Tertullian notes: "women past the age of sixty are chosen for that seat, women who are not merely the widow of one husband… but also mothers, and indeed, mothers who have raised children, so that by their own experience of the whole range of human emotions, they might easily know how to help others, by way of both counsel and consolation."[33] Another early document suggests that communities of widows emphasized a life of prayer: "It is neither right nor necessary therefore that women should be teachers, and especially concerning the name of Christ and the redemption of his passion. For you have not been appointed to this, O women, and especially widows, that you should teach, but that you should pray and entreat the Lord God."[34]

Regardless of what an Order of Widows might have looked like in apostolic times, Christian churches frequently supported communities of widows in later centuries. Fifth-century bishop Augustine of Hippo addressed an entire, much-read letter detailing what a life of holy widowhood might look like. In his letter, Augustine ponders Paul's words to the Corinthians, where Paul suggests that if a woman is widowed, it is better that she not remarry. By Augustine's day, there had been quite a bit of debate about the meaning of those words. Some had suggested, because of Paul's words, that marriage was evil, or at the least always and everywhere worse than holy virginity. Widowhood occupied a middle position, so long as a person didn't get remarried. By that view, widowhood was less good than holy virginity but more good than continued marriage.

While Augustine is willing to draw that kind of ranking between virginity, widowhood, and marriage, he also says that it cannot be the case that the simple adoption of a state of life necessarily means a person is good. One's state of life must be connected to practice and to virtue, via God's grace.

He writes that a virgin cannot rest assured in her chosen state of life, for example, because "she does not know whether any particular married woman is already capable of suffering for Christ, whereas she is not yet capable of that and it is a mercy to her that her weakness is not put to the test."[35] In other words, right belief and sincere desire to practice virtue make a married woman far better than a chaste virgin who is rude and lacking in humility.

Holy widowhood involved a life of vows and was therefore not a life that all widows entered into, as Augustine notes in section 16,9 of his treatise. Holy widowhood was meant to be one way that women, as members of Christ's body, were also members of his Bride, the Church—but they needed God's gracious gift in order to live such a life. He writes of Juliana's daughter, who wishes to be a consecrated virgin, and how they might live their holy life together: "That King, who is captivated by the beauty of his one bride, of which you are members. Do this together, she with virginal integrity, you with widow's celibacy, both with spiritual beauty."[36] Still, the importance of practicing virtue shows as important. For example, Augustine notes the virtues of Juliana's mother-in-law, also a widow living in Juliana's community:

> You have this elderly and holy woman with you, with you in your home, and with you in Christ. You can ask her advice about perseverance, how to combat one or another temptation, what to do to overcome it more easily, what precautions to take to prevent it from renewing its assault. From what she has already accomplished over a long time she will teach you, kindly in her love, caring because of her faith, and with the assurance that comes with age.[37]
>
> What is also crucial in this passage is that Juliana's mother-in-law is to be cherished and valued not only for her age but also for her long experience as a widow herself.

Writing slightly later, Cassiodorus even makes an analogy of the Church as widow:

> The church is called Christ's widow, because she is stripped of all worldly help and places her hope solely in the Lord.... She is called a widow because she is bereft of worldly protection and has placed her hope in her heavenly Bridegroom, who has transformed her darkness into beauty, her error into uprightness, her abrasiveness into devotion, and her frailty into total constancy.[38]

Cassiodorus finds the widow an apt analogy for the kind of dependency on God that the Church has on Christ. In Christ, we are all dependent.

Historian Katherine Clark describes how a theology of widowhood arose during the high Middle Ages in response to the writing of Saint Augustine on widowhood. Widowhood in that period perhaps occupies a middle way between marriage and celibate life: an opportunity for a married woman to become a chaste spouse of Christ.[39] Moreover, Clark argues that later, in the Middle Ages,[40] widows became revered as people who maintained a kind of "spiritual housekeeping" and who were prophetic voices in the Church—precisely because of their grief and mourning over departed spouses.[41]

As we shall see in the next section, the care of widows concerned the nineteenth-century Catholic Church as well, though in ways different from earlier configurations. Compared to some of the historical witness of Christian widows, contemporary widowhood is relegated to a position of being an afterthought in pastoral care and theological examinations in the United States. Those grieving the loss of spouses disappear, relegated to hiddenness. I think the task of Christians is clear: to take up the scriptural mandate and to consider widows and widowers as people who have much to contribute to the Body of Christ and whose memories, grief, or experiences should not be relegated to bereavement groups in a culture of death as choice.

Mother Elizabeth Ann Seton

But soon beyond the Tomb We'll meet to part no more
In His Name was all our trust He will hush each doubt and fear
And take His Wand'rers Home o yes my only love...[42]

(Poem by Elizabeth Ann Seton,
on her husband's death)

We turn, then, to a nineteenth-century woman whose witness to Christ in her own grief may prove helpful for widows/widowers, as well as for the church. Widowhood, combined with Christian faith, becomes Seton's specific way of living as Christ's disciple. Most importantly, Seton calls on Christians to take the proclamation of life, death, and resurrection seriously by taking grief seriously. Seton herself clearly grieves and remains in that grief in palpable ways. The poem she wrote (expressed above) describes Seton's sense of loss and separation from her husband and shows how she is reflecting on her faith in light of that grief. She and William, her husband, are both "Wand'rers" journeying toward God; someday they will no longer be separated.

One way of reading Elizabeth Ann Seton's biographical details is to see her life as a series of loss, over loss, over loss. There are many deaths and financial losses, but also the loss of the support of friends and family following her widowhood as well as her contentious decision to become Catholic. Abandonment, along with grief, become consistent themes in Seton's writing.

A Brief Biography

She was born Elizabeth Ann Bailey in New York City, in 1774. Her mother died when she was three, but Elizabeth developed a close relationship with her father. She grew up in the Protestant Episcopal Church and married William Seton, a relatively well-to-do merchant, in 1794. Together they had five children. She was very devout, and involved in numerous charities, including the Society of Widows at Trinity Episcopal Church. A few years after being married, William experienced some reversals of fortune in his merchant businesses. Close on the heels of that financial crisis, William began to suffer with tuberculosis, and Elizabeth's father died. William's struggles with tuberculosis put the family constantly on the edge of poverty; in October 1803 they traveled by ship with one daughter, Anna Maria (and left the other four) to Italy after selling off the last of their possessions, in the hope that he might recover in the warmer climate.

Instead, almost immediately upon arrival in Italy, her husband's illness grew worse. The family were quarantined because of a yellow fever epidemic in New York City. Though friends (the brothers Antonio and Filippo Fillichi, together with their wives) strove to make their lives comfortable and paid for a physician to attend the family, William died in Italy on December 27, 1803. Elizabeth buried him in the English Protestant Cemetery in Leghorn, where they had disembarked. She marked visits to his gravesite in her journal to Rebecca: "I have been to my dear Setons grave—and wept plentifully over it with the unrestrained affection which the last sufferings of his life added to remembrance of former Years, had made almost more than precious—When you read my daily memorandums since I left home you will feel what my love has been, and acknowledge that God alone could support..."[43] Seton feels utterly alone, except for the fact that God is there.

Elizabeth and her daughter had to then wait for a ship that could return them to America, so she lived for Italy for some months following William's death. While in Italy, Elizabeth reflected deeply on her husband's death and on God in a journal that she kept for William's sister Rebecca. She visited many of the churches and art galleries that her husband had advocated. She also finds herself both mystified by and strangely drawn to Catholicism, with its presence of Christ even in bread and wine. She wrote about the practice of reserving the sacrament of the Eucharist and reverencing it, wishing very much that she, too, could feel the presence of God as fully as she believes the Italian Catholics do:

> [W]hen they carry the B[lesse]d Sacrament under my Window while I feel the full loneliness and sadness of my case I cannot stop the tears at the thought my God how happy would I be even so far away from all so dear, if! could find you in the church as they do (for there is a chapel in the very house of Mr. F[ilicchi]) how many things I would say to you of the sorrows of my heart and the sins of my life—the other day in a moment of excessive distress I fell on my knees without thinking when the Blessed Sacrament passed by and cried in an agony to God to bless me if he was there.[44]

The young widow therefore began wrestling with whether to become Catholic. As I shall discuss below, her sense of the immanence of God became a very particular part of her theology of Christian discipleship, even as she grieved.

More disappointments awaited her in Italy. When they finally were able to board a ship back America in February 1804, Anna was diagnosed with scarlet fever, and mother and daughter were again forced to leave the ship. They again stayed with the Filicchis. Eventually, in April, they finally had passage back to America and were accompanied by Antonio Filicchi.

When Seton finally disembarked in New York City, she learned that her husband's sister Rebecca was very ill, and she died a month later. Seton was very much affected by the number of deaths she had encountered in short time. She wrote: "As for me, I think that, losing my Father, my husband and Rebecca all is finished. True, I look upon my little children as treasures, but with the fear of even placing the hope of happiness on objects that change so quickly and whose existence is so uncertain."[45] As we shall see further below, this uncertainty brings about more and more reflection on her life in God.

Moreover, Elizabeth's wrestling with becoming Catholic caused many friends and family to leave her. She was therefore very uncertain about whether

Catholicism was a good home. At one point in July 1804, she wrote to Bishop Carroll, the Catholic bishop of Maryland, saying that she

> Acknowledge[s] that the foundation of my Catholick principles is destroyed and I cannot see the necessity for my making a change—It is necessary to inform you that I have felt my situation in the most awful manner and as the Mother and Sole parent of five children have certainly pleaded with God earnestly and I may strictly say incessantly as it has been the only and supreme desire of my Soul to know the Truth.[46]

One of Seton's concerns was surely that she knew that if she did convert, she would be abandoned by family as well as people like her pastor at Trinity Episcopal Church, John Henry Hobart. She would be even more destitute as an abandoned widow.

Ultimately, Seton felt compelled by God. In March 1805, she was received into the Catholic Church. Some friends remained to sustain her, including Julia Scott, with whom she kept correspondence for life, and of course the Filicchi family. As she searched for some way to provide for her family, Seton eventually agreed to go to Catholic Maryland to found a school. Eventually, Seton and the other women who came with her become the Sisters of Charity (in 1808), a religious community, while also caring for her own children. (At one point she pleaded with the bishop to release her from being the leader of the community so that she could care for her children; the bishop refused.)

Over the next decades till her own death in 1821, Seton encountered death in many, many ways—her children, siblings, close friends, and so forth. Each death prompts writing and reflection in her journal; each death causes her to reflect on God's relationship with humans. Each death leads her inexorably toward the love of God and on greater and greater reflection. Seton left behind a number of Sisters of Charity to carry on her work, and the religious community continues still to this day.

There is no suggestion of an Order of Widows in Bishop Carroll's letters, at least not one like the communities suggested in the apostolic age. Still, Seton's community did become an Order of Widows of a sort, seemingly by default. The women in the Sisters of Charity adopted widows' garb as their clothing, and Seton tells that many of the women who joined the community were widows themselves. A number of widows joined the Sisters of Charity—Sister Margaret Farrell George, Sister Bridget Farrell, Sister Madeline Guerin, Sister Mary Xavier. The Sisters of Charity wore garb similar to that worn by widows in Italy at the time, as Seton described in her writing.[47] Other widows seem to have boarded at St. Joseph's, where the community lived, even if they did not become full members of the religious community.[48] Seton's attentiveness to her community seems both for the children they educate as well as for the plight of widows themselves.

One final point I want to make in this biographical section is to consider the historical context of Seton's writings. As we shall see in the next section, Seton's writing emphasized abandonment of the soul to God's will. This theme makes sense partly because of her encounters with the deaths of those she loved. Death is a kind of abandonment which caused her to turn to God, and abandon her soul to God. Yet Seton's writing also reflects the particularities of her American religious upbringing.

Historian Patricia A. Ward narrates American religion as integrating many distinct pieces, especially from its European roots. French Catholic mysticism, German Pietism, and Quietism all show in her book *Experimental Theology in America: Madame Guyon, Fénélon, and their Readers.* These strands of religious thought and practice appear across a range of religious traditions. A.B. Simpson, a popular late-century Presbyterian minister in Kentucky, discusses a particular version of Quietism, for example. Simpson stated: "The best thing about this stillness is that it gives God a chance to work and when we cease from our works, God works in us; and when we cease from our thoughts, God's thoughts come into us; when we get still from our restless activity, God worketh in us both to will and do of His good pleasure, and we have but to work it out."[49] The stillness Simpson advocates reflects themes of Quietism, which had some of its beginnings in Catholic mystical thought. For example, we might think of the writing of the 17th-century Jesuit Jean-Pierre de Caussade, author of *Abandonment to Divine Providence*, which emphasizes abandonment of the soul to God. Waiting in stillness for God to work is quite similar to the kind of patient stillness Seton advocates in her approach to others' deaths.

Seton's own life shows the kind of American religious diversity that Ward depicts. For example, historian Joseph Dirvin notes that Seton "wore a Catholic crucifix, looked kindly on the life of the cloister, subscribed to the doctrine of angels, liked Methodist hymns, the quietism of Quakers, and the emotionalism of Rousseau, read general Protestant works, practiced meditation, was inclined to the narrow Calvinism of her ancestors in the matter of sin and punishment, and attended the Episcopal Church."[50]

Mother Seton's writing is also directly connected to the work of her spiritual director, Simon Gabriel Bruté. Bruté was a priest and theologian in Maryland at the same time as Seton began her work in Maryland. He had been a French aristocrat (one who survived the Reign of Terror) who became a priest, having studied at St. Sulpice in Paris. At St. Sulpice, Bruté became acquainted with the spiritual writings of Pierre de Bérulle, who also emphasized abandonment of the soul to God. Later historians of spiritual life have named Bérulle's spiritual emphases as part of the "French School," which was influential on numerous theologians and missionaries. Bruté brought "French School" thinking to Maryland. He was a close confidante of Seton's, such that there is thus a line between Bruté's French brand of spirituality and Seton's own descriptions of her spiritual life.[51]

Proclaiming the Gospel of Surrender

In reflecting on her widowhood, Seton also thinks through her abandonment by other people, and she frequently describes a need to lose control, especially in the face of death, which we cannot control. The choice we make for God, however, is a choice to proclaim the Gospel, and this choice stands in stark contrast to the kind of choice of death I discussed above. Moreover, Seton's emphasis on surrender also helps bring into focus the place of Christian community for widows and widowers, as well as the place of widows and widowers in relation to the community.

Whether Seton herself was *good* at relinquishing control, especially the control of choice, is another question, and of course there are particular historical concerns related to thinking about choices here, especially the kinds of choices widows might be able to make. For example, historian and rhetorician Jenny Franchot thinks Seton aimed at controlling the illnesses in a certain limited way: "Hers was a language that sought to control illness by consenting to its presence everywhere, to use disease as an emblem not so much of civic disorder (as yellow fever functioned in the politically divisive 1790s) as of disordered subjectivity, independent of political era."[52] In Franchot's view, the fact that Seton becomes Catholic is a measure of her desire for for certainty and for rules, especially set against a Protestant worldview that was becoming increasingly individual and ephemeral. Seton's motherhood is also implicated. Franchot sees Seton as a very controlling mother, one who is disappointed in her sons' lack of spirituality but who dotes on her daughters who are appropriately obedient and godly.[53] As a side note along these lines, Seton could also have become a focus for my chapter on single parenthood. All of that said, I think that Seton's focus on having a widow's grief and facing death is more helpful for the contours of this book.[54]

Seton's theology has a strong sense of wanting to abandon the world for God, because she knows that world is not God. For Christians, this Christ/world distinction is always tricky, because while we proclaim that God is not part of this world, this universe, of course it is also the case that God meets us precisely here in the stuff of this world. The mystery of God's incarnation in

Jesus Christ cannot be taken apart from the mystery of Christ's ascension or the mystery of God's hiddenness. Seton's own life demonstrates the juggling between God and the world God loves.

It is important to know that Seton's sense of abandoning her will to God is, in part, who she has always been seeking in her spiritual life (in part due to those peculiarities of American religion that I described above). Prior to her husband's death and prior to becoming Catholic, Seton has an impulse toward wanting to abandon everything for God. For example, after her father's death, she notes that "with the calmness of a subdued spirit... now review with wonder and grateful praise that I live much less that I have lived through it."[55] Her observation stands in contrast to contemporary sensibilities: we cannot not make a choice between life and death, but rather in the face of another's death we surrender all to God and wait for God in the midst of grief.

Such a theme of God/world and abandonment to God continues as her life takes its course. As she sits by her husband's deathbed in Italy, in an era when pulling the plug is no kind of question on offer, she muses on William's capacity for surrender. Seton's theological thinking about God in moments of death continues in her experiences of her husband's death. As she waited by his death bed in Italy, she wrote: "No one ever saw my William without giving him the qualities of an amiable man. But to see the character exalted to the peaceful humble Christian waiting the will of God with a patience that seems more than human, and a firm faith which would do honor to the most distinguished piety, is a happiness allowed only to the poor little mother who is separated from all other happiness..."[56] She names herself as devoid of happiness, yet somehow also happy believing that William has surrendered his will in a way that she has not yet been able to do. She can see a particular kind of choice, which is a choice for God. It is not a choice for or against death as I suggested is part of our contemporary view of death and dying, but rather a choice for union with God.

Despite painting her husband's death in terms of happiness, Seton does not and cannot avoid the suffering that death brings. She clearly mourns her husband. In Italy, following her husband's death she visits the Uffizi art gallery one day (to pass the time while she waits for a ship to return her to her children in New York). Seeing the paintings and sculptures there causes her to reflect: "[I] felt the void of him who would have pointed out the beauties of every object, too much to enjoy any perfectly— '*Alone but half enjoyed*' 'O My God!''[57] She keens at the loss of her husband, her grief palpable.

Much later, in reflecting on her life prior to her husband's death, and comparing it to the life she has as Mother Elizabeth Ann Seton, religious leader of the Sisters of Charity, Seton proclaims the love of God:

> only be not insensible to the thousand countless motives we have to love the best of Beings and it will grow right at last,—that is if you will love. For my part I find so much contentment in this love that I am obliged to put on my consideration cap to find out how anyone can raise their eyes to the light of heaven and be insensible to it. I remember when Anna was six months old and every thing smiled around me, venerating the virtues of my Seton! And sincerely attached to him, accustomed to the daily visits and devoted love of my Father possessed of all I estimated as essential to happiness,
>
> alone with this Babe in the see saw of Motherly love frequently the tears used to start and often over flow, and I would say to myself while retrospecting the favours of heaven,—all these and heaven too?[58]

"All these and heaven too?" When she thinks of all she had, she finds herself amazed with the bounty and the love.

Yet, her 1810 widowed self has narrated her pre-widowed life as one that might be too in love with the world—including her husband and children—to be truly in love with God. Or at least, Seton knows that if it is real love, it will be love despite loss. She recalls that in holding her 6-month-old Anna, she would be

> sometimes falling on my knees with the sleeping suckling in my arms I would offer her and all my dear possession[s], Husband, Father, Home,—and intreat [*sic*] the bountiful giver to seperate [*sic*] me from all, if indeed I could not possess my portion here, and with him too—nor do I remember any part of my life after being settled in it that I have not constantly been in the same sentiment, always looking beyond the bounds of time and desiring to quit the gift for the giver.[59]

To contemporary ears (at least to mine), such a prayer seems almost to invite the deaths or abandonments of the people she loves, so this prayer is strange and terrible. Yet, Seton clearly does not mean to wish for death but rather for the gift of the love, the giver, God. God is all, such that Seton can do nothing other than to narrate her whole life, and all her loves, in relation to God's love. If the house, the husband, the children, are beautiful bounty, it is because they are God's gifts of love, which does not disappear because death has entered the scene.

Seton's life is a constant interplay between knowing God is there, believing God sets all to rights, but also encountering grief and abandonment in her own, very real, worldly life. In her move toward developing the religious community in Maryland, Seton writes about supposed friends and family who have abandoned her: "All the people are very silent—I cannot help it—to live forgotten and unloved is a Part of Christian Perfection—for the last part of it is not my greater fear—these dear beings around me breathe no other air but love.... *we* are in the Secret of his Tabernacle; and there is safety, and there alone, with true liberty and sweet content."[60] Again, God is all: Seton and the Sisters of Charity encounter love, even as they are often forgotten and go unloved.

That death and love are intermingled shows up again in Seton's own sense that we must all die each day—not the deathbed death, but death to whatever prevents us from surrendering to God. For example, in a letter to her good friend Julia Scott, Seton begs Julia to surrender her life to God:

> I will never preach to you, but I wish I could pour my heart in your bosom and tell you how sweet it is to have him our best friend, [our] dearest hope—do promise that you will pray to him for this Knowledge, you are sure of being heard with peculiar pleasure, he would leave his ninety nine in a moment if you would but be in earnest in begging his assistance.[61]

In the same letter, Seton clearly names self-surrender: "you and I must die dear daily—Oh do, do think of it.—poor Maria how much better an Inheritance you might leave her than riches."[62]

Alongside Seton's desire to join her will to God's comes the way that she reworks her understanding of family. In her journal to Rebecca Seton written while in Italy, Seton proclaims: "my poor high heart was in the clouds roving after my William's soul and repeating my God you are my God/ and so I am now alone in the world with you and my little ones but you are my Father and doubly theirs."[63] In another journal observation while in Italy, Seton compares her two homes: the earthly home and the home she has in God.

> Two days more and we set out for HOME—this mild heavenly evening puts me in mind when often you and I have stood or rather leaned on each other looking at the setting sun, sometimes with silent tears and sighs for that HOME where sorrow cannot come—'[64]

After her religious community has been established, she writes again of being a widow in the hands of God:

> You well know that he who works my fate has no need of any other help from me but a good will to do his will and an entire abandonment to

> his good providence. Let them plough, let them grind: so much the better; the grain will be the sooner prepared for its owner; whereas, should I step forward and take my own cause in hand, the Father of the widow and the orphan would say that I distrust him.[65]

God is all she needs, because God cares for widows and orphans.

Yet, because God cares for widows and orphans, Seton uses her love of God to make requests of her very human friends and family. Her frequent requests for friendship or funding or other needs carry the frank fact that she is a widow caring for this religious community of widows. In one letter to Antonio Filicchi, in which she underhandedly requests funding, she draws together care of widows and orphans with the command God gives to bestow that care, saying that God alone can repay him, for widows and orphans cannot.[66]

While her widowhood was not by choice, her decision to follow God was a choice, and her whole life becomes a way of living out proclamation of the Gospel message.

Proclaiming, Better

Seton's call to contemporary Christians is twofold. First, in the face of death she continually proclaims the Gospel, the life, death and resurrection of Christ. In contrast to a world that might rather avoid Good Friday, or at least think Good Friday isn't very significant, Seton leads Christians straight to the cross of Christ and to Good Friday. She believes there is Easter, but Easter goes hand in hand with Good Friday, suffering, and the death of Christ. Second, and because of her intimacy with God, she sees how Christian community might respond to widows. She is realistic enough to know that people might ignore widows (and widowers). Yet she is not afraid to call out people in the name of the Gospel.

How might contemporary Christians take note of such a call? One is to practice the kind of surrender to the Gospel Seton advocates. We need to witness that our primary choice in life, as in death, is for God and not for death. Prayer, contemplation, reading Christian holy people who write about suffering and death might all be communally focused ways of cultivating this surrender.

Second, I think we must revive an Order of Widows (and Widowers). In the introduction to this book, I mentioned that there would be interweaving between impermanent and permanent states of life. Mother Seton represents the interweaving of a kind of vowed religious life, together with widowhood. At the same time, the kind of order we might imagine could be distinctive from the forms of vowed religious life that Catholics, in particular, would recognize.

Some Christian communities have thought about how the elderly might be more integrated into their communities, and by association, include widows and widowers in that consideration.[67] While these are good considerations, widows and widowers comprise a broader group than "the elderly," and pose unique questions for the church. An Order of Widows and Widowers gives a more concrete place to the gifts that widowhood might offer. Perhaps such an order is as formal as the apostolic form seems to have been; perhaps it is less formally known, as in Seton's little band of widows that eventually became an order that encompassed far more people than just widows.

Some theologians have already called for such a revival, including the Catholic bishops gathered in 2015 at the Ordinary Synod on the Family. I think there might be interest and opportunity for such a move. When I have shared the writing of this chapter, more than one pastor or lay person has commented on how widows and widowers are the backbone of their congregations: setting up the spaces for worship, cooking the funeral dinners, praying for loved ones. Theologian Therese Lysaught describes older widows in particular in a description of the roles people play in Catholic communities, though I know similar activities happen among "older women" in non-Catholic traditions:

> It is older women who people daily Mass day after day. It is older women who faithfully nurture Eucharistic and Marian devotions. It is older women who work in church basements, preparing dishes for potluck suppers and cleaning up afterwards, embodying the virtue of hospitality. It is older women who visit the sick and elderly homebound, as well as practicing the other corporal works of mercy. It is older women who often clean the very church building itself.[68]

The great aspect of an Order of Widows and Widowers is recognizing the fact that widows and widowers do much of the work of the church.

Yet also, more than one widow or widower would be fascinated when I gave my talks about an Order of Widows: "How could we do this thing?" people would ask. I could see hope in peoples' eyes as they spoke of financial worry, but also a desire for human friendship. Part of recognizing widowhood is recognizing the ranges of ways widows and widowers can be destitute, and setting up some kind of communal housing. Perhaps each parish would own a house. An order might also include the kind of hospitality and charity that Elizabeth Ann Seton practiced in her own community, in arranging for the education of children. Therese Lysaught has named a range of other potential activities, including:

> An intensive practice of contemplative prayer, particularly for the community; wide range of charitable activities, particularly visiting the sick and homebound; Witness and catechesis, from assisting the staff of Catholic schools and CCD to adult education programs; Liturgical participation—leadership of presence in addition to serving as lectors, acolytes, Eucharistic ministers, and leading other forms of Eucharistic devotion; and Witnessing to a culture of life, drawing particularly on their own experiences of trial, illness, and suffering.[69]

It is imperative, in any case, for Christians to focus much more on widowhood and its particular concerns as well as gifts.

7

Grace: Divorce and Stanley Hauerwas

MANY WORDS HAVE been written, counsel given, and workshops tried in attempts to prevent divorce. The magazine column "Can This Marriage Be Saved?" still resonates with *Good Housekeeping* readers decades later. Retrouvaille (a retreat for divorcing couples) presents hope for failing relationships.

In an era when marriage is primarily understood as a relationship between two people that emphasizes love and well-being of the members of the couple, divorce troubles us. Divorce speaks to the failure of love and of our promises. More than that (but little acknowledged), the failure of a marriage creates ripples in other relationships, spreads beyond just the two people of the couple to encompass whole communities. As Pat Conroy, the author famous for such books as *The Prince of Tides*, writes: divorce is "a lurid duet that entices observers to the dance; the *pas de deux* expands, flowers into a monstrous choreography and draws in friends, children and relatives. Each divorce is the death of a small civilization."[1]

Divorce brings out the sociologists and statisticians telling us what is wrong with the culture, why marriage is good for people and society, how negatively divorce will affect the children. Everyone knows that half of all marriages will end in divorce—except that, in fact, it turns out we're wrong about that statistic. The number is more like 40 percent and on a decline—and the likelihood of divorce depends on all kinds of other things. Generation, race, age at getting married, all shift the probability of whether a couple will divorce. Nonetheless, we persist in believing half of all marriages end in divorce.

Christians don't often write about divorce.[2] I think there are two reasons why. First, the prospect of divorce messes with Christians' idolatries surrounding marriage, some of which I have already discussed in previous chapters: that God can help us find The One who will make life more or less perfect; that Jesus commanded us to live in nuclear families just like in the 1950s; that marriage is primarily about love, just like Jesus' love. All of these are idolatries because they put human love and human relationships in God's place, even as they give lip service to God.

The second reason is due to a key difference between divorce and the other single states of life mentioned in this book. Divorce signifies that a relationship has failed. When dating relationships or friendships end, there is not the same sense of personal failure.[3] For Christians, the sense of failure is felt even more deeply. Divorce is not merely the failure of a couple, it is the failure of Christian teachings about marriage and sexuality. Christian marriage hinges on two radical ideas: that I could stay with another person, even in and through all the changes a person makes throughout life; and that my sexual desire could be part of the basis of a relationship that is fruitful. Divorce disrupts Christians' radical claims about marriage.

When Christians *do* think about divorce, their responses come in two main guises. One is to join in a cultural frenzy about preventing divorce, along with various attempts to keep divorce out of their congregations. The other response is a move toward accepting divorce, and especially accepting divorcing people. Scripture scholar Richard Hays writes that the feeling among Christians is, "we must avoid being judgemental....To require people to stay in difficult marriages against their inclination would be to impose a harsh law contrary to the spirit of love."[4]

Nonetheless, in this chapter I am writing about divorce and divorcing people. I am not thereby saying that Christian teaching about divorce should be overturned. Yet I am writing about divorce as a state of life that witnesses to the life, death, and resurrection of Jesus Christ, and therefore as a state of life that says something important about Christian discipleship. I am asking a question similar to one that popular author Lauren Winner probes: "What is the witness of divorcing and divorced people in the church to the church?"[5]

In order to show how divorce and divorcing people do offer witness to the church, first I discuss New Testament passages about divorce, alongside how contemporary scripture scholars look at those passages. Then I detail contemporary Christian debate and writing about divorce more fully. I show how discussions of divorce are chiefly about reaffirming Christian theologies of marriage rather than posing anything particular about divorce. While, as I mentioned in Chapter 1, the flexibility and interconnectedness between impermanent states and the permanent states of marriage and vowed religious life do mean that thinking about divorce should mean we also think about marriage, in this chapter, I'm suggesting that there is very little interchange. This lack of dialogue is actually unhelpful for Christians. Specifically,

I suggest how the marriage theologies stemming from discussions about divorce lead to a debate about idealism versus being realistic, which is where the debate typically, and frustratingly, stops. The supposed story Christians must accept becomes one of either believing in a Christian theology of marriage (ideal) or accepting the messy lives of actual Christians who sometimes get divorced (real).

This supposed dichotomy between ideal and real is a false dichotomy. I demonstrate the falseness of this dichotomy by highlighting an author who has written about Christian life as well as his own divorce. Stanley Hauerwas, a professor at Duke University, has sharp critiques of an ideal/realist debate. I conclude with a discussion of Lauren Winner's description and discussion of her own divorce, as well as some thoughts for how Christians might continue on when it comes to encountering divorce in their midst. I think one of the particular characteristics that divorce teaches Christians is the nature of hope and the grace of God.

Christian Divorce Debates: Ideal versus Real

The New Testament scriptures that speak against divorce are often seen as ideal, and Christian communities choose to deal with the scriptures about divorce in many ways.

In Mark 10:2–12, for example, we find Jesus saying the strong words that became part of some denominations' wedding liturgies: "What God has joined together, let no one separate." Jesus speaks these words in response to questions from Pharisees about whether divorce is lawful. In the discussion that ensues, Jesus affirms that the Law of Moses permits divorce. Yet Jesus pushes for his followers to avoid divorce. Even more strongly, Jesus admonishes that those who divorce and remarry (both men and women) are committing adultery.[6] Scripture scholar Richard Hays provides the following commentary on the text: "Divorce is a sign of hardness of heart; those who follow Jesus are called to a higher standard of permanent faithfulness in marriage."[7]

One reading of Mark's gospel suggests that the very meaning of marriage is Christian discipleship and faithful service to Jesus. The fact that God becomes flesh and dwells among us changes Christian understanding of both marriage and divorce, and excludes the possibility of divorce if we are true believers. Therefore, divorce comes across as antithetical to Christian discipleship and is prohibited by some Christian communities.

Matthew 19:3–12 is similar to Mark 10 in that Jesus reiterates his statement that people should not separate what God brings together. However, in Matthew Jesus adds some exceptions: in cases of *porneia*, men may divorce women. Scholars have not settled on what all *porneia* might mean, but there is a tendency to see *porneia* as referring to many different kinds of "sexual immorality."[8] Jesus also mentions divorce in his Sermon on the Mount (Matthew 5:31–32) and in a very similar passage to this one in Luke 16:18. The lengthy Sermon on the Mount is where we find the Beatitudes, the Lord's Prayer, and numerous other conversations about what it means to be Jesus' follower. In the Sermon on the Mount, Jesus boldly states: "Do not think I have come to abolish the law or the prophets; I have not come to abolish them, but to fulfill them." Then he follows up this bold claim by referring to statements about what Jewish law allows and takes the law even further. One example is, "You have heard it said, an eye for an eye, but I tell you, Do not resist an evildoer. But if anyone strikes you on the right cheek, turn the other also." [9] This much-debated passage has shaped Christian conversation about nonviolent practice, war, and the death penalty, among others. Jesus' idea of fulfillment of the law is to take law and reshape it.

Similarly, on divorce Jesus says, "It was also said, 'Whoever divorces his wife, let him give her a certificate of divorce.' But I say to you that anyone who divorces his wife, except on the ground of unchastity, causes her to commit adultery; and whoever marries a divorced woman commits adultery." While the law permits divorce and remarriage, Jesus' fulfillment of the law suggests not only that divorce is wrong, but that remarriage is not a permissible action for Christians. These texts all suggest an idealistic view that relationships can and must never fail.

A final passage on divorce comes in Paul's first letter to the Corinthians (7:10–16). This comes in the lengthier passage I have already discussed in Chapter 2 of this book, Paul's words about remaining widowed or unmarried. Paul writes, "To the married I give this command—not I, but the Lord—that the wife should not be separated from her husband (but if she does become separated, let her remain unmarried or else be reconciled to her husband), and that the husband should not send his wife away."[10] While Paul does not go as far as Matthew, Mark, and Luke in describing remarriage as adultery, he does clearly discourage divorce and remarriage.

Moreover, Paul writes that Christians ought not even divorce their spouses who do not share their belief in Jesus Christ. He states that if the unbelieving partner wishes to divorce, then let them divorce, for "It is to peace that God has called us."[11] Christians might not seek divorce, but if a spouse who does not share in Christ's peace seeks a divorce, then let the divorce happen. Richard Hays' gloss on Paul's words is to suggest, "participation in the community of faith is the most fundamental commitment, more basic than marriage. . . . God has called us (i.e., the church, the community of God's elect people) to peace."[12]

To sum up: scripture scholars have "virtual consensus that Jesus was unequivocally opposed to divorce."[13] Marriage is meant to be a way of following Jesus. The caveat is that not all Christians need get married, which is perhaps supposed to make the teachings about marriage more palatable. Divorce might happen for some, perhaps especially in instances of *porneia*, but when divorce happens, Christians should be encouraged not to remarry.

How Christians Attempt to Live these Scriptures: The Marriage Ideal

Taken together, these strongly worded texts show Christian marriage as a commitment of fidelity that cannot (very easily) be broken. Christians have developed practices over the centuries that strongly mitigate against divorce and aim at helping people maintain marriages. Some communities have actively or implicitly shunned those who are divorced. In the contemporary period, Christians have articulated additional reasons why divorce might necessarily happen—especially in cases of abuse.[14]

In the Roman Catholic Church has developed a practice of annulment—a communal process of determining whether a marriage met the requirements for being sacramental or not. It is important to note that annulment is not, strictly speaking, a Catholic version of divorce. Annulments look at the relationship as it existed at the beginning, when the couple sought to be married. Divorce, a government court–guided process, looks at the relationship as it is now. Divorce seeks to divide the goods of marriage—its property, children, and so forth. Annulment does not say that a relationship never existed, but it does say that a sacramental marriage as understood by Christians did not exist. When a Catholic who has been granted an annulment marries again, that Catholic is viewed as having been married only once sacramentally. The Roman Catholic Church further withholds communion from Catholics who are divorced and remarried (though Catholics who are divorced and not remarried may still receive it). During the era of Christendom, political regimes also supported Christian stances against divorce via law and cultural ostracism.[15]

Such practices can lead to people feeling a great sense of shame and failure in the midst of their divorces. Pope Francis famously called for two bishops' synods to discuss Catholic doctrine on families, and people's pastoral responses. Many divorced and remarried Catholics hoped for changes to doctrine, specifically changes that would allow divorced and remarried Catholics to receive communion even without having had their first marriage annulled. That doctrinal change did not happen; however, the pope asked for pastors to discern with couples and possibly grant exceptions in some cases.[16]

Contemporary Christians often respond to divorced and divorcing people with similarly strong words. For example, Henry and Ella Mitchell, both leaders who served at United Methodist and Reformed Christian seminaries, wrote a sermon together on divorce that describes the pastoral care advice they typically give to couples. They suggest that when divorce happens, it's often "because at least one of these divorcers fully intends to remain hard and resistant to the very idea of uniting on God's terms."[17] Some hardness of heart requires divorce, such as physical abuse. The Mitchells think that most of the time, what couples need is the knowledge that marriages can be renewed. Couples need the restored hope that God can provide. "[W]hen we see families fail, it is all too often true that the power of Christ just hasn't been fully tried by two sincere seekers."[18] The Mitchells emphasize an image of marriage that puts Christ at the center. They suggest that when Christ is there, the love just simply "flows."[19]

When confronted with divorce, many Christians respond as the Mitchells do: they try to emphasize the significance of marriage for Christians. Moreover, they wonder how Christians might form their church communities so that the incidences of divorce become lower. Pastoral care therefore emphasizes the period before marriage, especially engagement, in an attempt to pre-empt divorce.

Pastoral care is not the only arena where the emphasis is on pre-empting divorce rather than focusing on the meaning of divorce itself. For example, Richard Hays concludes his examination of New Testament scriptures on divorce by asking, "How can we in the church form our life together so that the marriages in our midst do become signs of the mystery of grace? How can we enable our marriages to resist the corrosive cultural influences that make divorce seem inevitable?"[20] These are good and important questions, yet these questions do not really touch on care of divorcing and already divorced adults. These are preventative questions, meant to help a community establish helpful anti-divorce practices.

For some Christians, the hope is that by providing stronger understandings of marriage and better communities, Christian couples won't find themselves in the position of getting a divorce at all. The difficulty comes when divorce does, in fact, happen—and the ideal visions become tarnished. What then? The whole of the Christian vision seems to come crashing down from its pedestal, making the ideal seem unworkable and impractical. Moreover, as much as I sympathize with the impulse to reinvigorate a Christian theology of marriage (and truly, this is important and necessary work), this impulse has the effect of dismissing the presence of divorcing people, for the most part. Richard Hays begins his chapter on divorce by asking, "Can the church bless divorce? If so, under what conditions?"[21] While he answers these questions to an extent, the force of Hay's work is much more on identifying a theology of *marriage*. He makes important observations, such as that marriage is a practice of Christian discipleship and that "the church must recognize and teach that marriage is grounded not in *feelings* of love but in the *practice* of love."[22] His chapter concludes with a homily that emphasizes particular ways Christians practice marriage. The most Hays says about divorcing people and their experience is, "the community of the church must seek to find ways to provide deep and satisfying *koinonia* and friendships for those divorced persons who choose not to remarry in order to devote their lives to the service of God outside the married state...."[23]

Where does this leave divorce—and the questions Hays raises about the extent to which the church can bless divorce? I think Hays is right to suggest that the church should not be about the task of blessing divorce, as in accepting divorce as an action that is God-given. Yet I think there is still space to think about what Christians are to make of divorce and how to think about relationships that fail, or still more, how—in the midst of failure—we can still bear witness to Christ.

Too Idealistic?

In response to authors that address divorce by developing theologies of marriage, some Christians respond to the idealism they perceive by promoting (in their view) a more realistic view of marriage. What "more realistic" means is that people's experiences of marriage form and shape Christian theology about marriage, divorce, and remarriage.

In what follows I narrate some of the theologians who speak against idealistic marriage in favor of closely examining peoples' experiences. I also complicate their sense of what is "realistic." While I think experience can be important (for example, I make use of people's experiences in this book in order to show a cloud of single witnesses!), a focus on experience is just as troubling, if not more so, than a focus on what ideal marriage looks like.

Roman Catholic theologian Bernard Cooke writes, "in our theological study of Catholic marriage, it is essential that we remain constantly in contact with *what is*. There is no place where divine saving intent is revealed apart from the lives of humans...."[24] Cooke goes on to investigate people's lives, including the fact that many people in the twenty-first century get divorced and remarried. So, for example, against the idealistic Roman Catholic view of first marriages as sacramental if they have not been annulled, Cooke wonders whether second marriages might also contain the ingredients of sacramentality. Cooke's view of the sacrament is "the concrete social reality of couples whose commitment to intimate sharing of life together bears witness to the mystery of God's transforming love for us humans."[25] He sees that marriages that people enter into after divorce, even if they have not sought annulments, have the key ingredients of sacramentality. Human relationships help Christians see Christ, but Christ meets us in our hopes as well as our failures. There is little or no reason, in Cooke's view, for the church to refuse to see that remarriage is a possibility and that sacrament is not limited to a person's first marriage.

One example of what Cooke means is the story of Anna Cannon. In a personal account of how she tries to be a faithful Catholic in spite of her divorce, Cannon describes her "whirlwind romance" that resulted in a church-sanctioned wedding. This sacramental marriage "lasted four profoundly damaging years, in which I was exposed to mental cruelty and abuse as well as serial infidelity, and ended six months after our daughter was born."[26] As often happens in divorces, Anna found herself impoverished for a while but eventually found a good job and a relationship with a man who became her life partner. When she began living with that man, she also began not to receive communion each week at mass. She did not, however, go through an annulment process; her parish priest ended up blessing the marriage without an annulment. Anna compares the grace she receives from her present relationship with the unbearable nature of her first, church-sanctioned sacramental marriage, and names her second marriage as one capable of bearing the marks of the sacrament in ways that the first marriage did not.

Another response scholars have taken is to raise questions about scripture interpretation in relation to divorce. Some scripture scholars dismiss the New Testament canon or find the words insufficient because, in their view, the situation of early Christians was far different from Christians today. For example, Mary Rose d'Angelo suggests Christians should not worry about the divorce texts I discussed above because early Christian writers like Mark and Matthew spoke from "early Christian sexual asceticism."[27] Sexual renunciation in that context meant freedom, but in our context sexual renunciation is not freeing. Because the scriptures deal with sexuality in ways particular to first- and second-century Christians, "They by no means express an ideal for marriage."[28] D'Angelo instead advocates seeking other scriptures that can supplant the troubling ones about divorce. She suggests this passage from Galatians: "All you who have been baptized into Christ have put on Christ: there is among you neither Jew or Greek, neither slave nor free, no 'male' or 'female.'" This is Christ's new ideal, one that suggests new ways of understanding human relationships to the point that divorce gets overshadowed by Christ's new alternatives.

In a different vein, Peter Carrell suggests that there are "significant shifts" in thinking about marriage that change how we read scriptures today. The three shifts he identifies include (1) greater acceptance of divorce and remarriage, (2) marriages based on gender equality, and (3) the fact that singleness "is not valued as an alternative to marriage to the degree that Paul endorsed in 1 Cor[inthians] 7."[29]

From a realist point of view, pastoral care focuses on the divorced or divorcing couple almost entirely. The well-known pastoral care manual by Howard Clinebell states that a central problem for divorced and divorcing Christians is that "our society has few organized resources for helping divorcing women and men do their grief work, learn and grow from their painful experiences."[30] Clinebell recommends three main goals for pastors working with divorcing people: (1) to help people deal with the pain of divorce, (2) "to help divorcing people learn and grown from the experience,"[31] and (3) to find the best ways to guide children through their parents' divorces so that the impact on them is minimal. Clinebell's third point is significant, because consideration of children is frequently missing in discussions of divorce, as I discuss below. Clinebell's specific communal solution was for pastors to offer support groups for divorcing people, which is especially helpful because churches have traditionally been places of judgement for divorcing people.

In aid of helping divorcing people through pain, some Christians have advocated for special prayers and blessings over divorces. Secular culture has even developed a ritual known as the "divorce party."[32] Christians appear to have joined in at times, by blessing divorces. Episcopal bishop John Shelby Spong suggests a "Service for the Recognition of the End of a Marriage" in which a divorcing couple "[stood] before the altar and the congregation, 'asked each other for forgiveness, and pledged themselves to be friends, to stand united in caring for their children, and to be civil and responsible to one another. . . .' "[33] The service concludes with the presider affirming the couple's new covenant. (Richard Hays wonders wryly whether a couple that can make such affirmations might actually also be able to work out and sustain the original marriage covenant in the first place.)

Michael Lawler also speaks on the theme of idealism and realism in a book on what is versus what ought to be. Lawler argues that theologians need to pay attention to sociologists and others who present data on what currently *is* the case among humans. We then sift through what is, and think theologically to consider what *ought* to be. Lived experience needs to guide what ought to be, in other words.

In Lawler's estimation, "the church's practice with respect to divorce and remarriage is not founded exclusively on the words of Jesus. Much of it is founded on the re-reception of the words of Jesus nuanced in the socio-historical contexts through which the church has passed in its journey to the modern world."[34] That is to say, in Lawler's view, people have always interpreted Jesus' words in relation to their own contexts. In the early twenty-first century, Christians are reinterpreting Jesus' words in light of their new understandings of marriage and family, and they see that divorce and remarriage are sometimes necessary for Christians and need to be reconfigured.

These several commenters' complaints speak something true about both the present state of marriage and the cultural shifts surrounding marriage. It is important to be truthful about the state of marriage now as well as throughout history. Christians do no favors by trying to pretend that the particular ideal family as we hold it to be (that is, the nuclear family) has been the ideal throughout history. Christians also do no favors by sidestepping the very real pain that divorced and divorcing Christians experience in the process of divorce, as well as from the community's response to that divorce.

Yet, many of these authors make at least two mistakes. One mistake is to suggest that marriage and divorce are aspects of Christian life that deserve to be moving targets because the time in which we live is different. We think differently about marriage now, so therefore we can summarily avoid what scripture says about marriage and divorce.

While it is undoubtedly true that we live in an age where marriage has different meanings than it has often had, historians would argue we should not get too comfortable with marriage as we *think* it existed in previous generations. That is, the "ought" of our supposed idealism is not the only ought that exists. There is also a historical "ought" that Lawler, d'Angelo, and Cooke, presume. Families have always been messy and have generally not followed the "nuclear family" model made so familiar in 1950s sitcoms.[35] When it comes to divorce, in fact, in the 1940s about one in three marriages ended in divorce—perhaps a surprising figure when a more common story is that the1960s is the decade that started a divorce revolution. Historian Stephanie Coontz also describes how, in the 1970s and 1980s, there was a concerted effort from several quarters to make divorce unacceptable. Divorce was evidence, in some people's views, of a selfish society gone wrong; many times, divorce culture is blamed on the feminist revolution (among others).

Coontz disputes a view of divorce as so easily equated with individualism:

> I have met only a tiny handful of divorced parents who didn't worry long and hard about the effects of divorce on their children. . . . And while it's true that a few pop psychologists have made irresponsible

claims that divorce is just a 'growth experience,' I don't believe we are really a culture that 'celebrates' divorce.[36]

Still, Coontz says: "[L]et me be clear. Ending a marriage is an agonizing process that can seriously wound everyone involved, especially the children. Divorce can interfere with effective parenting and deprive children of parental resources. Remarriage solves some of the economic problems associated with divorce but introduces a new set of tensions...."[37]

A second mistake that many of the scholars quoted above make is to speak as though the divorcing couple lives in a vacuum, without reference to children or to others in their communities. The lack of discussion of children is especially concerning. For example, Judith Wallerstein's research has famously described the effects of divorce on children both in the short term and the long term.[38] While there are issues with Wallerstein's research—particularly the question of whether other factors related to divorce, like loss of income, demonstrate the negative effects of divorce on children—most researchers have found that there are negative effects of divorce on children. In the short term, older siblings might take on heavy burdens of being parents for their younger siblings, or even parenting their parents. Such a burden comes in addition to the emotional toll of divorce. Children feel lonely, angry, like they're the cause of the divorce, and find themselves "weighed down by the responsibility for making all the decisions themselves" when it comes to school and grades and sport and other day-to-day life experiences.[39] Similarly, adult children from divorced families often find themselves without role models. Family get-togethers and vacations are warm memories for children of intact families (even when these children also noted "open antagonism"), but children of divorce rarely mention vacations or family get-togethers. These kinds of memories are missing from their storehouse of childhood memories that help form and shape adults and their adult functioning and development. While there are scholars like Ross Thompson and Paul Amato, who describe the resilience of children of divorce, their findings also generally support Wallerstein's work. Divorce has its effects, and those effects continue for years. Children find ways to adapt, and sometimes are successful, but that does not change divorce's effects.[40]

It is important to note that Wallerstein and others do study so-called "high conflict" relationships, relationships where patterns of physical abuse and emotional abuse comprise day-to-day life, where children fare worse. Maintaining a high-conflict marriage over divorce negatively impacts children in these relationships. That said, Wallerstein suspects most marriages are not high-conflict relationships. Wallerstein's own thought is that in non-abusive relationships that are "not so explosive or chaotic or unsafe," people might strongly consider remaining "unhappily married."[41] He suggests that the proverbial axiom that children feel their parents' unhappiness and are therefore unhappy too is not true: "It depends on whether the parents are able gracefully and without anger to make the sacrifice required to maintain the benefits of the marriage for their children."[42] That said, Wallerstein is realistic, recognizing that many adults will be unable to make that kind of sacrifice. For these adults, Wallerstein suggests being excruciatingly realistic about the need for further education (for example), more support, and to consider very carefully how to parent their children so that they remain the parents (rather than this role being passed along to eldest children, often girls).

The impulse toward a real/ideal dichotomy, or the is/ought dichotomy, stems from at least two important desires. One is the desire to follow Christ as revealed to us in scripture, including in the strong words about divorce. The second is the desire to be generous, hospitable, and loving to people in pain. The question to ask is whether these two desires are as separate as the idealist/realist dichotomy seems to suggest. Is God present, even in the pain and suffering of divorce? Can divorcing people speak words of witness to the church about God's presence?

Stanley Hauerwas: The Character of Christian Life

Stanley Hauerwas is a theologian at Duke University whose writing has been directed against American liberalism, and particular at the idealist/realist (or in Lawler's terms, is/ought) that American liberalism suggests. "Liberal" here does not mean Left, as it does in American politics (that is, "liberal" in relation to being liberal and conservative means something different than what Hauerwas means). Rather, liberalism refers to a particular view of human life together that emphasizes individuality, freedom, autonomy, and universal tolerance.

For Christians, there should be several difficulties with American liberalism, and especially that it subverts the Gospel of Christ while pretending to be the standard-bearer of "Christian values." For example, Hauerwas has often told seminary students in his introductory ethics courses that having an American flag in the sanctuary is an act of idolatry. The presence of the flag suggests that "America" and its ideals are stronger than Christ. Christ is not Lord of one nation, but Lord of the whole creation, including other nations and peoples—having a flag in the sanctuary does not proclaim Jesus as the Lord of all creation.

One of the key features of liberalism is that it pretends to be objective—it pretends to give what "is" the case. Liberalism pretends to be the umbrella under which all people—and especially all religions—can seek to have their disagreements arbitrated, because liberalism is open to all perspectives and is tolerant of all. In the face of claims that religion causes violence, liberalism offers freedom from that violence by proclaiming separation of church and state. The American government offers liberalism par excellence.

Yet, Hauerwas points out how people never notice that liberalism itself is only supported by violence, especially the violence of war. America cannot be the free, tolerant society it seeks to be except by promoting other societies like itself through violence. Liberalism presumes that only its versions of tolerance are the ones that matter. "[Christians] began to say that their task was to create societies where no one ever has to die for what they believe; therefore, Christians became identified with people of goodwill—wishing everyone well. And that is exactly to buy into the liberal presumption that there really is a common morality that we all share and that we all know how to work for."[43]

Hauerwas suggests that Christians have been given the gift of the church—a Christian community that spans the time since Jesus Christ. The gift of the church enables Christians to offer a counter-politics to the dominant politics we experience in daily American life. The church gives Christians a way of living political life that shows people an "otherwise" for how to live. For example, against the violence of war, Christians can be communities of peace. Against a culture that supports killing of children via abortion, Christians can suggest that children are signs of hope. Against an American culture that is individualistic, Christian Eucharist forms people into seeing each other as community—even people that we might not otherwise consider worthy to be our dining companions, such as the disabled.

Hauerwas's emphasis on the Christian community called "Church" has left many wondering where this church is that Hauerwas sees. Indeed, many people's experience of their local congregations is *not* of a nonviolent community of people seeking to live the Gospel but rather of racist, sexist, legalistic people. Is Hauerwas' view of Christian community too much of an "ought" rather than an "is"?

Ought versus is, and ideal versus real is exactly the charge Michael Lawler makes against Stanley Hauerwas. "The church as it *ought to be* can enshrine Christian values properly, but unfortunately the church as it *is* in history does not do so properly. In Hauerwas's judgment, the church as it ought to be, read as Hauerwas believes it should be, has not yet happened in its two-thousand-year history."[44] Lawler goes on to suggest that philosopher Alasdair MacIntyre is far more correct to suggest that there is no such thing as a perfect ideal.

He cites MacIntyre: there "'is a mélange of moral thoughts and practice... fragments from the tradition—virtue concepts for the most part—are still to be found alongside characteristically modern and individualist concepts such as those of rights or utility.'"[45] Lawler continues on to suggest that "in the real world," virtues learned in church overlap with virtues learned in non-church contexts. There is no pure churchly world or community, in other words.

The funny thing is, Hauerwas might agree with Lawler that Alasdair MacIntyre's point is a good one—a crucial point, in fact. We do indeed live in a fragmented world where moral thoughts and practices stand fragmented and intermixed with each other. So of course, the church and its members do not live in a perfect world that is cordoned off by perfect concepts and words. Faced with so fragmented a world, it seems that all we humans can do is choose our own best way of narrating whether and how the fragments fit together. In Lawler's view, there is a collective sensibility[46] that many people share as they seek to draw the fragments together.

Yet this is also where Hauerwas would say that Lawler has MacIntyre wrong.[47] The fragmented world is a tragedy. We humans do have to figure out how to continue on, even in a world that is fragmented and pluralistic. Lawler's way of continuing on, even of making the problem disappear because all he has to do is make Catholic teaching conform to peoples' sociological experiences, is not MacIntyre's way, on Hauerwas' view (nor is it Hauerwas' way).

Rather, for Hauerwas, we learn to continue on by learning to live truthfully in our various communities. Sometimes, this means attempting to tell truth to people who may not want to hear it. Hauerwas has learned from the philosopher Ludwig Wittgenstein that we learn multiple languages—that is, we learn that words have multiple meanings in many different communities, and we learn how to use words well according to the particular communities in which we find ourselves. Words shape our vision of the world, and they shape the kinds of actions we think we can do. The work of Christians is the difficult work of naming the particular words and actions that bear witness to Christ. This work is difficult precisely because we live in a fragmented world, a world in which our language and actions have multiple uses and meanings, and it can be excruciatingly difficult to know whether a person is glorifying God or not.

For example, in the book, *Christians Among the Virtues,* Hauerwas and his co-author Charles Pinches describe courage, one of the virtues that Christians and non-Christians seek to cultivate in their lives. What courage means, and what it looks like in action, differs depending on the communities in which people reside. For the pre-Christian philosopher Aristotle, a soldier on the battlefield is an example of a courageous person. That solider does not necessarily lack fear, but has learned to respond to his fear rightly. Moreover, "death on the battlefield . . . stands as the paradigm of courage for Aristotle precisely because it gives the genuinely courageous person the chance to offer the one great good that unifies all other particular goods, that is, his life, for an even higher good: namely the common good of the state."[48] In Aristotle's vision, the best example of courage is the soldier on the battlefield. More importantly, the reason the battlefield soldier's death is the best example of courage is because the greatest aim of human life was "the common good of the state."

By contrast, when the thirteenth-century theologian Thomas Aquinas writes about courage, the best example of courage is the Christian martyr. Like the soldier, the Christian martyr is willing to die for the best thing, but for the Christian the best thing is not the common good of the state but life in Jesus Christ. The martyr's action is markedly different from the soldier's. While both people die, the Christian is "required patiently to persevere in the face of persecution."[49] "Martyrs, in effect, have to be ready to lose to their persecutors, dying ingloriously. They can do so only because they recognized that neither their life nor their death carries its own (or anyone else's) weight of meaning; rather, that is carried by the God who supplies it."[50]

Hauerwas and Pinches go on to wonder how these two visions of courage relate to contemporary American political life, especially in an America whose soldiers (many of whom are Christian) die for America. These soldiers' courage is still courage, but it is not the same as the courage that Christ asks when he calls on his followers to take up their crosses and follow him. American Christians have too often conflated the two kinds of courage, seeing the soldier's death as an act of courage that bears witness to Christ. In fact, the soldier is witnessing to the ideals of America. That courage is a "semblance of courage," which may help us learn a little about Christian courage, but it does not display the truth of courage as we have it from Christ who dies on the cross. Thus Hauerwas and Pinches attempt to name truth about Christian courage to American Christians who may be all too willing to conflate the kinds of courage—and too willing to presume that what we do and say as Americans in relation to war, violence, and politics, is necessarily what Jesus meant.

Christian Marriage, Christian Divorce

Marriage and *singleness* are two words that are similarly distinctive for Christians, in Hauerwas' account. To live a life of singleness is to bear witness to the fact that marriage and family are not the most important activities in a Christian's life, and, moreover, marriage is not required to live a Christian life. Hauerwas writes: "We must remember that the most significant thing the single give up is not sex. What the single give up are heirs, grandchildren named Joel Adam Hauerwas, and they do so because they now understand that they have been made part of a community that is more determinative than the biological family."[51] Other, more dominant, communal understandings of marriage see marriage and family in romantic ways: that marriage is chiefly about falling in love. Marriage confirms the couple's love.

Rather, Hauerwas points out that Christian teaching about marriage (even if we have often forgotten it) emphasizes that marriage is a vocation Christians hold in the "more determinative community" of the church. "That the church is a more determinative community than a marriage is evidenced by the fact that it requires Christian marriage vows to be made with the church as witness."[52] Couples getting married take vows for lifelong fidelity and monogamy, which, at the beginning of the marriage, no couple could possibly quite understand, yet the church stands both as witness and as the community that helps shape and form people to live their marriages well. Moreover, the church is asking the question "whether you are the kind of person who can be held to a promise you made when you did not know what you were promising."[53] (Note—the marrying couple do not pledge "love" precisely, though the attempts to live faithfully and monogamously surely help people try to cultivate the virtue of love).

So Hauerwas would vehemently disagree with Lawler's insistence about is/ought as a workable principle in naming a theology of marriage. The is/ought distinction doesn't serve Christians at all. The dichotomy especially doesn't enable people to serve Christ. How can we make an is/ought distinction about Jesus? The Son of God most definitely ought not to have died on the cross, and yet he does die on the cross. For that, Christians sing "O Happy Fault" at every Easter Vigil service, proclaiming how wonderful it is that Adam and Eve sinned, so that Jesus could come to die on a cross. Christians proclaim the happiness of the cross, the dying of a savior.

How, too, can we make an is/ought distinction about Christians and their life together? If life together isn't bearing witness to Christ, then it simply isn't a Christian life. Is/ought doesn't help people speak truth to each other, nor does it help Christian communities find ways to help each other live and love as Jesus commands us to do.

To say that does *not* mean that (a) Christians have a unified or universal vision of what it means to follow Christ or that (b) Christians and Christian communities always bear witness to Christ. Hauerwas is often misunderstood to be saying something like (a) and (b) above. Communities, and the people within them, can fail and often do. Those theologians like Katie Grimes, who name the excruciating and non-Christ-like racist actions of Christian communities that supported and undergirded slavery, are helping the church to be more truthful about itself and its members.[54]

In one essay, in fact, Hauerwas states:

> While I have drawn on some motifs derived from communitarian thinking, my concerns always have been how to exhibit the power that theological convictions have had, can have, and should have, for how Christians should understand their care for one another.... Indeed, I think that underwriting the commonly made contrast between liberalism and communitarianism can result in blurring the theological issues.[55]

Community is not the end result of Hauerwas' theology, but rather communities are the ways we humans can do certain things that we simply can't do alone, such as worshipping God. (While I might pray, and therefore worship God on my own, the language I am using and even my very knowledge of God is a gift of the fact that I am and have been part of Christian communities.) In relation to the themes of this chapter, it becomes apparent that we cannot marry alone, we cannot survive alone, we cannot divorce alone. Those are facts; how we tell the story of those facts in relation to belief in God is what is crucial for Christians.

Hauerwas writes about pain, failures, and loneliness, as part of his belief in God. (One wonders if his detractors read all the real life stuff that Hauerwas writes, when it comes to pain, suffering, failure, disability, and so forth.) His writing on pain and failures turns out to be important for Christian thinking on divorce, as I shall show in the next section.

Hauerwas' Divorce

As I mentioned earlier, the difficulty of divorce for Christians is that it names failure. Not just the individual couple's relationship—indeed, to push the pain and failure of divorce solely on the couple would be cruel and untruthful. Divorce also, and most especially, names a failure of Christian community to live as though it believes in Christian marriage.

In what follows, I will try to make clear that Hauerwas' understanding of church is not a lofty ideal (similar to the ideals I mentioned in the first section) that can be gotten around, if and when real life gets in the way. I will describe Hauerwas' divorce alongside his writings on reality and failure. Further, I discuss Lauren Winner's divorce, and her searching through Christian tradition, as an example of thinking about reality and failure.

In the end, I suggest that rightly being able to offer pastoral care to divorcing people means, first of all, acknowledging Christians' failures (and mostly *not* the failures of divorcing people, by the way). Thinking about failures also opens a way for removing the relative silence about divorce. It opens a way for seeing divorced and divorcing people as people who have gifts to offer the church, if we other members of the community can see them as gifts.

Hauerwas' account of divorce must be seen hand in hand with his account of his first wife's illness. Anne had manic-depression and would have "three or four episodes a year.... Episodes would come in diverse and colorful forms. I knew we were in trouble, for example, when she began to read Robert Graves's *The White Goddess*. I wanted to tell her not to read further, because I knew it would trigger an episode in which she would become 'the white goddess,' which is exactly what happened."[56] He describes the gradual progression of the disease, the frightening nature of its impact on her, him, and his young son Adam, the chaos, the despair, the struggle to survive despite not knowing what would happen. Yet he also names how "life did not stop" because of her illness, nor did the marriage—they all strove to survive, a very difficult thing to do. Indeed, "during the years that Anne's illness dominated our lives, I discovered the gift of friendship."[57] Colleagues and congregation members befriend him and his family; he comes to the know the significant truth that marriage cannot be lived in a vacuum, but requires a community.

As he considers making a move from the University of Notre Dame, where he spent many years on the faculty, to Duke University, he writes: "Anne was still not well. I had to make the decision without her. 'Do whatever you want,' she said. What I wanted was for her to love me. What I wanted was for us to have a life together. What I wanted was for Adam to have a mother."[58] None of those things would happen at Notre Dame (any more than at Duke). Hauerwas describes making the move to Duke even as Anne finds herself in and out of manic-depressive episodes, in and out of caring about the move.

Just before the first semester began at Duke, Anne "went crazy... convinced she needed to return to South Bend to save Jim [Burtchaell—a priest at Notre Dame that Anne had fallen in love with]. It seems he was possessed by demons and only Anne could exorcise them." Hauerwas describes trying to get her to the medical center, to get treatment. "She was angry that I had the power to have her committed. What could I say? I did have the power, though I had never actually used it. She continued to maintain that I was her jailer. It was clear that any hope of our beginning a more 'normal life' was gone."[59] Moreover, Anne thought that "she was ill because she was married to me."[60]

"I was in pain, but I could see no alternatives. One of the reasons I could see no alternatives was, interestingly enough, rather self-interested. I worried that if I found a way to 'escape' from the marriage, I might lose the critical edge that seemed to make my work compelling."[61] They tried all the usual things people try in fixing ailing relationships. As time spun out, Adam headed to Haverford College, Anne tried numerous new combinations of drugs, they went to marriage counseling. One day, Anne "walked out midway in the third session, declaring that she was not coming back. In fact, she said she was going to leave me.... She did not seem to be crazy. I finally told her to do what she had to do."[62]

She left. She left after a 24-year marriage, left behind the house with the cats. She returned to South Bend, Indiana, still determined to marry the priest, Fr. Jim Burtchaell, and wanting a divorce as quickly as possible. Hauerwas writes, "I got a lawyer in Durham to prepare a separation agreement. Anne was ready to sign the agreement, but I did not want the divorce to be contested, and I wanted to make sure Anne would not be destitute. So I also hired a good lawyer in South Bend to act on her behalf. Even though my lawyer protested, the separation agreement obligated me to pay Anne monthly alimony. She signed the agreement."[63]

I tell this poignant story in part because some of Hauerwas' friends and colleagues have wondered what Anne's presence in Hauerwas' life and written memoir means for his life and work. Gerald McKenny wrote a letter to Hauerwas (which Hauerwas later commented on in a subsequent lecture) in which McKenny asks, "Is Anne one of the strange members of the Christian community whose presence with us teaches us how to be Christians, or is she the surd that resists your story, refusing to be assimilated into it and therefore reminding you of the limits of any account of Christian discipleship, including yours? My sense is that she is the latter and you did not really let her play that role."[64] (A surd is a mathematical term referring to an irrational number that refuses to be simplified.)

Jonathan Tran, a student of Hauerwas, gamely takes up McKenny's question in an essay that featured as part of a retirement celebration for Stanley Hauerwas. Tran focuses on Anne Hauerwas' mental illness alone as the surd, as the question of whether mental illness is a limiting factor for Christian community, charity, generosity, friendship, and so forth. On my view it is not only the mental illness but the whole of the relationship between Anne and Stanley that raises the question: what are the limits of the church?

Yes, in fact, the Christian community excludes. There are some limits to Christian community, for it is not a universal community, but a community of people who share in the life of Jesus Christ. The shared language and community Christians have together admits some affinities and analogies with those who stand beyond that community—but that also means that there are some words that cannot be named as Christian, that do not get to be shared by just everyone. Yet those limits do not make Christian community absurd. In just the same way, the kinds of puzzles that Anne's life and mental illness bring to bear on her marriage and parenting do not mean that her life exposes an idealism in Hauerwas' thought. To the contrary, Anne's presence shows the messy humanness of what it is to live together. As Tran notes, "insofar as Anne spoke in ways we could not make sense of, she remained beyond us. But this doesn't make her a surd. It just makes her human—that is, someone who shares in our human life in words; this is true even if her share issued without sense."[65]

Divorce, just as much as the craziness and incomprehensibility of mental illness, stands outside Christian community in a sense. Divorce is not a word Christians can make much sense of—as evidenced both by scripture and by the current debate that Christians have. I suggested in the above sections that our theology about divorce tends toward two options: either divorce is shoved aside in favor of speaking about a theology of marriage, or theologians try to do away with the scriptures in order to provide a space for divorce to be a word that belongs to Christian community. It is small wonder that divorced and divorcing people feel excluded, often, from their communities—quite simply because divorce represents something puzzling and more than a little bit irrational for Christian community.

Exclusion must not be the last word, however. God's story is a story of being present to God's people, even in the midst of the strange and unexplainable. Tran goes on: "The presence of Anne Hauerwas in his life tells us that the church Professor Hauerwas imagines Israel promising, Christ establishing, the Holy Spirit enabling, and God completing is a gift difficult to bear...."[66] But maybe it is the case, Tran wonders, that the church itself is a surd, "random and unexplainable," naming some as outsiders, yet, "none of that should be a problem for those who find themselves inside a story where random and unexplained events have been ordained as the norm."[67]

Tran turns to pain as a way of describing his point further—pain is something humans all suffer and yet something that remains mysterious. "When we are in pain we want to be helped. But it is exactly at this point that one of the strangest aspects of our being in pain occurs—namely, the impossibility of our experiencing one another's pain."[68] While we can tell others we are in pain, they cannot bear that pain for us, which makes us isolated from each other even as we reach out to each other. This is excruciatingly difficult to bear. Yet being with each other even in the midst of suffering and pain is one of the vocations Christians have.

The point is that life the church has to offer is not triumphalist. We do not get to pretend everything is wonderful. Instead, we proclaim that in it all, God is with us. As Tran writes:

> If we have asserted Christian unity over against non-Christian division, the coherence of our liturgy over against liberalism's incoherence, or the church's peace over against the world's violence, if we have proclaimed any of these without also at least intending the difficult conditions under which that coherence, liturgy and peace come about, the inestimable constraints and entailments, then we have yet to understand that the church's coherence, liturgy, and peace come as a sword, that the terms of the Kingdom's coming are nothing less than the end of this present age.[69]

God asks Christians to be the Body of Christ, that is, to be that sword that Jesus came to bring. That means being Christian occurs in the midst of pain. Yet that sword does not negate all the other things that the Body of Christ also means. For Hauerwas, the Body of Christ especially relates to friendship. Hauerwas responded to Tran's essay by noting, as he has often done, the importance of friendship. "It is one thing to be lonely by oneself. It is quite another thing to be lonely with someone...."[70]

In his presidential address to the Society of Christian Ethics, Hauerwas spoke on the theme, "Bearing Reality." "We create hells for ourselves and others fueled by false hopes anchored in the presumption of our significance. We are wounded by sin, we are wounded by our illusions of control, we are wounded by our inability to acknowledge the wounds our desperate loves inflict on ourselves and others."[71] The church does not obliterate the difficulties of our lives; the church, too, has "histories that involve cruelties so horrible there is no way to undo what has been done." No—we live with our difficulties and tragedies, and despite it all we believe in the hope God offers to us in Christ. This offering is grace for us, the knowledge that God is with us despite everything. How can we call this too idealistic?

Divorce stands as a jarring word in the midst of many Christian words. Divorce rightly also makes Christians question their own (sometimes smug) sensibilities about what it means to be married. But in some sense, divorce is not unique. Divorce is one of the many difficulties and tragedies that Christians bear and that Christian community is called to bear, nonetheless.

A Coda: Lauren Winner on Divorce

On that note about the difficulties that Christians bear, even as we also bear hope, I want to conclude this chapter with notes from Lauren Winner, a well-known author on Christian spirituality, and say more about what this gift of hope might mean. Unlike Hauerwas, whose story of life with Anne

Hauerwas invokes pathos and perhaps admiration for how long Stanley Hauewas endured marriage—Winner's divorce contains little or no pathos. Her divorce is representative of more of the divorces in the United States. Winner states plainly: "What needs to be said here about my marriage is, I think, only this: I was very unhappy for a long time, and all my explanations for that unhappiness seem pat and flat and deceptive."[72] Winner finds herself confronting the fact of her divorce—"the point I this: I came to believe that I simply could not stay married. I came to believe that I could not do this thing I had said I would do."[73]

Her own divorce—along with her mother's death from cancer—propels Winner into the "middle" of her spiritual life. She is in the middle of faith, as many of us are, though we may get to the middle by other means. God seems absent post-divorce, and Winner does not know how to restore her previously happy, joyously church-going self. Winner still goes to church, only now it is grudging. Occasionally, she catches glimpses of God. One Christmas, she finds herself meditating on the fact that she is in a "baptismal line" with all manner of sinners—the "embezzler and the adulterer and the prig." She'd rather not be there, but at the same time it feels like relief, because she is in the same crowd as everyone else, and they're all in line for God. She is given grace to see that her failure does not place her outside Christian community, but rather she is at its center.

Winner's mid-faith crisis is painstaking and slow. She learns to sit with loneliness, to see what it can teach her. She meditates on boredom, and pilgrimage, and keeps at her research and her work. Perhaps it was in this middle that she wrote what she calls a *lectio divina* on divorce. What she means by that is the following:

> [I]n traditional *lectio*, a person reads a biblical text following a four-part pattern of prayer and reflection as she reads: first, read and notice which word or phrase your attention is drawn to (or better, which word or phrase the Holy Spirit brings to your attention); second, read and ask what God is offering you in this reading and noticing and attention-drawing; third, read and ask yourself, and God, how you might wish to respond to what is being offered; fourth, read and dwell contemplatively (in the company of the text) with God.[74]

In this case, the *lectio* is the divorce itself, and all that surrounds the divorce.

"To suggest that divorce can teach the church something is not to argue that divorce is 'a good' as such, or a gift created by God in a way that precisely parallels marriage and singleness."[75]

So what can divorce teach us? Similar to Lawler, Winner thinks experience can be part of theological conversation. Yet in contrast to Lawler, this divorce is no mere experience, but rather "self-knowledge." Self-knowledge is a process of becoming self-aware of one's own limits and "complicity in sin. This is the kind of self-knowledge that may faithfully be part of Christian conversations about divorce."[76] But also, divorce teaches the church something about human frailty and about the power of resurrection. Sometimes relationships that seem on the brink of failure nevertheless survive; sometimes the resurrection is manifested mostly in the people who, having gotten divorced, learn to survive the pain of divorce.

Winner proclaims that we Christians have our own divorce ritual, one that stands in contrast to the popular divorce parties and to Bishop Spong's divorce blessing that I described above: it is our collective habits of confession. This is confession not only of sin (and not only individual sin, but the community's complicitness in being unloving, or allowing unloving behavior.) Confession is also, and most especially, confession of faith in God who is good. This is what Winner proclaims about God: "God will not be broken by remaining in a failing relationship; men and women sometimes will be."[77]

Bit by bit, as Winner confronts the middle of her spiritual life, she also finds that the nothingness, the blank wall she felt about God in the aftermath of her divorce has begun to change. Subtle changes begin to happen. Winner finds a quote from theologian and pastor Sam Wells: "a saint can fail in a way that the hero can't, because the failure of the saint reveals the forgiveness and new possibilities made in God, and the saint is just a small character in a story that's always fundamentally about God."[78] Winner does not presume to be a saint, but she does begin to see that her story—even the story of her divorce—is a story that is fundamentally about God. I think that the church needs a story similar to Winner's and Hauerwas'—to try narrating the grace of God in the midst of divorce.

Grace, Better…

Divorce does signify the failure of myriad relationships. The loss of a marriage is troubling, but even more so is the fact that Christian community so often seems unable to grapple with failure. What are Christians to do with failures? In the ideal/real dichotomy, failure becomes a moving target. Either you can dispel failure by providing the best images of marriage possible (while often not providing the kind of support that can sustain marriage), or you can make failure disappear by catering to people's experiences and changing doctrine.

Both responses are illusory, preventing people and communities alike from reflecting theologically about divorce.

Perhaps one better response is that of some Orthodox Christians, who have liturgies for second and third weddings, each of which is more penitential than first wedding liturgies. Scriptures shared in these second marriage rites emphasize God as faithful, forgiving, and compassionate. This kind of liturgy stands as an answer for how Christians can help each other bear witness to Christ even as we acknowledge that we fail.[79] The liturgies present hope even as they acknowledge pain and failure.

In the Western church, there are beginning stirrings of new ways to see ourselves as the Body of Christ, divorced and married together. Pope Francis calls Christians to see themselves, whether divorced, remarried, married, never-married, and so forth, as part of Christian community, all together standing in need of God's grace:

> It is a matter of reaching out to everyone, of needing to help each person find his or her proper way of participating in the ecclesial community and thus to experience being touched by an "unmerited, unconditional, and gratuitous" mercy.... Here I am not speaking only of the divorced and remarried, but of everyone, in whatever situation they find themselves.[80]

As opposed to seeing perfection versus imperfection, or seeing all kinds of relationships as "perfect," the pope asks us instead to recognize each of us, regardless of state of life, as standing in need of mercy.

How to acknowledge that we fail—and acknowledge that we all fail, not only the ones with failed marriages, but also the ones who seem to have perfect marriages—that is the hard work to which Christians are called. This does require that we learn how to confess our failings and to forgive each other. It is not only the couple who is divorcing that needs to learn forgiveness, but the community who needs to seek forgiveness from the divorcing people that it has failed, and from all the other ways it fails its people. Such forgiveness is different from the forgiveness Bishop Spong articulated above; there is no new covenant that is proclaimed between two divorcing people. Rather, there is simply recognition of the covenant Christians already proclaim: God is with us. Against our temptations to believe we are good or perfect, have perfect relationships, or can manipulate our thinking to believe that our relationships are good no matter what (Matthew 10: 38—"Jesus said to him, "Why do you call me good? No one is good but God alone."), God in

Christ asks all people instead to fall into grace. The richness of mercy and grace should be offered to people who fail, and those who have found that mercy and grace in the midst of failure should be encouraged to offer such witness. This most especially includes privileging the voices of those who are divorced.

8

Sufficiency: Single Parenting and Dorothy Day

SINGLE PARENTING AND the related concept of co-parenting (typically referring to a variety of shared custodial arrangements in cases where being a single parent is the result of divorce) are not often seen as forms of singleness, even though the word *single* comprises part of the term. In this chapter, when I refer to single parenting I mean not only parenting arising from never-married, divorced, or widowhood status, but I also include military spouses and spouses of incarcerated people, both of whom are likely to be raising children for significant periods of time without the active presence of the other spouse. As we shall see in this chapter, however, it is usually only certain kinds of single parents that receive a focus—the ones who are single parents because of out-of-wedlock pregnancies, or divorces, or other life events that Christians see as shameful. That kind of focus is short-sighted, however and doesn't enable Christians to respond well and rightly to all parents, including married parents.

Single parenting already comes with at least one relationship in evidence, the parent–child relationship. Single parenting thus seems not to fall under Paul's categorization of singleness as being anxious about the things belonging to the Lord (from Chapter 2), because parents are very much anxious for their children. Readers might even interpret Paul's letter to the Corinthians as *advocating* being anxious about family matters by describing what a married man or woman might do.

Being anxious to be a good parent is a major facet of contemporary Christian thought. Christians take family and child-rearing very seriously. For many Christians, the way they choose to raise their children *is* a means of Christian discipleship. Surely seeing Christian parenting as part of Christian discipleship is good—and it is! The difficulty, I argue, is not in seeing Christian parenting as part of Christian moral practices and witness to Christ. Rather, the key difficulty is in how Christians describe parenting, especially by rhetorically creating two tiers of parenting: a tier for parents who are able to achieve near perfection, and a tier for parents who cannot. Perfect parenting—or as I name it in this chapter, *supernatural* (superheroic) parenting—is chiefly defined by parents' abilities to be self-sufficient.

For example, the evangelical Protestant Quiverfull movement[1] encourages parents to embrace as many children as God is willing to send them; Catholics who call themselves "providentialists" might have similar aims. Alongside having as many children as possible, Quiverfull also strongly encourages home schooling as the best means of handing on the faith as well as for keeping the family as free from worldly influences as possible. Quiverfull parenting practices provide a specific way for women (in particular) to be good Christian disciples. While Quiverfull is a relatively small group, theologian Emily McGowin has shown that the way Quiverfull articulates good parenting as a way of defending their families from worldly attacks is merely a stronger form of the family/discipleship connection seen in mainstream evangelical, mainline Protestant, and Catholic groups.[2]

For instance, among Christians more generally, intact marriage is touted as the desirable, promoted form of parenting; while numerous studies do support the importance of two-parent families, the ways Christians describe and use two-parent families can have a detrimental impact on single-parent households.[3] As I shall strive to show below, single parenting is understood as second-best, and in some cases not even as a manifestation of Christian discipleship. As in the other chapters in this book, my concern is to shine a spotlight on single parenting and to raise two questions: how single parents *can* and *do* witness to Christ and Christ's church, and how Christians generally might think differently about single parenting when doing ministry.

This chapter is organized in the following way. First, I narrate single parenting in America, but then show how single parenting is part of larger conversations about parenting generally. I suggest that single parenting can be detrimental for parent and child alike, and it is quite often the people who are already marginalized by disability, race, and gender that especially feel the detrimental aspects of single parenting. Then I discuss in more detail what I have hinted at above: parenting (whether single or married) is a strong moral force in both secular and Christian American contexts; in fact, I refer to contemporary Christian views on parenting as "supernatural parenting" for how much is at stake in rightly parenting children.

Next, because parenting is a juggernaut in a range of contemporary moral debates (including debates about things that seem to have little to do with parenting as such), I show how single parenting has been negatively conceived and impacted, especially by describing the "welfare mothers" crisis of the 1990s—a crisis that extends well into our present day. I draw out some of the theological themes resulting from these contemporary moral debates.

Finally, I turn to the guide for this chapter, Dorothy Day. Dorothy Day was a single mother who became single precisely because she became a Catholic. She founded Catholic Worker and its associated houses of hospitality, working ceaselessly on behalf of the poor, and practiced hospitality to the point of allowing all who showed up on her doorstep, no matter their station, a place to stay and food to eat. Day's theological reflection on nature and grace helps put contemporary parenting in its proper context as related Christian discipleship: that is, she suggests a better way to think about supernaturality, parenting, and discipleship.

A View Toward Twenty-First Century Parenting

In describing single parenting in twenty-first century America, the image that must predominantly come to mind is of a woman as head of household. Single parenting has a distinct gendered aspect (just as do many other single states of life). A staggering 76 percent of households headed by a single parent are women. The impact of gender is twinned with a significant economic burden: poverty rates are much higher for single-parent, and especially single-mother households. Almost twice as many households headed by single mothers are in poverty (43%) compared to 24 percent of single dads.

While some studies have suggested that people's overall views of single parenting are changing as the number of single-parent households rises, single-parent stigma continues to exist.[4] Furthermore, when people are asked about their attitudes toward single mothering and single fathering, more people have negative views toward single mothers than single fathers.[5] This stigma may exist in part because of the association between single parenting and unwed pregnancy—an unfortunate connection to make, in part because a slight majority of single mothers are divorced, separated, or widowed (51 percent) compared to mothers who have never been married (49 percent).[6]

This gendered aspect affects my writing in this chapter because I focus largely on the central problem: discussions of single parenting emphasize single mothers, their poverty, and the particular and mostly negative attitudes associated with single mothers. I think single fatherhood needs more protracted discussion; some of my conclusions in this chapter will likely relate to single fatherhood as well, but I am advisedly focused on women in this chapter.

The online site "Single Mother Guide" collates statistics about single mothers even further. Poverty associated with single parenting is highly correlated to racial/ethnic identity. In a 2009 report on single parenting and race, 18.5 percent of white children lived in mother-only households, while the percentages were 25.7 percent of Latino/a children and 50 percent of African American children in mother-only households. About one in every two Native American, Hispanic, and African American households exists at or below the poverty line; for white female-headed households, the number is slightly more than one in three existing at or below the poverty line. Among households headed by Asian women, the number is one in four. Among all homeless families in the United States, about three-quarters are single-mother households.[7]

The high poverty rate exists despite the fact that about two-thirds of single mothers hold employment, though nearly a quarter of single mothers are unable to find jobs for the whole year, and a single mother's income is significantly lower than that of married mothers. Forty-five percent of single mothers receive food stamp assistance.[8] Sociological research on single parents, especially mothers, shows that usually, when poverty is not a factor, children do not see the same detriments as those born to impoverished mothers.[9]

An additional concern, which impacts both male and female single parents, is that single parents are often heading households with children who have significantly different needs than most children. Disability is one major factor leading to parents' divorce; up to one-third of single-parent households of both genders have children with physical, mental, or developmental disabilities.[10] While this is not precisely a gendered concern, it is part of the landscape of single parenting, and because of the high number of single-mother headed households likely impacts women far more than men.

Christians ought to be especially concerned about the sociological data, for they suggest many troubling considerations for single parents and their children. Most especially, the data suggest single-parent households often already feature people who are at the margins of society. Marginalization is likely a cause of some single parenting situations and exacerbates already existing concerns regarding race, gender, and disability.

Numerous theologians have used scripture to describe how God is with and for the poor and marginalized, and it is a particular focus of Pope Francis' papacy.[11] God's particular concern for marginalized people does not negate God's relationship with those who are not poor. Yet power and wealth can hide marginalized people from view, which in turn obscures a good vision of God.

Single parenting must be part of rightly understanding Christian community. As we shall see later in this chapter, Dorothy Day's vocation with Catholic Worker springs from such a view of God and goes hand in hand with her twin Christian witness as a single parent.

Before turning to Day, however, it is important to see how Christians often have not supported single parents and have instead strongly supported what I call "supernatural" parenting. That is, Christians have made too much of right parenting to the point that parenting has sometimes become an idol, much as I have described marriage in other chapters.

Supernatural Parenting

Part of the stigma associated with single parenting has to do with present-day debates about what it means to be a good parent. What it means to be a good parent has become a multifaceted issue, at the center of which is the surety that good parents make for good children. While parents clearly have an impact on their children and should aim to be good parents, the arguments about what constitutes a good parent have taken on so lofty a tone that a good parent would, in my view, have to become a superwoman or superman—supernatural in a kind of secular way—as I attempt to show below.

We might begin with the Mommy Wars of the 1990s, a decidedly gendered cultural argument that involved debates about whether to be a stay-at-home mom or a career mom, for the sake of the children. Those "wars" have expanded in intervening decades to involve much more widespread disagreements, as journalist Mollie Hemingway notes:

> Now the wars engage a wide range of questions. Is it better to raise children in the city or suburbs? Should you breast feed or use formula? If formula, what type? How much should you nurse? Do you want to join a "nurse-in" to protest bans on public breastfeeding? Are Cesarean sections evil and overused, or modern-day medical miracles? How much effort should be made to avoid products containing the chemical Bisphenol-A? Does an environmentally conscious consumer purchase disposable or cloth diapers? Is it your civic duty to send your children to public schools? Or is it an unconscionable act of abandonment when you live where I do—in Washington DC?[12]

Hemingway points to the ways that, in contemporary grappling with parenting, nearly every parenting decision has become a critical moral choice upon which a person's children, family, and even an entire society rise or fall. The aspect of "critical moral choice" has been especially evident in debates such as whether to allow children to walk to and from school alone.[13]

The world of Mommy Wars is often, as journalist Sandra Tsing Loh writes, a matter for an increasingly smaller group of middle- and upper-class women who can choose not to work. In a review of Leslie Morgan Steiner's book, *Mommy Wars: Stay-at-Home and Career Moms Face Off on their Choices, their Lives, their Families,* Loh caustically writes:

> There are, in fact, great varieties of American mothers left out of Steiner's anthology. They're women for whom work is not a "lifestyle choice" but a necessity—a financial one, gauchely enough, and not an emotional one. Why do they work? To keep the electricity on. Such women would include, oh, single-mother waitresses, hotel maids, factory workers, grocery-store cashiers, manicurists, even countless low-level white-collar functionaries, from bank clerks to receptionists to data processors.[14]

Loh makes a good argument, though it is also important to note that financial reasons may well be involved in a "choice" *not* to work as well: women from lower economic strata sometimes make a decision not to work precisely because child care is expensive and—despite that it is difficult to make it on one person's salary—it is easier to make it on one salary without child care than to make it on two salaries with child care.

Attributing moral concern to parenting has been present in many ways and in many times, especially in how parents are blamed for how poorly children behave—or are perceived to behave. Theological ethicist Amy Laura Hall has discussed in detail how early twentieth-century Christians linked American preferences for good hygiene and good genes with good parenting; clean homes bred good, polite children, as noted in several Christian magazines. Advertising from such ordinary household products as Lysol and Seven-Up demonstrated the importance of good housekeeping for well-bred children, especially those who had the right genes. Of course, well-bred clean children equated with being white and wealthier; African Americans, Appalachians, and other marginalized groups were criticized in part for poor hygiene, which stemmed from poor genetic background. Thus Hall indicts Christians for colluding with a racialized proclivity for having perfect children.[15]

Historian Kathryn Lofton notes that in the United States, the past century has particularly centered on children's behaviors and the ways that parents shape and mold those behaviors (or not). That focus has in turn significantly placed a burden on parents and their responsibilities. Lofton focuses on the mid-twentieth century and how parenting became intertwined with religious thought, political sentiments, and sometimes both together. In the mid-1950s, for example, Dr. Spock's popular book promoted parenting that supported children's own will to learn, while in the 1960s and 1970s, some religious thinkers (such as James Dobson, founder of Focus on the Family) took a stand against Dr. Spock's advice by advocating more and greater parental control. When that sense of parenting is combined with American and Christian ideals about nuclear families, parenting becomes a very isolated activity.

Though she writes a history, Lofton has our morally minded society in mind when she observes: "Amid the current debate about toddler breastfeeding and supermothers, about nannies and quality time, about the new slacker dads and the old midwifery, there is a constant hum of one truth: practicing parenting is central to American life and determinative of the American moral imagination."[16] From pre-born life and whether to parent (in vitro fertilization and contraception), from questions of abortion to the delivery table and questions of birthing, to schooling, helicopter parenting, and the ways parents affect a person's ability to be a fulfilled, functioning adult (or, by contrast, led a person to do domestic violence or other crimes), parenting remains at the forefront of major moral and political debates.[17]

Supernatural parenting, as in superheroic parenting, presents itself as a series of moral choices. Morality becomes almost solely a matter of making a choice, which must be made with appropriate (anxious) study and reflection. Make the right choices, and the gates will be wide open for parents and children; make the wrong choices, and you and your child both will be stuck in the mire of failure and inability to succeed in life.

There's something theologically amiss in that all-consuming view of perfection. Mollie Hemingway attempts to de-escalate the Mommy Wars and the sense of Christian parenting perfection. She draws from the sixteenth-century Protestant reformer and father of Lutheranism, Martin Luther.

> How should Christians think about the Mommy Wars? Vocationally.... Martin Luther used [vocation] to talk about every Christian's calling to particular offices, through which God works to care for his creation.... Parenting is one of the most important vocations we can be given.[18]

Yet Hemingway is conflicted. While parenting is an "important vocation" she isn't sure how to square her sense of parenting's importance with the fact that people argue vehemently about breastfeeding and bottle feeding. She makes her argument along familiar lines. Allow rational people the space to parent in their own ways, even if different from my own. In a pluralistic society, we dare not impose our own parenting beliefs on others. Hemingway adds a Christian spin: "So long as I am not sinning, I am free to parent my children as I see fit."[19]

Such a statement actually serves to escalate rather than de-escalate the Mommy Wars. Part of the difficulty with Hemingway's attempt to de-escalate the parenting arguments is that because we live in a world that moralizes parenting choices, Christians may well narrate formula feeding or other particular parenting choices as sins. For example, Emily McGowin writes in detail about Christian homeschooling movements, both Catholic and Protestant, which emphasize secular education as a sinful, inappropriate arena in which to learn to be a Christian disciple.[20] In Protestant circles, and in the past few decades for Catholics as well, marriage has thus come to be seen as discipleship par excellence, a means of determining how well parents measure up to being disciples, especially by looking at the fruits of their parenting: how well their children are able not to be sinners. Prominent pastor Voddie Baucham has famously described a baby as "a viper in a diaper," alluding to the sinful nature of children and the responsibilities good Christian parents have in stamping out all sin from their children.[21]

Another drawback of Hemingway's live-and-let-live picture is that it suggests that a *good* family needs to be self-sufficient and know within itself how to live. It presumes a well-to-do nuclear family that is independent of other families and needs little in the way of help from others, because our parenting choices ought to be our own.

Supernatural Single Parenting? The Second Tier

In much Christian writing, single parenting lessens the possibility of the supernatural parenting I have briefly described above. In fact, single parents become a point of contrast to other parents, a second (and less desirable) tier in a two-tiered system: there are the (married) parents who have a hope of perfection, and everyone else. Christian accounts of single parenting that I have examined express great sympathy for single parents and a need to provide ministries for them. Underlying the rhetoric of ministerial care, however, is a narrative that single parents have households that are already broken. The moral choice presented to parents has already been made, often before a child has ever been conceived (especially in the case of unmarried single parenting). The choice that has been made is a choice for abject failure. It is the dual-parent family that represents more than a best practice for being a family, but a kind of perfection and an ability to achieve parenting in godlike standards.

It doesn't help that single-parent households often arise from divorce or pregnancy out of wedlock, which adds to the sense of failure surrounding single parenting and also impacts the kind of help Christians believe they can or should offer.

For example, *US Catholic* magazine published several articles about single mothers, including one where writer Heidi Schlump discusses the impact of a focus on nuclear families: "Catholic single moms may have added guilt from their church's emphasis on the 'traditional' nuclear family...."[22] Part of the experience of imperfection is the fact of a rising number of Catholic single mothers being fired by the church because they failed to be a "positive Catholic example,"[23] where the subtext was clearly not only that the women interviewed were single parents but were also unmarried. These single parents lost their livelihood—which in turn meant that the Christian help offered to single mothers cannot be jobs, at least not jobs in the church. The author of the essay worried that such negative associations might be ironically promoting a culture of abortion that favors single, childless, women. Of course the issue is complicated: the church also does not want to promote a hint that premarital sexual activity is okay, especially in cases where the single parents are teachers in Catholic schools. Being a good example is important, but in this case the key example might be that of using the church's authority to say to all people, "Don't ever mess up, especially sexually, or we won't help you."

Other Christian thinking follows similar trajectories. In *The Christian Educator's Handbook on Family Life Education*, David Miller states baldly: "Divorce and single parenting have arrived."[24] While he goes on to state, "There can be no rational objection why the Christian community should not respond to the needs of single parent families," the way he states the case suggests that indeed, some Christians have objected and withheld help, especially since single parenting is so closely associated with divorce. The Christian Broadcasting Network makes a similar argument, clearly aimed at getting Christians to respond to the needs of single mothers even if and when they disagree with why women are single mothers in the first place. At CBN, the advice comes with a decidedly paternalistic flavor: "Whether they are unwed or divorced, many single moms need parenting advice, financial instruction, emotional support via networking, and Spiritual growth opportunities."[25] Missing from that list is any material support: they need advice, but not jobs; they need a Christian view of perfect parenting, but not the kinds of material goods that might enable "Spiritual growth opportunities" to be had.

Perhaps it is no surprise, therefore, to find that welfare reform of the 1990s emphasized self-sufficiency as a major criterion for measuring the relative health of a single-parent family and remains a significant criterion today. To put the matter in sharp contrast: women who can accomplish supernatural versions of parenting are women who have the financial means to be self-sufficient, at least economically speaking, and who therefore can speak from a position of power when it comes to viewing their own way of life as positive, even if it stands in great contrast to other families around them (such as Mollie Hemingway cited above). Poor women, however, have the paradox of being asked to become "self-sufficient" by the institutions (churches, government, and so forth) that seek to help, while simultaneously those women are forced to maintain that particular institution's vision of what self-sufficiency means. In what follows, I highlight the self-sufficiency narrative by focusing on welfare reform debates, debates which engulfed Christians left and right as they wrestled with finding a proper balance between Christian values and worldly affairs. In welfare reform, while single-mother households might become "self-sufficient" in the sense that mothers have jobs, they are not able to pick and choose what they themselves view as the best parenting strategies; by contrast, wealthier women have many more choices for parenting strategies.[26]

Theologian Julie Maddalena offers a brief history of how self-sufficiency relates to parenting, especially single parenting, in the welfare debates. Maddalena tells the story of single, poor women who must seek jobs in order to support their families throughout American history. At various times and places, but especially during the Industrial Revolution as well as the mid-twentieth century, women in poverty were narrated as threats to the dominant, mostly middle-class view that nice ladies shouldn't have to work outside the home and should, rather, predominantly be present to their children at home. Maddalena argues that middle class, apparently Christian, values come to the forefront in the early 1990s, when "the claim of the moral good of self-sufficiency was directed with increasing intensity toward poor mothers and their children in the months leading up to the welfare reforms promised by presidential candidate Bill Clinton."[27]

We can see this kind of self-sufficiency narrative in a brief history of welfare reform in the 1990s. "Welfare" came to be a nasty term in the 1980s and 1990s, but it had not always been the case. A *Saturday Evening Post* article in 1949 asked: "Who is against welfare? Nobody...."[28] In those days, welfare meant a wide number of benefits for a broad range of the public. In the 1980s, however, welfare became a symbol of racial division on the Left and overly permissive government spending on the Right. Political scientists reflecting on the 1980s write, "Progressive revisionists argued that 'Democratic doctrine went off track during the Johnson years [of the 1960s],' turning toward divisive policies that favored the very-poor and racial minorities over the working class, white mainstream. . . ."[29] Conservatives had the view that "[b]y rewarding irresponsibility, the Aid to Families with Dependent Children (AFDC) program had fueled racial stereotypes, bred pathology among the poor, undercut public support for anti-poverty efforts, and put liberals at an ongoing political disadvantage." White voters believed they were spending money that not only did not benefit themselves, but instead benefitted an abstract "welfare queen"—usually a picture of an African American single mother who reputedly had children simply in order to receive the welfare check and was simultaneously addicted to crack or heroin or other substance that endangered the lives of her children as well as the public at large. Yet, in fact, even to this day, the vast majority (91%) of people receiving income assistance in some way are not substance abusers, but are either disabled, children, or members of the working poor. Over 56 percent of government spending supports people who have jobs but whose wages are too low wages to support them or their families. Some of these include fast-food workers (52% are enrolled in at least one government aid program), home care workers (48%), child care workers (46%), and part-time college faculty (25%).[30]

The idea that welfare programs exacerbated a racial divide promoted a call for welfare reform in the 1990s. Democratic president Bill Clinton, together with a Republican Congress, developed new welfare legislation that featured time limits for receiving some kinds of aid, as well as work requirements. The aim of seeking jobs was, ultimately, to reduce women's dependence on government assistance in favor of achieving better incomes and work that could sustain families. The Temporary Assistance for Needy Families program (TNFA, begun in 1996) was the result, a program that has a five-year lifetime maximum for receiving aid. Some hoped that

> the welfare restrictions—time limits and work requirements—would do more than revamp one discredited program. [They] would help create a political climate more favorable to the needy. Once taxpayers started viewing the poor as workers, not welfare cheats, a more generous era would ensue. Harmful stereotypes would fade. New benefits would flow. Members of minorities, being disproportionately poor, would disproportionately benefit . . .[31]

The opposite seems to have happened: people these days are as likely as in the 1980s and 1990s to disparage people receiving welfare. A 1989 Gallup poll showed that 61 percent of Americans believed that "welfare benefits make poor people dependent and encourage them to stay poor," while a 2002 Pew study shows that 53 percent of Americans think "the current welfare system" makes things worse "by making able-bodied people too dependent on government aid," and 71 percent in a 2003 Pew study think "poor people have become too dependent on government assistance." Political scientists Soss and Schram further find that American attitudes have not changed; changing welfare policy has not affected Americans' racist, dominant views that welfare assistance equals assisting African Americans who are drug addicts.[32]

Attitudes toward the poor did not change, but neither did attitudes toward single mothers. Historian Linda Gordon argues that at least since the 1890s, single mothers have been seen as a sign that society is falling apart.[33] Gordon connects the nineteenth-century activism surrounding single mothers (which was frequently championed by white middle class women, as in Hull House) to the 1930s developments of government assistance. Gordon argues that there was a disparity from the very beginning in the way that single mothers were treated and could receive welfare benefits, contrasted with the elderly, who received Social Security entitlements—a disparity that Gordon finds continued to the 1990s.

When it came to work, single mothers dramatically entered the workforce in the 1990s and showed some gains in being able to spend more money on their households.[34] Yet, theologian Julie Maddalena concludes that the program meant to reduce welfare assistance among single mothers actually consigned women to low-paying jobs and barely subsistence wages for the long term. While welfare reform did and does reduce government assistance, it does not reduce the number of impoverished households.

Moreover, families are left unsupported. Women taking maternity leave are penalized, prevented from receiving funds, yet the time they take off from work is counted in the five-year maximum for benefits. Further, the amount of money the program allows for child care does not remotely begin to cover the actual cost of child care, such that financially it does indeed make more sense simply to "pay" women to raise their own children rather than subsidize day care.

Maddalena also demonstrates how fear of poverty has defined welfare-reform conversations, since the prevailing assumption was that poor women were having lots and lots of babies. In fact, the birth rates for poor, middle class, and wealthy women in this period remained largely the same.[35] In Maddalena's view it is poverty, intersecting with gender and social norms about what counts as a (self-sufficient) family, that constitutes the chief concern rather than how many children each individual woman has. Maddalena raises further concerns stemming from her work in feminist theology: that the TNFA program presumes that poor women with children simply need to find wealthy benefactors to support them, thereby more permanently reducing "single welfare mothers."

E.J. Dionne suggests a link between the high wages of union workers and the kind of family it could sustain, in contrast to single parent families:

> But there are many others [families] where the woman "is a single parent, or her husband is unemployed, or her husband isn't seeing the kind of wage growth that his father did and can't afford to support the family on his own." This points to a contradiction that few conservatives want to confront. When trying to win votes from religious and social traditionalists, conservatives speak as if they want to restore what they see as the glory days of the 1950s family. But they are reluctant to acknowledge that it was the high wages of (often unionized) workers that underwrote these arrangements.[36]

Dionne and Maddalena suggest that welfare reformers advocated that poor women seek jobs, even as they supported and advocated for middle class women *not* seeking jobs, for the good of their children.

The welfare reform story I have described above shows one major way in which single parenting is at the center of many moral debates taking place in contemporary American politics and life. Single parenting is rife with presumptions and shaming: one of the first presumptions is that single parents ought to get married, or people simply ought not to get pregnant and have children unless they can "afford" children—and even then, single parents need to think sufficiently about the negative effects of being a child in a single-parent household. This presumption moralizes all single parenting, and often prevents Christians from providing generous and helpful responses to people in need. Single parenting may be just as much a result of a spouse's military service or other job, a spouse's death, physical or emotional abusive relationships, and many other points that do not get considered when Christians are consumed with an unhelpful and single-sided narrative about single parenting as the result of premarital sex or divorce. It is further not clear why moral questions about premarital sex and divorce need to be linked to moral questions about being parents.

As I have mentioned in many other chapters, such presumptions and shaming idolize the idea that a person can "choose" relationships like marriage and children. Just as people must come to terms with the fact that marriage relationships aren't choices in the same way that I choose what toothpaste to buy (see Chapter 2 for more on this), so too being unmarried or becoming unmarried (via divorce or widowhood) and having children aren't equivalent to choices in the sense of consumer buying and spending. Yet the welfare reform debates, with their direction connection to buying and spending, makes precisely this link. The welfare reform debates seemed to separate deserving single parents from undeserving single parents: that is, parents who had gotten married and used artificial contraception, but had children and an abusive spouse nonetheless and were lucky to leave. The flip side of the narrative is that undeserving single parents are those who bring it on themselves and therefore should have little or no part in receiving governmental assistance.

As I said initially about supernatural parenting: such parenting relies on an idea that we make individual choices about best parenting practices and that we reap what we sow in terms of the good of our children. Such narratives collude with the kinds of welfare practices suggested above, because they enable us to believe that the main solution is marriage, with a close second being finding a well-paying job (which may or may not exist). Such narratives also link to the point Hemingway observed, "So long as I am not sinning, I am free to parent my children as I see fit." Parents can be self-sufficient unless and until they step into sin. That view suggests a live-and-let-live ideal, which works well for wealthier, middle class, often white women, but less well for others who don't fit into those categories.

Another aspect of supernatural, superheroic parenting is in the ways people want to categorize each other. Above, I named single parents as part of a second, lower, tier of parenting, compared to the first tier of intact married-parent families. A helpful way of examining these tiers is to connect them to the idea of the church/world relationship, with which Christians have wrestled for the whole of Christian history. How should the church relate to the world, and to worldly concerns? We worship Christ who, after all, told us to be perfect as our heavenly Father is perfect. Yet we also worship the Word Incarnate who came to live in our midst. Christians have had a difficult time reconciling these. (See the previous chapter for a discussion of idealism and realism, which touches on similar points.)

In the mid-twentieth century, the Protestant theologian H. Richard Niebuhr's book *Christ and Culture* attempted to help Christians navigate church/world relationships in modernity. Niebuhr argued that there are five basic ways Christians have lived out relationships with the world: Christ against culture, Christ of culture, Christ above culture, Christ and culture in paradox, and Christ the transformer of cultures. Niebuhr gave historical examples of all five types of Christians as he saw them, while clearly privileging Christ as transformer of culture. For example, Niebuhr sees Mennonite and Quaker Christians as representative of "Christ against culture," for these are groups that, in Niebuhr's view, tend to withdraw entirely from political life by not voting or participating in military service, and which develop alternative methods for economic life and children's education.[37] He did not see such withdrawal from political life as useful, especially for witnessing to Christ; that withdrawal seemed too perfectionistic, too little engaged in the world. Instead, Niebuhr preferred to think in terms of the more active-sounding idea of transformation of modern cultures and modern-day problems.

Christians since Niebuhr have used his, or similar, types to describe Christians who seem to be exhibiting too much perfectionism about the ways they followed Christ. For example, Catholic moral theologian Kristin Heyer writes about "perfectionist" Catholics who engaged in the kind of radical discipleship Dorothy Day offers (as discussed later in this chapter). Day and others like her (Michael Baxter, Michael Budde) are perfectionistic because they advocate countercultural practices, like pacifism, that seem to require absolute separation from contemporary politics. Such separation seems to be a denial of a Christian belief that "grace builds on nature" and that God can enter into and engage us, even in our messy, sinful contexts.[38] In Heyer's view, America is a suspect entity for radical Christians like Day. By contrast, theologians like Heyer see engagement as necessary. As theologian Benjamin Peters notes: "For many 'public' theologians . . . the tendency is to see the Church as engaging with American society and culture—or the 'public'—not as a means of necessarily offering grace, but rather of making American society and culture aware of its graced character."[39] Critics of Dorothy Day and other radical Christians, such as David O'Brien, say the radical worldview is "sectarian" since it is overly concerned with a supernatural world in which a select few experience and encounter God, in ways that admits little of the real life most people experience. O'Brien writes that "by defining issues and responses in Christian terms, advocates [of sectarian Catholicism] become marginalized in the larger public debate. Respected, even admired, they are not seen as offering an appropriate or reasonable way in which the American public as a whole can evaluate problems and formulate solutions."[40]

Benjamin Peters argues that commenters like Heyer and O'Brien rely overly much on the idea of human sufficiency: that God has graced us sufficiently that we can make good, even Christ-like, changes to our world.[41] That is the kind of sufficiency, I would argue, that welfare reformers also sought. If welfare mothers could become self-sufficient, that would be great for them and their children, and hence for society. Here was a time when Christians, both liberal and conservative, sought to evaluate problems of single mothers, alongside their secular counterparts. What happened instead is that the sufficiency narrative engulfed single mothers with a sufficiency narrative that has in fact left them (among others) lagging far behind other parents.

The critique that radical Christians are isolationists who don't really impact broader culture isn't quite fair, and it is precisely the contemporary parenting tropes that expose this point. Nowadays, it isn't only Anabaptists who develop alternatives for children's education; it's also white middle class parents seeking refuge from failing inner city school systems through other solutions, like private school or homeschooling. Or, consider the kind of isolation most of us experience in our generally segregated communities and churches. Michael Emerson, a sociologist at Rice University, reports "congregations have long been hyper-segregated. As of 2007 (our most recent data with such detail), 85 percent of congregations in the United States were comprised of at least 90 percent of one group. As of 2010, just 4 percent of all congregations claimed to have no racial majority."[42] Emerson thinks the numbers are changing, slowly, yet the reality is still that "Because group members cannot understand and feel the needs of another group as completely and deeply as those of their own group, reliance on love, compassion, and persuasion to overcome group divisions and inequalities is practically impossible." The experience of most churches in America mirrors a secular reality: white, and wealthy, flight exists; wealthier, often white, people still leave behind schools and communities in favor of living in more favorable situations (for them).[43] These segregated realities also impact single parents, though there has been far less conversation about that impact.

Those who cannot lift their children into the first tier of parenting perfection, especially single parents, become part of a marginalized second tier. There is the extraordinary family and the merely ordinary family, which often cut not only along single parenting lines but also along racial and economic lines.

What contemporary ideas about supernatural parenting do *not* do is enable people to critique the starting assumptions. Is striving to be a superhero or a self-sufficient parent (single or married)—even the kind of parent who has zest for forming children to be good Christians—really good Christian discipleship?

In trying to answer this question, world and church—nature and grace—still matter, of course, and we shall need to consider a theology of nature and grace very carefully. Yet I think we also need to return to Dorothy Day and explore her sense of radical discipleship more closely, especially in light of the fact that she herself was a single mother. I think it is the case that her views of single parenting actually show a way forward in the midst of a self-sufficiency narrative, a way that can be very much aware of the real, lived lives of even non-radical Christians.

Dorothy Day: A Woman of Family

Dorothy Day is a fascinating person to study regarding that question of good Christian discipleship, single parenting, and formation of children, especially since members of her own Catholic Worker movement have found her to be a poor example of good motherhood. Like the people I describe above, Day, too, is caught up in a narrative in which her parenting is utterly insufficient, in which she can never measure up as a mother.

Day herself has quite a different theological argument to offer, however. Against a narrative of self-sufficiency, Day argues for an insufficiency of self, which in turn requires a broader vision of family, community, and parenting. She acknowledges that her single parent family with daughter Tamar would not have been typically understood as the kind of family that Christians often meant (and still mean) when they think about the term, Day defiantly declares that "I *am* a woman of family."[44] Against a two-tiered vision, Day offers a vision of natural love and parenting, in which we come to know the supernatural love of God (and vice versa); there cannot be two tiers, because we are all standing insufficiently in the love of God. I begin my discussion of Day's theology by first discussing her biographical details, then continuing with descriptions of her theology of nature and supernature.

A Life of Radical Discipleship

Dorothy Day (1897–1980) grew up in a nominally Christian (Protestant) middle class home. As a young adult, she was attracted to philosophical ideas that highlighted concern for workers and the poor. She was a journalist who wrote about the plight of workers, including their riots, protests, and impoverished situations. Day also joined movements and protests herself, including the fight for women's right to vote and worker's rights. Throughout her twenties she was unsettled, and developed several relationships with men, including one that involved a pregnancy and ended with an abortion. Being unsettled also meant she dabbled in religious practices but remained uncommitted to any particular religious group.

Eventually, friends convinced her to settle a bit, and she moved to a house on Staten Island. She fell in love and had a common-law marriage with Forster Battingham, who fathered her child Tamar. In her autobiography *The Long Loneliness*, Day describes the happiness she has with Forster as a "natural happiness" and a natural peace. "It was a peace, curiously enough, divided against itself. I was happy but my very happiness made me know that there was a greater happiness to be obtained from life than any I had ever known."[45]

Her encounter with natural happiness and peace lead her to consider whether there is a greater happiness and peace. Dorothy writes, "I have that it was life with him that brought me natural happiness, that brought me to God."[46]

This natural happiness that catches Dorothy up into happiness with God extends to Dorothy's pregnancy and the eventual birth of her daughter. From the beginning, Day's motherhood is intertwined with her burgeoning urge for God. Day describes the birth of Tamar in terms of overflowing love—a love that could not be fully contained even by the small baby, but that needed a Someone. "To think that this thing of beauty, sighing gently in my arms, reaching her little mouth for my breast, clutching at me with her tiny, beautiful hands, had come from my flesh, was my own child! Such a great feeling of happiness and joy filled me that I was hungry for Someone to thank, to love, even to worship, for so great a good that had been bestowed upon me. That tiny child was not enough to contain my love. . . ."[47]

Despite her deep love for Forster and her knowledge that Forster could not see his way clear toward being a father or toward religion, Dorothy knew she would become baptized herself. The very fact of becoming Christian pushes Dorothy away from even the unmarried, yet somewhat standard family life she has, because she knew she and Forster would end up separating if she inched toward Catholicism. "Becoming a Catholic would mean facing life alone and I clung to family life. It was hard to contemplate giving up a mate in order that my child and I could become members of the Church."[48] Yet at the end, Dorothy says, "I knew that I was going to have my child baptized a Catholic, cost what it may. I knew that I was not going to have her floundering through many years as I had done, doubting and hesitating, undisciplined and amoral. I felt it was the greatest thing I could do for a child."[49]

Day becomes baptized a couple of years after her daughter's baptism, the move that irrevocably ends her relationship with Forster. She became a single mother, one who is dearly in love with her daughter, but she had not yet begun the work with Catholic Worker that would also define her life. In 1931, Dorothy Day wrote an essay for *Commonweal* that describes four-year-old Tamar's reluctance to go to bed, a touching account of her parenting. Day describes Tamar discussing a drawing she has made for her mother, as Tamar consciously avoids bed: "Here is a picture of a man, a man dancing and telling a whole lot of stories. He's playing on his catarrh too, and singing songs. Are you listening?" Dorothy states that she is listening, that she is looking at the drawings, that she is there. Dorothy continues her description of Tamar as the young girl draws out bedtime with a demand for kisses, for water, and finally, with the crazily insightful questions that young children ask at bedtime. Then, suddenly, Tamar is asleep, without Day quite realizing that it happened, as she was reading and writing.

The mother-daughter relationship changes, however, as Day becomes converted by other events, most especially her encounters with socialists and communists protesting against the injustices and hunger of workers. Day wonders: "I could write, I could protest, to arouse the conscience, but where was the Catholic leadership in the gathering of bands of men and women together, for the actual works of mercy that the comrades had always made part of their technique in reaching the workers?"[50] Dorothy subsequently meets Peter Maurin, who introduces her to Catholic social teaching and Catholic concern for workers and the poor.

Maurin and Day began the Catholic Worker movement via a newspaper in 1933, and also established houses of hospitality where people could come and find food and shelter. The Catholic Worker movement also advocated for farming, as a means of support but also as a place where people could go on retreat, and promoted nonviolent resistance in World War II, the Cold War, and the Vietnam War. Throughout her life, Day brought together her advocacy for the poor with her spiritual fervor.

Day and the Single Parenting Debate

Day's biographical sketch would be incomplete, especially in this chapter, without a sense of how her co-workers describe her parenting. Day's single parenting has even inspired a poem, written in the voice of her daughter, Tamar:

Go ahead. Tend to them.
Bowls lined up. Soup. Bread.
As a little girl,
I hated the smitten poor who followed you,
Hauling their sun-boiled faces and stench.
But see how you have forced me
to become one? How else to be loved by you?[51]

In Juliana Baggott's poem Tamar is pregnant with her ninth child and finds herself close to penury. Baggott depicts Tamar wondering about her place in Dorothy's heart and emphasizes the love the Dorothy gave to "the smitten poor" who—at least in poetry—are loved more than Tamar, unless she, too, can prove herself worthy.

Baggott's depiction of Dorothy is a rather common view of Dorothy Day's parenting—including from some members of Catholic Worker houses who suggest that love of the poor and love of family is incompatible. Just as we saw with welfare reform and its attendant notions of parenting sufficiency, Day, as single parent, is unable to carry out two crucial aspects of parenting. On the one hand, parents are supposed to provide for children's material needs; on the other hand, parents are supposed to nurture their children and be present to them. To Dorothy's detractors, she was somewhat able—with quite a lot of begging and getting by—to provide for Tamar's schooling, food, and shelter; whether she was able to provide for Tamar's emotional and spiritual needs is quite another question.

Larry Holben is one Catholic Worker who suggests that it is far easier to be a Catholic Worker if a person is single—which for him means both not-married and also not with children. Holben is quick to state that Dorothy Day was not a "good role model" as a mother, unable to be present to Tamar in the ways that she needed.[52] Holben describes other children of Catholic Workers, too. Among other Catholic Worker children, some describe a desire to follow in their parents' footsteps in some way, whether that is running a Catholic Worker house (Tom Christopher Cornell and Deirdre Cornell have both followed in their parents' footsteps in running the Peter Maurin Farm in New York state), or living simply. Others reject their parents' lifestyles, seeing and disliking the ways it put them at odds with their friends (Ralph Dowdy, another parent living at the Peter Maurin Farm, described his sons' rejections of a simple lifestyle).[53]

Katherine Yohe has written a careful essay discussing Dorothy and Tamar's relationship. Yohe helpfully attends to several points in Dorothy's and Tamar's mother/daughter relationship and aspects of Day's parenting. Day suggests that her single parenthood took a definitive change when she started the Catholic Worker. As Yohe describes it, prior to Catholic Worker, even with putting Tamar in daycare, Day still had whole days and moments with Tamar all to herself. With Catholic Worker, that changed—"her 'working day' began with early Mass and ended at midnight. 'She was no longer my only one. I should have known what to expect when Peter Maurin stood over her sick-bed when she had measles, indoctrinating the doctor.'"[54] As Yohe describes it, that lack of having Tamar all to herself—and the practice of treating others the same as her daughter—made Holben and others quite concerned about Dorothy's ability to parent.

Yet I think it is also important to note that Tamar's own experiences of Dorothy are more complex. Tamar Henessey says in an interview: "I loved the Catholic Worker. It was so exciting. I wouldn't have missed a moment of it."[55] She clearly displays some of the tension, too: a sense that Day expected "everybody to be like saints."[56] But Tamar muses: "I mean, who can measure up to that?"[57]

Still, Tamar's own description of her life stands in contrast to the poem mentioned above, which is that she liked and appreciated the rural vision that both Day and Peter Maurin advocated. Yet there was a personal cost. Tamar observes: "I tried to hold on to those values. I tried to live simply. I tried to follow the Catholic faith. It did not turn out well. Right now I seem to have lapsed."[58]

Day's Theology of Natural and Supernatural Parenting and Family

I shift, here, to a description of Day's theology by recalling that Dorothy's natural love for her child overflowed to love for God: "The final object of this love and gratitude was God. No human creature could receive or contain so vast a flood of love and joy as I often felt after the birth of my child."[59] Yet, Dorothy's child displayed only one facet of her love of God. Her other love was "the life I had led in the radical movement... I wanted to be poor, chaste and obedient. I wanted to die in order to live, to put off the old man and put on Christ. I loved, in other words, and like all women in love, I wanted to be united to my love."[60]

Several people helped her think through her various loves, but two stand out: Father Hugo and Father McSorley, both priests and both leaders of the retreats that Dorothy advocated for herself and her communities. Day quotes, at length, a selection from Fr. John Hugo's book, *A Sign of Contradiction*, where the priest is discussing the importance of "the comparison between sexual union and the Beatific Vision..."[61] "The retreat"—the "dreaded retreat," as Tamar put it, formed part of what some have called Day's second conversion.[62]

The retreats involved a week of conferences (four talks per day), prayer, and opportunities for silence and reflection. Theologian Ben Peters has examined both Hugo's writings and the notebooks Day kept during her retreats in order to show how Hugo's understanding of natural and supernatural love worked. He summarizes the first two days of the retreat as follows:

> [T]he first part of the retreat presented an understanding of the nature-supernatural relationship that formed its theological foundation—the natural life understood as distinct from both that which is supernatural and sinful. The implication of this understanding is that all Christians are called to detach from the things of the world—to mortify their habitual attachments to created goods and the motives which these attachments informed.[63]

Hugo was careful to note that human nature couldn't be separated from God—that is, from supernatural ends. That is, humans are called to become saints, to participate fully in the life of God. The natural stuff of this world is not evil, Hugo emphasized, but that didn't prevent the natural happiness of this world from becoming an end in itself.

What we are to do, then, is first to allow God to "prune" us: "the vine is pruned so that it can bear fruit, and this we cannot do ourselves."[64] Second, we are to "sow" our money, our goods, and our time, with the faith that we will receive back more than we sow. Hugo used the term *sow* in reference to how a Christian should respond to God. Love of God is not opposite to love of neighbor and of the world. Indeed, Dorothy wrote in her retreat notes that contempt for the world was 'Opposite to love of God, like convex and concave go together cannot be separated. Must have right idea of this harsh world. Holy indifference."[65]

Peters observes: "For those who embraced the retreat, it offered a way for ordinary Christians—laity and secular clergy alike—to strive to live a holy life in the context of early twentieth-century American culture and society."[66] The way for ordinary Christians to live this holy life was in what Hugo named the "duty of the present moment," which is to be attentive to the present moments in which we live. This involves contemplative prayer intertwined with human activity: every moment is a prayer for union with God in one's action.

Dorothy was enraptured by Hugo's discussion of the natural and supernatural. Indeed, we can see Hugo's influence, above, in her retroactive description of her love for her common-law husband Forster, as well as her love for her daughter. That natural happiness was good, not evil. Dorothy saw it as wholly good. Yet that natural love pointed her beyond itself, to something greater—to God. If natural love became the stopping point for a person, that person ran the risk of loving the things of this world while not knowing God. "Samples" of natural life tend us toward God, unless we allow the natural stuff of life to become the end of our loves.

As Benjamin Peters puts it, one of the significant points is that "Building on the idea that all are called to the life of holiness presented in the Sermon on the Mount, Hugo argued that the Christian life was not two-tiered and so it made no distinction between the *extraordinary* life of a vowed religious and the *ordinary* Christian life of the laity."[67] Ordinary people have a vocation to holiness, a call to become a saint. Humans become fully human by glorifying God—and because God is Love, glorifying God becomes love and loving action. One of the key points that Fr. Hugo emphasized, and that Day took from the retreat, was the idea of the priesthood of all believers. In an era of clericalism, Day found the priesthood of all believers to be refreshing.[68]

The retreat was divisive to the Catholic Worker movement and its houses of hospitality. Fr. Hugo famously called on people to give up their worldly attachments—their cigarettes and booze—in love for others. Some experienced this call as a move toward austerity that also fostered guilt. One early member of the community, Stanley Vishnewski, writes of community resentment toward the unbaptized, for *they* could "enjoy all the creatures and comforts of this world and enjoy their eternity in Limbo," while Christians were "headed straight to Hell."[69] Natural love came across as a horrible aberration of God's love. The retreat seemed too unyielding and exacting. When Dorothy wanted to establish a house dedicated toward retreats at a Catholic Worker establishment, she therefore found some opposition.

A different view of the retreat comes from Catholic Worker Julian Pleasants:

> I didn't agree with the giving up things at all. Father Hugo said that the best thing to do with good things was to give them up. And I just didn't think that was Dorothy's attitude at all. She didn't want to give them up, she wanted to give them away. It was a totally different approach. Dorothy liked her good literature, her good music, and she never really felt that obligated. I think she got out of the retreat only the notion that you had to be *ready* to give them up. She took what worked for her and hoped other people would take what worked for them.[70]

Dorothy's own encounter with the retreat was one of refreshment, however, and her experience of others in her community who also made the retreats was that they felt likewise.

The retreat shines through in Dorothy's writing, especially in her discussions of her single parenting and her view of family. Day's view of family especially becomes expanded far beyond love for her daughter (which, as we have seen, was a great, beloved aspect of her life to begin with). In her 1948 diaries (published as *On Pilgrimage*) Day describes her life as a mother, grandmother, and lover of all people:

> What else do we all want, each one of us, except to love and be loved, in our families, in our work, in all our relationships? God is Love. Love casts out fear.... We want with all our hearts to love, to be loved. And not just in the family but to look upon all as our mothers, sisters, brothers, children.[71]

Yet Dorothy did not denigrate families, including families that were more standard nuclear families; an important component of Catholic Worker philosophy is that family is a basic unit of society. In her book on Therese of Lisieux, Day describes the twin purposes of society and home, first by drawing on her Catholic Worker colleague and second by meditating on homes:

> Peter Maurin, the peasant, said that our aim, if we love our brothers, is to make that kind of a society where it is easier for people to be good. The Martins [Therese's parents] well knew that the beginnings of peace, the beginnings of a good society are in the home. . . .[72]

Yet we might say that family becomes paradoxical, for Day. On the one hand, she speaks of the possibility of having a community of families living together, ordering their lives in a way similar to a monastery. On the other hand, Day writes of a man, Victor, who "wished all the work of the Catholic Worker to center around the family" because "we had said the family was the primary unit of society."[73] Victor moved to Easton farm with his family and created a very strict community of families, rather than continue hospitality to the (often single) poor who showed up. Dorothy notes some of the difficulties that the tension between being single and being a member of a family brought to Catholic Worker houses. One group of single men moved out of an apartment they had recently rented and furnished, so that a family could move in; the family left a week later, taking all the furnishings. At another house, a married couple was given a place to stay in a house of hospitality but refused to give other rooms to single people who later arrived in need to hospitality.[74]

Day experiences such tension in her own life, and meditates on whether such tensions exist for her daughter as well. Dorothy's description of herself with Tamar in 1936 is, "To think of the little time I have with her, being constantly on the go, having to leave her to the care of others, sending her away to school so that she can lead a regular life and not be subject to the moods and vagaries of the crowd of us!"[75] In *The Long Loneliness*, Day further speaks to the constant hum of relationships and people coming and going that generated Tamar's sense of family. Dorothy's observation points to many relationships, and not just the relationship between mother and child. Dorothy is well aware of her and Tamar's dependence on others. Part of Day's own witness to her Christian community and to her daughter is that she cannot be "self-sufficient."

Still, the tensions existing between individual and family led her to focus far more on family than on the individual. Once a priest criticized her writing, suggesting that if she were really a "woman of family" her writing "about community and personalism would have more validity."[76] While she took the criticism, on reflection Day exclaimed: "How can anyone put over on me the idea that I am a single person? I am a mother, and the mother of a very large family at that. Being a mother is fulfillment, it is surrender to others, it is Love and therefore of course it is suffering."[77]

Day knows that her life is not self-sufficient. She relies on generous others for carrying out her work in Catholic Worker, as well as for caring for her daughter when she must be away giving talks. The lack of self-sufficiency that Day knows and practices in her life becomes a source for the title for her signature book, *The Long Loneliness*, and is inspired by Tamar. When Day began to write the book, Tamar wrote to her

> ...about how alone the mother of young children always is. I had also just heard from an elderly woman who lived a long and full life, and she too spoke of loneliness. I thought again, 'The only answer in this life, to the loneliness we are all bound to feel, is community. The living together, working together, sharing together, loving God and loving our brother, and living close to him in community so we can show our love for Him.[78]

Tamar's reflections generate more of Day's own reflections on community, and I think it is significant that the points about loneliness and community come from her daughter, herself a young mother of many children who sees her own lack of self-sufficiency.

For Day, the retreats are an antidote to two-tiered, stratified thinking about parenting and families, in which some families are nearly perfect and self-contained, and others are a mess and all-too-dependent. For example, at the end of *The Long Loneliness*, she says: "We have all known the long loneliness and we have learned that the only solution is love and that love comes with community."[79] This is Dorothy's very practical response to how to love God, for in her notes from one retreat, she writes, "How can we love our husbands, our children, our mothers? All other loves I have must be a sample of the love of God. All the world and everything in it must be samples of the love of God. We must love the world intensely, but not for itself."[80] Love of the world, love in community, are insufficient, without God.

Sufficiency, Better

Dorothy Day represents a radical way of Christian discipleship, a way of life that many Christians have rejected as being impossible for them to follow. A dominant theological response to people like Dorothy Day is to argue that they so advocate separatism, even "apocalyptic sectarianism" as Catholic historian David O'Brien put it, that Day's life and witness can be celebrated but simultaneously safely ignored. It is significant that such a view of Day's life comes both from George Weigel (commonly called a conservative Catholic) as well as David O'Brien (commonly called a liberal Catholic), who agree with each other on very little but do agree that Day represents an apocalyptic strand in Christian tradition that is not helpful for most people.[81]

Yet we would do well not to be quite so heavy-handed in dismissing Dorothy's fierce discipleship or her example as a single parent. Dorothy spent much time (months at a time, in fact) with Tamar and with her grandchildren). Dorothy's discussion of "the world" is nuanced, of course, with a focus on "the good and the better." Worldly separation is less the point than seeing all of life imbued with holiness. Consider, for example, Dorothy's discussion of sex in April 1948: "All things must be restored to Christ; our bodies were redeemed too. Children should be learning healthy and holy attitudes unconsciously as well as consciously from infancy so that they can fuse the natural and supernatural in every part of life."[82] Every moment, the moments of sex, the moments of being with your child who is pretending that a wash basin is a hat, the moments of having to work to provide for your family, all of these are moments, too, when love of God can be cultivated.

What Dorothy Day offers as a witness to Christian life is the gift of knowing that we are not self-sufficient. What single parents, too, might especially bring as gifts to the community is a reminder that self-sufficiency is a lie. The church needs to respond with a clear "yes" to those among us who stand in need of child care, money, food, companionship, and so forth. In a contemporary society that, in a certain way, reveres child-parent relationships such that to be a parent requires a kind of perfection that we might well see as saintly—Day's decidedly unsaintly parenting, by today's standards, is perplexing. Yet it might also be the case that Day's wrestling with what it means to care for one's "own" in contrast with caring for the least of these might be a helpful notion for contemporary parenting—single or otherwise.

The two tiers of the parenting divides cannot stand. Not only do the parenting divides separate us humans from each other—when, instead, we could be helps to each other—the parenting divides foster a false sense of holiness. As we saw above in the discussion of welfare reforms, that holiness gets especially depicted as self-sufficiency. We cannot be "sufficient" parents any more than we can be sufficiently and fully human, or fully love, on our own.

This is true whether we are single parents, married with children, or live out some other state of singleness. In other words, supernatural parenting belongs to single parents as much as to dual-parent families, but this supernatural parenting is the kind that Day describes. Thinking in terms of supernature is meant to direct our thought and work toward God. Two-parent families need to acknowledge, fully, the fact that self-sufficiency simply doesn't exist—and name the expansive communities of which they are already a part. Two-parent families rely on others outside their nuclear families just as single-parents do. Single-parent and two-parent families thus become all part of one Body of Christ. Then, both two-parent and single-parent families are more free to see family as leading us all toward the love of God.

Yet, while Day exhorts Christians to the self-*in*sufficiency exemplified by Christian community, Day also knows that community is a mixed blessing. Day knows that community is not perfect when she describes all the people who take over the various Catholic Worker farms, without a care for the communities they are disrupting. Indeed, the benefit of knowing and experiencing community, including Christian community, as a mixed blessing is that we understand it, too, to be insufficient apart from God's love. As Dorothy has it: "The only reason the love of parents, the love of a spouse, the love of children, and the love of friends are precious is because they in some way resemble God's love. All human love derives from God and is meant to direct us back to God."[83]

In short, we are all imperfect, yet God loves us anyway and we respond to that love. In this expansive view of God as love, Day also gives us the realistic view of the failure of humans to be properly loving to each other. Thus the proper response of Christians to the family ideal is to say, "This is good only because it points to better," and to acknowledge that all people are in need of the love of God because family is insufficient.

Conclusions

WE ARE SURROUNDED by many single witnesses of the faith. I said in Chapter 1 that this book was meant to provide a beginning for thinking about theologies of singleness. Now, at the end of this book, I am quite certain I have not said all that there is to say about Christian singleness and that there is much rich theological work remaining. In this conclusion I set out some of what I think has been learned, alongside some possible future directions for the church at large and for its theologians.

First, I hope I have shown that Christian traditions have been thinking about theologies of singleness in many ways, but that contemporary American Christians have not often recognized that fact. That is, I think Christians in many times and places have been far more reflective than we contemporary American Christians about singleness in its many forms. It is simply too broad and bold a brushstroke to paint Christian thought about singleness as stating something like, "Single? Okay, no sex for you. Lonely? Go join a monastery!"

Christians have rightly emphasized marriage (and, depending, vowed religious life) as significant, and (often) sacramental. The lifelong character and the vows people make are both important practices that help people foster Christian virtues. In holding out marriage and vowed religious life as significant, Christians have made the mistake of implying that marriage and vowed religious life are the only true choices for following Christ. Or, alternately, everybody who is not married or in vowed religious life becomes grouped into a shapeless conglomerate mass of the people who are baptized but who have not made lifelong vows. A theology of baptism is crucial for Christian identity and a sense of vocation in the life, death, and resurrection of Christ, but it doesn't reflect the many important distinctions between, say, widowhood and being engaged, that Christian theologians have made down through the centuries.

Simultaneously, an emphasis on sex prohibition has tended to make people think the only important point to learn or understand about non-vowed states of life was "don't have sex." This in turn has meant that Christians have, collectively, spent a lot of time and energy focusing on trying to get people not to have sex, and often with unsuccessful results (for example, abstinence-only education!)[1]

I hope that this book has shown other, better ways of thinking about singleness. One of the aspects of researching for this book that most surprised me was how often Christian communities have had particular prayers or worship services for states of singleness. From betrothal services to lifelong friendship vows to penitential wedding rites for those who have divorced and will be remarried, Christians have been making use of rituals to mark the importance of impermanent single states of life. The popular phrase "*lex orandi, lex credendi*" (usually translated as "the law of prayer is the law of belief") in use in so much theology over the past few decades might here indicate the particular and significant importance of single states of life in the past, quite simply because singlenesses have been part of our communal prayer and worship.

I was also surprised by the number of states of singleness in which women are disproportionately affected, and often in negative ways. Divorced and widowed women are far more impoverished than men, for example. Women are more likely to be single heads of households than men, which in turn is more likely to negatively impact their ability to find well-paying work. Never-married women are more likely to be described in negative tones than men: the terms *spinsters* and *old maids* tend to have more derogatory overtones than the male *bachelor*.[2] In fact, given the impact of single states of life on women, it's rather surprising that states of singleness haven't been more prominently discussed among scholars concerned about gender. (This is in addition to the fact that, given that singleness impacts almost half the US population, its surprising singleness isn't more discussed as a whole.)[3] The gendered nature of single states of life suggests, to me, a possible reason for why singleness isn't more often discussed. Christians so often want to remember and include those who are marginalized because God cares for those who are marginalized. Given the gender concerns about singleness, Christians ought to be focusing much more on women and singleness. Feminist theologians, especially, ought to be taking up states of singleness more often in their considerations of gender bias as it intersects with being unmarried.

Similarly, I found that questions relating to same-sex marriage impacted a wide variety of states of singleness, even when LGBTQ+ status didn't seem to relate directly. The nature of loneliness described in Chapter 1, for example, takes shape in a context of Justice Kennedy pitying single gays and lesbians.

Questions about divorce link to same-sex attraction and how often Christians see homosexuality as being hand-in-hand with the destruction of marriage and family. It would be worth thinking more about discrimination toward LGBTQ+ people in relation to discrimination against single people, regardless of their sexuality.

What least surprised me was the fact that many of the guides mentioned in this book sought some form of specific Christian community for their states of singleness. I think this is, in part, due to loneliness, as several of them acknowledged. But these communities are no "lonely hearts" clubs. These were not mere age-related clubs, or dating services for never-marrieds, or bereavement groups for widows. Rather, the Christian community each person sought was meant specifically to enable further and deeper Christian discipleship and the life of the church more broadly, especially as it touched on their specific state of life. Elizabeth Ann Seton's group of widows endeavored to serve children at their school and related ministries. Dorothy Day's Catholic Worker movement enabled her to think about family more broadly and to bring up her daughter in the midst of a very large household whose purpose was to live with the poor. Augustine sought out a monastic-like community with his mother, son, and friends, shortly following his conversion to Christianity and chastity, which helped him solidify his commitment to Christian life ("My memory harks back to our sojourn there, and it is my delight, Lord, to acknowledge before you what inward goads you employed to tame me, how you laid low the mountains and hills of my proud intellect and made of me an even plain....")[4] Aelred had his monastic community, but more importantly saw spiritual friendship as an important friendship to nurture even and especially within larger communal structures. Stanley Hauerwas narrates his divorce and remarriage in relation to the loosely-gathered group of Christian friends who surrounded and supported his family.

Christian community has appeared as informally as small households of married and unmarried people living together, or as formally as the more well-known religious communities of monks and religious sisters and brothers. As we have seen, some of the guides I mentioned in this book ended up moving from their informal single state of life to a vowed religious state.

Christians ought to be far more supportive of people seeking a variety of communities in which to practice Christian life. The stories of Tim Otto and Wesley Hill, who desire the support and strength of Christian community, should stand before the church as a call to live in different ways than we do (with our focus on nuclear families each living in one household). The widows I visited at one parish were hungry for Christian community in which people could live together and share financial and emotional burdens, as well as the joys of daily life.

Yet community cannot become an end in itself. As I mentioned in Chapter 1, Bonhoeffer noted that community can very much become an idol, especially in the face of loneliness—just as marriage becomes idolatrous sometimes, too, when it becomes an end in itself. Marriage is not, by itself, a direct path to Christ. Community is not, by itself, a direct path to Christ. Singleness is not, by itself, a direct path to Christ. At times and places, Christians have been guilty of overprivileging marriage or singleness or community as ways of "achieving" God.

God will not be "achieved," though. Rather, God seeks us out in our marriages, vowed religious life, and all the varieties of singleness. Our commitment to love God and neighbor take on different tones or emphases depending on our states of singleness, marriage, or vowed religious life. Yet each state provides strong ways for Christians to live out their chief commitment to Jesus Christ and witness to the Body of Christ as well as to the world. Impermanent states of singleness are quite capable of revealing Jesus Christ to others in important ways. Impermanent states of singleness are well able to speak truth about God, especially when the church as a whole fails to remember or practice grace, love, perfection, and so forth. We all, single and married alike, would do well to learn more from each other about the love of God as revealed in Jesus Christ. My hope is that others will now tell stories and offer theologies from other singular witnesses in Christian tradition.

Notes

CHAPTER 1

1. The verses in question are 7:36–38, where Paul admonishes those who are "not behaving properly toward your fiancée," or more literally, "your virgin." Some have read in this text the possibility of a form of *syneisaktism*, or "spiritual marriage," which would have involved living together but would not have involved sexual activity. Paul clearly separates *syneisaktism* from getting married, which is why I am naming it here as a form of cohabitation. See, for example, Liesbeth Van der Sypt, "The Use of 1 Corinthians 7:36–38 in Early Christian Asceticism," in *Asceticism and Exegesis in Early Christianity: The Reception of New Testament Texts in Ancient Ascetic Discourses*, Hans-Ulrich Weidemann, ed. (Gottlingen, Germany: Vandenhoeck & Ruprecht, 2013).
2. Pope Francis, *Amoris Laetitia*, paragraph 197.
3. Pope Paul VI, *Lumen Gentium, Dogmatic Constitution on the Church*, November 21, 1964, http://www.vatican.va/archive/hist_councils/ii_vatican_council/documents/vat-ii_const_19641121_lumen-gentium_en.html, §7.
4. A couple of references may suffice. The baptism rite for United Methodists includes the words: "The Holy Spirit works within you, that being born through water and the Spirit, you may be a faithful disciple of Jesus Christ." Accessed September 15, 2016, http://www.umc.org/what-we-believe/baptism. Similarly, the Presbyterian Church-USA states: "In baptism, we are called to a new way of life as Christ's disciples, sharing the good news of the gospel with all the world." Accessed September 15, 2016, https://www.pcusa.org/news/2016/1/21/what-presbyterians-believe-baptism/.
5. *The Catechism of the Catholic Church* §2230: "When they become adults, children have the right and duty to *choose their profession and state of life*. They should assume their new responsibilities within a trusting relationship with their

parents, willingly asking and receiving their advice and counsel. Parents should be careful not to exert pressure on their children either in the choice of a profession or in that of a spouse." Accessed September 15, 2016, http://www.vatican.va/archive/ccc_css/archive/catechism/p3s2c2a4.htm.

6. *Obergefell et al v. Hodges, Ohio Director of Health et al* (US S.C. 2015). Accessed August 20, 2015, http://www.supremecourt.gov/opinions/14pdf/14-556_3204.pdf.
7. Michael Cobb, "The Supreme Court's Lonely Hearts Club," *The New York Times*, June 30, 2015. Accessed November 20, 2015, http://www.nytimes.com/2015/06/30/opinion/the-supreme-courts-lonely-hearts-club.html?_r=0.
8. Ibid.
9. In conducting the research for this book, I found that the ways Christians celebrate or denigrate singleness is connected to cultural practices. That is one of the reasons why I have chosen to focus on contemporary American Christianity and singleness. That said, voices from other nationalities and cultures show up on occasion, especially when they have been influential on American practice or thought.
10. Pew Research Center, "Marriage." Accessed September 9, 2016, http://www.pewresearch.org/data-trend/society-and-demographics/marriage/.
11. See US Census Bureau, "Median Age at First Marriage: 1890–Present," https://www.census.gov/hhes/families/files/graphics/MS-2.pdf.
12. US Census Bureau, "Facts for Figures: Unmarried and Single Adults Week." Accessed September 9, 2016, http://www.census.gov/newsroom/facts-for-features/2015/cb15-ff19.html.
13. Michael Cobb, *Single: Arguments for the Uncoupled* (New York: New York University Press, 2012), 192.
14. Kate Bolick, *Spinsters: Making a Life of One's Own* (New York: Penguin Books, 2015); Rebecca Traister, *All the Single Ladies: Unmarried Women and the Rise of an Independent Nation* (New York: Simon and Schuster, 2016).
15. Anthea Taylor, *Single Women in Popular Culture: The Limits of Postfeminism* (London: Palgrave Macmillan, 2012), 26.
16. Cobb, *Single: Arguments for the Uncoupled*, 13.
17. Taylor, *Single Women in Popular Culture*, 20.
18. "Millennials in Adulthood," Pew Research Center, March 7, 2014. Accessed September 10, 2016, http://www.pewsocialtrends.org/2014/03/07/millennials-in-adulthood/.
19. See Meg Murphy, "Why Millennials Refuse to Get Married." Accessed September 10, 2016, http://www.bentley.edu/impact/articles/nowuknow-why-millennials-refuse- get-married.
20. D'Vera Cohn, "Love and Marriage," Pew Research Center, February 13, 2013. Accessed September 10, 2016, http://www.pewsocialtrends.org/2013/02/13/love-and-marriage/.

21. Jilian Straus, excerpt from *Unhooked Generation: The Truth About Why We're Still Single*. Accessed July 16, 2009, http://www.unhookedgeneration.com/excerpt.php.
22. Briallen Hopper, "On Spinsters," *LA Review of Books*, July 15, 2015. Accessed July 26, 2016, https://lareviewofbooks.org/article/on-spinsters/#!.
23. Justin Wolfers, David Leonhardt, and Kevin Quealy, "1.5 Million Missing Black Men," The Upshot in *New York Times* Online, April 20, 2015. Accessed July 26, 2016, http://www.nytimes.com/interactive/2015/04/20/upshot/missing-black-men.html.
24. Ralph Richard Banks, *Is Marriage for White People?: How the African American Marriage Decline Affects Everyone* (New York: Dutton, 2011), 14.
25. See also Kevin L. Smith, "The Challenge of Matriarch: Family Discipleship and the African-American Experience," *Journal of Discipleship and Family Ministries* 2.2 (2012): 34–40.
26. Banks, *Is Marriage for White People?*, 140–141.
27. Melissa Murray, "Black Marriage, White People, Red Herrings," *Michigan Law Review* 111.977: 977
28. Hopper, "On Spinsters." Emphasis mine.
29. Albert Hsu, *Singles at the Crossroads: A Fresh Perspective on Christian Singleness* (Downer's Grove, IL: Intervarsity Press, 1997), 25.
30. Ibid., 174.
31. Barry Danylak, *Redeeming Singleness: How the Storyline of Scripture Affirms the Single Life* (Wheaton: Crossway, 2010).
32. Owen Stracham et al., *Whole in Christ: A Biblical Approach to Singleness* (Louisville: Danvers Press, 2015).
33. Al Mohler, "The Mystery of Marriage." Cited in Colón and Field, *Singled Out*, 90.
34. Gary Thomas, *Sacred Marriage*, 21. Cited in Colón and Field, *Singled Out*, 91.
35. Christine A. Colón and Bonnie E. Field, *Singled Out: Why Celibacy Must be Reinvented in Today's Church* (Grand Rapids: Brazos Press, 2009), 79.
36. http://www.boundless.org/, accessed December 10, 2015.
37. Colón and Field, *Singled Out*, citing The Barna Group, 2006 and 2007.
38. Augustine, *Holy Virginity*, in *Marriage and Virginity*, ed. David G. Hunter, trans. Ray Kearney (Hyde Park, NY: New City Press, 1999), 6. I discuss the idea of all Christians being both married and single in much more detail in my book, *Water is Thicker than Blood: An Augustinian Theology of Marriage and Singleness* (New York: Oxford University Press, 2008), especially Chapter 4.
39. I am one of these theologians, too. My first book, *Water is Thicker than Blood: An Augustinian Theology of Marriage and Singleness* (New York: Oxford University Press, 2008), tried to make some of these points. But while I tried to name what this might look like, I don't think I went quite far enough in resetting the terms of theological discussion about marriage and singleness. I was concerned not to return to a time of over-idealization of singleness (especially vowed singleness)

as a means of discipleship, such that I did not highlight enough what single people offer to the Body of Christ.

40. Saint John Paul II, *Familiaris Consortio,* apostolic exhortation, http://w2.vatican.va/content/john-paul-ii/en/apost_exhortations/documents/hf_jp-ii_exh_19811122_familiaris-consortio.html. He goes into far more detail in his Theology of the Body talks; see *Man and Woman He Created Them: A Theology of the Body* (Boston: Pauline Books and Media, 2006).
41. I discuss this further in Chapter 1 of *Water is Thicker than Blood.* See also Julie Hanlon Rubio, *A Christian Theology of Marriage and Family* (Mahwah, NJ: Paulist Press, 2003).
42. Stanley Hauerwas, "Sex in Public: How Adventurous Christians Are Doing It," in *The Hauerwas Reader,* John Berkman and Michael Cartwright, eds. (Durham: Duke University Press, 2001), 499.
43. Andy Crouch, "Family Values," in *Called to Community: The Life Jesus Wants for His People,* Charles E. Moore, ed. (Walden, New York: Plough Publishing House, 2016), 229.
44. Nicole Flores [Henry], "Latina/o Families: Solidarity and the Common Good," *The Journal of the Society of Christian Ethics* 33.2 (2013): 67.
45. Global cultural understandings are outside the scope of my book but remain fascinating to read, for example, Laurel Cornell's essay, "Why are There No Spinsters in Japan?" *Journal of Family History* (Winter 1984): 326–339.
46. Emily Stimpson, *The Catholic Girl's Survival Guide for the Single Years: The Nuts and Bolts of Staying Sane and Happy While Waiting for Mr. Right* (Steubenville, OH: Emmaus Road Publishing, 2012).
47. Colón and Field, *Singled Out,* 11.
48. Ibid., 222.
49. Michael Lipka, "Why America's 'Nones' Left Religion Behind," Pew Research Center August 24, 2016. Accessed September 12, 2016, http://www.pewresearch.org/fact-tank/2016/08/24/why-americas-nones-left-religion-behind/.
50. Fan Zhong, "The Future of Sex is Already Here," *W Magazine* (11 October 2016), http://www.wmagazine.com/story/future-sex-emily-witt-book.
51. Ibid.
52. Matthew 5:48.
53. Elizabeth Abbott, *A History of Celibacy* (New York: Scribner, 2000), 136. See also JoAnn McNamara, *Sisters in Arms: Catholic Nuns Through Two Millennia* (Cambridge, MA: Harvard University Press, 2000) for a similar but more detailed argument.
54. Ibid., 161. It should be said: trying to live these vows is difficult, and Christians have advocated communal living for most people attempting to follow this path; in community, a person is formed in being obedient to others and in learning how to practice celibacy and poverty over a lifetime. One of the most famous

founders of monastic communities is Saint Benedict of Nursia, who authored the *Rule of Saint Benedict* for his monastic communities. This rule of life is still influential in Benedictine and other religious communities today. Saint Benedict wrote his rule for monks who wished to make a start toward life in God. He worried about people who had no community in his rule for his monks: "Two or three together, or even alone, without a shepherd, they pen themselves up in their own sheepfolds, not the Lord's. Their law is what they like to do, whatever strikes their fancy. Anything they believe and choose, they call holy; anything they dislike, they consider forbidden." (Chapter 1 of the *Rule of Saint Benedict*, Timothy Fry, ed. (Collegeville, MN: The Liturgical Press, 1980.) Saint Benedict admitted there might be a few people who could be anchorites or hermits: those who had already been formed in the monastery and could therefore be tried on their own. Most people, however, couldn't be solitary, but they could undertake the rigors of spiritually attempting perfection if they were in community. So in Benedict's view, being unmarried didn't mean "no relationships" in the contemporary sense I described above; it meant communal relationships without sexual activity.

55. Benjamin Kahan, *Celibacies: American Modernism and Sexual Life* (Durham: Duke University Press, 2013), 142.
56. Ibid., 10.
57. See Chapter 3 of his book.
58. Kahan, *Celibacies*, especially Chapter 4.
59. Crunkashell, "Single, Saved, and Sexin': The Gospel of Getting your Freak On," *Crunk Feminist Collective*, February 3, 2011. Accessed September 14, 2016, http://www.crunkfeministcollective.com/2011/02/03/single-saved-and-sexin-the-gospel-of-gettin-your-freak-on/.
60. See, among his many works, Adrian Thatcher, *Marriage After Modernity: Christian Marriage in Post-modern Times* (New York: New York University Press, 1999); *Thinking About Sex* (Minneapolis: Fortress Press, 2015). I cite others later in this book.
61. There are numerous examples, of course. A smattering of examples include Chris Hobart, "A Single-Minded Focus on Loneliness," *The (Hobart) Mercury*, March 30, 2011: 22; Whitney Caudill, "Being Single: How to Handle Loneliness," *The Huffington Post*, August 6, 2013, http://www.huffingtonpost.com/whitney-caudill/being-single-how-to-handle-loneliness_b_3461062.html; "I'm Lonely and Other Things that Suck about Being Single," *Your Tango*, January 28, 2016, http://www.yourtango.com/233213/10-heartbreaking-truths-about-loneliness-single-people-dont-say.
62. See Magnhild Nicolaisen, and Kirsten Thorsen "Who Are Lonely? Loneliness in Different Age Groups (18–81 Years Old), Using Two Measures of Loneliness." *International Journal of Aging & Human Development* 78.3 (2014): 229–257

Accessed September 15, 2016; Tova Band-Winterstein et al., "The Experience of Being an Old Never-Married Single: A Life Course Perspective," *International Journal of Aging and Human Development* 78.4 (2014): 379–401.

63. Katie Hafner, "Researchers Confront an Epidemic of Loneliness," *The New York Times* (September 5, 2016). Accessed September 13, 2016. http://www.nytimes.com/2016/09/06/health/lonliness-aging-health-effects.html?_r=0.
64. Lauren Winner, *Still: Notes on a Mid-Faith Crisis* (New York: HarperOne, 2012), 57–58.
65. Candida Crewe, "The Unspoken Truth about Being an Average Single Mother… It Can Be So Lonely," *The Daily Mail* (July 7, 2016): 55.
66. Hafner, "Researchers Confront an Epidemic of Loneliness," http://www.nytimes.com/2016/09/06/health/lonliness-aging-health-effects.html?_r=0.
67. "Is Single Life Something to Lament or Celebrate?" Tell Me More (February 15, 2012). NPR.
68. Bella DePaulo, *Singled Out: How Singles are Stereotyped, Stigmatized, and Ignored, but Still Live Happily Ever After*, (New York: St. Martin's Press, 2006).
69. Cobb, *Single: Arguments for the Uncoupled*, 18.
70. I do not think that Cobb or DePaulo take seriously enough the "marriage penalty"—the fact that people who marry and have similar incomes end up paying more because they have gotten married. See Tax Foundation at taxfoundation.org for more information.
71. Barack Obama, *Dreams from my Father: A Story of Race and Inheritance* (New York: Three Rivers Press, 1995, 2004), 91; cited in Cobb, *Single: Arguments for the Uncoupled*, 13.
72. Cobb, *Single: Arguments for the Uncoupled*, 31.
73. See also Laura Kipnis, *Against Love: A Polemic* (New York: Pantheon, 2003).
74. Marilynne Robinson, "Further Thoughts on a Prodigal Son Who Cannot Come Home, on Loneliness and Grace," interviewed by Rebecca M. Painter, *Christianity and Literature* (2009): 492.
75. Dietrich Bonhoeffer, *Life Together*, Translated and with an Introduction by John W. Doberstein (San Francisco: Harper San Francisco, 1954), 76.
76. Ibid., 77.
77. Ibid.
78. Katherine Holden, Amy Froide, and June Hannam, eds., "Introduction," *Women's History Review* 17.3 (July 2008): 319.

CHAPTER 2

1. Janelle Nanos, "Single By Choice," *Boston Magazine*, January 2012, http://www.bostonmagazine.com/2012/01/single-by-choice-why-more-of-us-than-ever-before-are-happy-to-never-get-married/.

2. Jessica Keating, "Single By Default: When a Vocation is Not a Vocation," *America Magazine*, September 2016. Accessed September 16, 2016, http://americamagazine.org/issue/single-default.
3. "Bachelor," *Oxford English Dictionary*, definition 4. http://www.oed.com/view/Entry/14313.
4. Richard Allestree, *The Ladies Calling*, Project Cambridge, http://anglicanhistory.org/women/calling/virgins.html, II.i.5.
5. Howard Chudacoff, *The Age of the Bachelor: Creating an American Subculture* (Princeton, NJ: Princeton University Press, 1999), 1.
6. Ibid., 4.
7. Ibid., 255.
8. Ibid., 260–261.
9. Natalie Schwartzberg, Kathy Berliner, and Demaris Jacob, *Single in a Married World: A Life Cycle Framework for Working With the Unmarried Adult*, 1st ed. (W.W. Norton & Company, 1995).
10. See, for example, David Reisman, *The Lonely Crowd, Revised Edition: A Study of the Changing American Character* (New Haven: Yale University Press, 2001).
11. Kate Bolick, *Spinster: Making a Life of One's Own* (New York: Crown, 2015), 72.
12. Ibid.
13. Reverend Scotty MacLennan, *Finding Your Religion: When the Faith You Grew Up With Has Lost Its Meaning* (New York: Harper Collins, 1999), 1.
14. This paragraph and the following four paragraphs are modified from a public lecture I gave on choice: "Choosing God: Thoughts on Religious Freedom and the Meaning of Life," Loyola Maryland University, October 29–30, 2012. Available online at https://www.academia.edu/1991792/Choosing_God_Thoughts_on_Religious_Freedom_and_the_Meaning_of_Life.
15. Wikipedia, "Freedom of Religion." Accessed November 23, 2015, http://en.wikipedia.org/wiki/Freedom_of_religion.
16. For example, the most recent Amnesty International report on human rights violations discusses largely Hindu persecution of Muslims in the Indian state of Gujarat. Amnesty International, "Annual Report: India 2011." Accessed October 25, 2012, http://www.amnestyusa.org/research/reports/annual-report-india-2011?page=4. Violence against the Muslim minority has been ongoing; about 2000 Muslims were killed there in the early 2000s. It is also worth noting that scholars of religion have significant questions about what counts as "religion." It is not clear, for example, that Hinduism is a "religion" in the same way that Westerners imagine Christianity and Judaism to be "religions." There is a tendency to name as religion anything that smacks of what Westerners think is "spiritual" and related to God. Such a knee-jerk reaction overlooks that for many cultures, what counts as "religious" cannot be intelligibly separated from what counts as "politics" or "economics" and so on.

17. The number of colleges and universities impacted by questions about consent and sexual assault, in relation to Title IX concerns, is far too numerous to mention here. Some sampling of stories include: Amanda Hess, "How Drunk is Too Drunk to Have Sex? Universities are Struggling to Determine when Intoxicated Sex Becomes Sexual Assault," *Slate*, February 11, 2015, accessed November 24, 2015, http://www.slate.com/articles/double_x/doublex/2015/02/drunk_sex_on_campus_universities_are_struggling_to_determine_when_intoxicated.html; Hanna Kozlowska, "Yes Means Yes: The Big Consent Debate," *New York Times* October 15, 2014, accessed November 24, 2015, http://op-talk.blogs.nytimes.com/2014/10/15/yes-means-yes-the-big-consent-debate/?_r=0; Peter Schworm, "Harvard's View on Consent at Issue in Sexual Assault Policy," *Boston Globe* November 17, 2014, accessed November 24, 2015. https://www.bostonglobe.com/metro/2014/11/17/harvard-sexual-assaults-policy-fuels-debate-about-consent/IRpfu05MkjbHohN8ETErbK/story.html.
18. Jon Zimmerman, "We're Casual about Sex and Serious about Consent. But is it Working?" The Washington Post October 13, 2015, accessed November 24, 2015. https://www.washingtonpost.com/news/in-theory/wp/2015/10/13/were-casual-about-sex-and-serious-about-consent-but-is-it-working/?utm_term=.3845999e24fb.
19. Lauren Winner, *Real Sex: The Naked Truth About Chastity* (Grand Rapids: Brazos Press, 2005), 12.
20. Rusty Reno, *In the Ruins of the Church: Sustaining Faith in an Age of Diminished Christianity* (Grand Rapids: Brazos Press, 2002), 117.
21. Scott Paeth, "Is it Time for a New Sexual Ethic?" *Against the Stream*, February 7, 2013. Accessed September 17, 2016, http://scottpaeth.typepad.com/main/2013/02/is-it-time-for-a-new-christian-sexual-ethic.html.
22. See my discussion in Chapter 1 of *Water is Thicker than Blood: An Augustinian Theology of Marriage and Singleness* (New York: Oxford University Press, 2008), especially pp. 5–10.
23. *Catechism of the Catholic Church*, §2230. Emphasis in text.
24. For more on this see Jana Bennett, "Singular Christianity: Marriage and Singleness as Discipleship," in *Leaving and Coming Home* (Eugene, OR: Cascade Books, 2010), 85–100.
25. Wendell Berry, *Sex Economy, Freedom, and Community* (New York: Parthenon Books, 1993), 120.
26. Ibid., 121.
27. Ibid., 133.
28. William Cavanaugh, *Being Consumed: Economics and Christian Desire* (Grand Rapids: Eerdmans, 2008), 17.
29. Amanda Scherker, "14 Times Women Were Sexed Up for Absolutely No Logical Reason," *Huffington Post* (September 17, 2014). Accessed August 31, 2015,

http://www.huffingtonpost.com/2014/09/17/women-sexist-media_n_5792960.html?utm_hp_ref=women-and-advertising.

30. David Matzko McCarthy, *The Good Life: Genuine Christianity for the Middle Class* (Grand Rapids: Brazos Press, 2004), 59.
31. Ibid.
32. Ibid.
33. Ibid., 60.
34. Bolick, *Spinsters*, Chapter 4.
35. Bella DePaulo, *Singled Out*, 186–187. Emphasis mine.
36. For example, being President of the United States. See DePaulo, *Singled Out*, 198.
37. See Stephanie Coontz, *The Way We Never Were: American Families and the Nostalgia Trap* (New York: Harper Collins, 1992), especially Chapter 1.
38. See Julissa Cruz, "Marriage: More than a Century of Change," National Center for Family and Marriage Research (2013), https://www.bgsu.edu/content/dam/BGSU/college-of-arts-and-sciences/NCFMR/documents/FP/FP-13-13.pdf.
39. Michael Cobb, "The Supreme Court's Lonely Hearts Club," *The New York Times*, June 30, 2015. Accessed November 20, 2015, http://www.nytimes.com/2015/06/30/opinion/the-supreme-courts-lonely-hearts-club.html?_r=0.
40. For this kind of reading, see R.C.H. Lenski, *The Interpretation of St. Paul's First and Second Epistles to the Corinthians* (Minneapolis: Augsburg Publishing House, 1963), Chapter 7.
41. Jerome writes, "When you come to marriage, you do not say it is good to marry, because you cannot then add *than to burn;* but you say, It is better to marry than to burn. If marriage in itself be good, do not compare it with fire, but simply say, It is good to marry. I suspect the goodness of that thing which is forced into the position of being only the lesser of two evils. What I want is not a smaller evil, but a thing absolutely good." *Against Jovinianus*, I.9.
42. His conversion takes place in Acts 9:1–19.
43. Margaret MacDonald and Leif E. Vaage, "Unclean by Holy Children: Paul's Everyday Quandary in 1 Corinthians 7:14c," *The Catholic Biblical Quarterly* 73 (2011): 526.
44. Daniel Boyarin, *A Radical Jew: Paul and the Politics of Identity* (Berkeley; Los Angeles: University of California Press, 1994), 192.
45. For example, the Essenes; see Calvin J. Roetzel, *The World that Shaped the New Testament* (Atlanta: John Knox Press, 1985).
46. Another scholar, Yonder Moynihan Gillihan, writes that Paul's uses of the words "unclean" and "holy" show that Paul was influenced by his rabbinic past, since those words mark much rabbinic writing. See "Jewish Laws on Illicit Marriage, the Defilement of Offspring, and the Holiness of the Temple: A New Halakic Interpretation of 1 Corinthians 7:14," *Journal of Biblical Literature* 121 (2002): 711–744.

47. For an excellent overview of Alexander the Great and the rise of Hellenistic culture, see Roetzel, especially Chapters 2 and 3.
48. David Wheeler-Reed, "Paul on Marriage and Singleness: Reading 1 Corinthians 7 with the Augustan Marriage Laws." (Dissertation, Toronto: University of Toronto, 2013), 2.68–69.
49. Horace, *Odes and Epodes*, ed. Jeffrey Henderson, trans., Niall Rudd, LCL Vol. 33 (Cambridge MA: Harvard University Press, 2004), 263. See also Michèle Lowrie, *Horace and Augustus*, 86.
50. See Horace, *Ode* IV.15.
51. See, for example, Andrew Wallace-Hadrill, *Augustan Rome* (London: Bristol Classical Press, 1993), especially pages 66–70.
52. See some of these examples in Bonnie MacLachlan, *Women in Ancient Rome: A Sourcebook* (London: Bloomsbury, 2013).
53. Jouette M. Bassler, "Limits and Differentiation: The Calculus of Widows in 1 Timothy 5.3–16," in *A Feminist Companion to the Deutero-Pauline Epistles*, Amy-Jill Levine, ed. (Cleveland: The Pilgrim Press, 2003), 129.
54. Thanks to Meghan Henning and David Wheeler-Reed for help in thinking through this question.
55. 1 Corinthians 2:2.
56. On the importance of the church to Pauline theology, see Luke Timothy Johnson's' brief essay in Thomas R. Schreiner, et al., *Four Views on the Apostle Paul* (Grand Rapids: Zondervan, 2012), pp. 65–96.
57. "God decided, through the foolishness of our proclamation, to save those who believe."
58. Robert Grant, *Paul in the Roman World: The Conflict at Corinth* (Louisville: Westminster John Knox Press, 2001), 34.
59. Leander Keck, *Paul and His Letters*, second edition, revised and enlarged (Minneapolis: Fortress Press, 1988), 92.
60. F.W. Grosheide, *Commentary on the First Epistle to the Corinthians: The English Text with Introduction, Exposition and Notes* (Grand Rapids: Eerdmans Publishing Company, 1953), 177.
61. See further Anthony C. Thiselton, *The Living Paul: An Introduction to the Apostle's Life and Thought* (Downers Grove, IL: IVP Academic, 2009), Chapter 1.
62. New Revised Standard Version (NRSV). All scriptures are taken from the NRSV unless specifically noted.
63. Some have wondered if early Christians had some kind of nonsexual living arrangement that involved virgins living together, and they wonder too if Paul here is advising those Christians who cannot treat their virgins well to go ahead and marry them. Liesbeth Van Der Sypt notes there were actually three possibilities in answer to the question of marriage: no because virginity is preferred, yes because marriage and virginity are both possible states of life for following God,

and a third, more curious "yes" that marriage was possible between two celibate people. Celibate "spiritual" marriage (*syneisaktism*) was a sometime state of life in some Christian communities, especially in the early Middle Ages. Liesbeth Van der Sypt, "The Use of 1 Corinthians 7:36–38 in Early Christian Asceticism," in *Asceticism and Exegesis in Early Christianity: The Reception of New Testament Texts in Ancient Ascetic Discourses*, Hans-Ulrich Weidemann, ed. (Gottlingen, Germany: Vandenhoeck & Ruprecht, 2013), 148–159.

64. See Reidulf K. Molvaer, "St. Paul's Views on Sex According to 1 Corinthians 7:9 and 36–38," *Studia Theologica* 54 (2004): 45–59.
65. This point was developed in personal conversations with Meghan Henning.
66. Molvaer, "St. Paul's Views on Sex," 50.
67. Morna D. Hooker, *Paul: A Short Introduction* (Oxford: One World Publications, 2003), 126.
68. Ibid., 131.
69. Dale B. Martin, *Sex and the Single Savior: Gender and Sexuality in Biblical Interpretation* (Louisville: Westminster John Knox Press, 2006), 65.
70. Ibid., 66.
71. Ibid., 68.
72. See David G. Hunter, "Asceticism, Priesthood, and Exegesis: 1 Corinthians 7:5 in Jerome and His Contemporaries," in *Asceticism and Exegesis in Early Christianity: The Reception of New Testament Texts in Ancient Ascetic Discourses*, Hans-Ulrich Weidemann, ed. (Gottlingen, Germany: Vandenhoeck & Ruprecht, 2013): 413–427.
73. *In ep. Ad Cor Primam* 7:5 (CSEL 81/2, 71-72), cited in Hunter, "Asceticism, Priesthood, and Exegesis," 423.
74. Hunter, "Asceticism, Priesthood, and Exegesis," 423.
75. Laura Smit, *Loves Me, Loves Me Not: The Ethics of Unrequited Love* (Grand Rapids: Baker Academic, 2005), 36.

CHAPTER 3

1. Linda Waite, "Cohabitation: A Communitarian Perspective," unpublished paper (1999) cited in Adrian Thatcher, *Living Together and Christian Ethics* (Cambridge: Cambridge University Press, 2002), 54. Adrian Thatcher takes Waite's point further to argue that Christians need to interpret different kinds of cohabiting relationships differently, such that some more committed cohabiting relationships that are clearly aimed toward marriage might not be seen as "fornication," to use his term. Thatcher furthermore argues for reviving betrothals as a gradual process of entering into marriage, a point I discuss further in Chapter 4.
2. It is possible for both dating and cohabitation to form part of more committed relationships (and it is also possible that an uncommitted relationship might

move to being a more committed one, and vice versa). More committed relationships focus on establishing emotional and physical bonds between people and expect sexual relationships to be largely monogamous, even though these relationships might not attain the kind of commitment and understanding of sexual activity that Christians tend to mean when they discuss marriage.

3. For example, Paul's letter to the Colossians, Chapter 3: "[12] As God's chosen ones, holy and beloved, clothe yourselves with compassion, kindness, humility, meekness, and patience. [13] Bear with one another and, if anyone has a complaint against another, forgive each other; just as the Lord has forgiven you, so you also must forgive.[14] Above all, clothe yourselves with love, which binds everything together in perfect harmony. [15] And let the peace of Christ rule in your hearts, to which indeed you were called in the one body. And be thankful. [16] Let the word of Christ dwell in you richly; teach and admonish one another in all wisdom; and with gratitude in your hearts sing psalms, hymns, and spiritual songs to God."
4. See Stephanie Coontz, *The Way We Never Were: American Families and the Nostalgia Trap* (New York: Basic Books, 2000).
5. Though I will note that the argument about women not needing the economic benefits of marriage applies largely to white and/or middle class women, especially those who are childless.
6. See, for example, Jessica Bennett and Jesse Ellison, "The Case Against Marriage," *Newsweek* June 11, 2010, http://www.newsweek.com/case-against-marriage-73045, accessed March 5, 2016; Olivia Blair, "Oprah Winfrey Could Not Have Had the Life She Built if She Had Got Married," *Independent* November 18, 2015, accessed March 5, 2016, http://www.independent.co.uk/news/people/oprah-winfrey-claims-she-could-not-have-had-the-life-she-has-if-she-were-married-a6739401.html.
7. See, for example, Hera Cook, *The Long Sexual Revolution: English Women, Sex, and Contraception* (Oxford: Oxford University Press, 2004).
8. See, for example, Sigmund Freud, *Three Contributions to the Sexual Theory* (New York: Bartleby.com, 2010).
9. Cook, *The Long Sexual Revolution*, 339.
10. See http://casualsexproject.com and an interview with the author at *Nerve*, "This Woman is Collecting Thousands of Casual Sex Stories to Learn More about How We Hook Up," May 22, 2014. Accessed August 25, 2016, http://www.nerve.com/love-sex/this-woman-is-collecting-thousands-of-casual-sex-stories-to-learn-more-about-how-we-hook-up.
11. A random selection of examples readily available via search engines: Dear Abby, "Man in Relationship Wants More than Sleeping on the Floor," August 17, 2016, http://www.uexpress.com/dearabby/2016/8/17/0/man-in-relationship-wants-more-than; Andrea Thompson, "Would You Use an App for No-Strings Sex?"

Marie Claire, April 18 2016, http://www.marieclaire.co.uk/blogs/544766/the-top-3-apps-for-no-strings-sex.html.

12. Mark Regnerus and Jeremy Uecker, *Premarital Sex in America: How Young Americans Meet, Mate, and Think About Marrying* (New York: Oxford University Press, 2011), 24.
13. Zhana Vrangalova, "Is Casual Sex on the Rise in America?" *Psychology Today*, April 25, 2014. Accessed March 11, 2016, https://www.psychologytoday.com/blog/strictly-casual/201404/is-casual-sex-the-rise-in-america.
14. Carl Rodrique et al., "The Structure of Casual Sexual Relationships and Experiences Among Single Adults Aged 18–30 Years Old: A Latent Profile Analysis," *Canadian Journal of Human Sexuality* 24.3 (2015): 220.
15. Ibid., 220–221.
16. Lauren Winner, *Real Sex: The Naked Truth About Chastity* (Grand Rapids: Brazos, 2005), 48.
17. Ibid., 79.
18. See, for example, Susan Sprecher et al., "Premarital Sexual Standards and Sociosexuality: Gender, Ethnicity, and Cohort Differences," *Archives of Sexual Behavior* 42 (2013):1395–1405.
19. See Hanna Rosin, *The End of Men (and the Rise of Women)* (New York: Riverhead Books, 2012).
20. See especially Chapter 2 of Donna Freitas, *The End of Sex: How Hookup Culture is Leaving a Generation Unhappy, Sexually Unfulfilled, and Confused About Intimacy* (New York: Basic Books, 2013).
21. Ibid., 5.
22. Mark Regnerus and Jeremy Uecker, *Premarital Sex in America: How Young Americans Meet, Mate, and Think about Marrying* (New York: Oxford University Press, 2011), 133.
23. Freitas, *The End of Sex*, 114.
24. Ibid., 1–2.
25. Peggy Orenstein, "Playing at Sexy," *New York Times Magazine*, June 13, 2010. Accessed March 11, 2016, http://www.nytimes.com/2010/06/13/magazine/13fob-wwln-t.html.
26. Rick Rojas and John Surico, "A Guardian is Accused of Holding 2 Teens Captive for Years," *The New York Times* January 12, 2016. Accessed March 11, 2016, www.nytimes.com/2016/01/13/nyregion/a-guardian-is-charged-with-holding-2-teenagers-captive-in-queens-for-years.html.
27. Stacey Little and Nancy Rivard, "Airline Trafficking: Signs for Spotting Human Trafficking in Transportation," podcast audio interview, *In Public Safety: Relevant Insight by the Experts*, http://inpublicsafety.com/2014/12/transportations-critical-role-in-fighting-human-trafficking/.

28. Nicholas Kristoff, "Every Parent's Nightmare," *The New York Times*, March 10, 2016. Accessed March 11, 2016, http://www.nytimes.com/2016/03/10/opinion/every-parents-nightmare.html.
29. "Humans for Sale: The Fight to End Human Trafficking," CNN.Com, July 21, 2015. Accessed March 11, 2016, http://www.cnn.com/2015/07/20/us/sex-trafficking/.
30. Freitas, *The End of Sex*, 90.
31. See, for example, Christine Stark and Rebecca Whisnant, *Not For Sale: Feminists Resisting Prostitution and Pornography* (North Melbourne, Australia: Spinifex Press, 2004); Pamela Paul, *Pornified: How Pornography is Transforming our Loves, Our Relationships and Our Families* (New York: Times/Henry Holt, 2005); Ariel Levy, *Female Chauvinist Pigs: Women and the Rise of Raunch Culture* (New York: Free Press, 2005).
32. Scott R. Braithwaite et al., "Is Pornography Consumption Associated with Condom Use and Intoxication During Hookups?" *Culture, Health, and Sexuality* 17.10 (November 2015): 1155–1173.
33. Freitas, *The End of Sex*, 89.
34. See Michel Foucault, *The History of Sexuality: An Introduction*, Vol. 1 (New York: Vintage Books, 1990).
35. Angie Manzano, "A Different Kind of Feminism: Feminists Resisting Prostitution and Pornography," *Off Our Backs* 35.7/8 (July 1, 2005), 25.
36. Dawn Eden, *My Peace I Give You: Healing Sexual Wounds with the Help of the Saints* (Notre Dame, IN: Ave Maria Press, 2012), 109.
37. Pope Paul VI, *Humanae Vitae*, §17, http://w2.vatican.va/content/paul-vi/en/encyclicals/documents/hf_p-vi_enc_25071968_humanae-vitae.html.
38. Beth Felker Jones, *Faithful: A Theology of Sex* (Grand Rapids: Zondervan, 2014), 83.
39. Ibid., 84.
40. Colón and Field, *Singled Out*, 88.
41. Mark Regnerus, "The Pornographic Double Bind," *First Things*, November 11, 2014. Accessed January 29, 2016, http://www.firstthings.com/web-exclusives/2014/11/the-pornographic-double-bind.
42. Robert Wuthnow, *After the Baby Boomers: How Twenty- and Thirty-Somethings are Shaping the Future of American Religion* (Princeton: Princeton University Press, 2007), 139–140.
43. An interesting and insightful discussion of the biblical texts related to premarital sex is found in Jennifer Knust, *Unprotected Texts: The Bible's Surprising Contradictions about Sex and Desire* (New York: Harper Collins, 2012). Knust points out that some texts show premarital sex as a good, while other texts show premarital sex as prohibited. In short, the Bible cannot be used as a sexual morality manual with clear sets of rules.

44. Duncan Dormor, *Just Cohabitating? The Church, Sex, and Getting Married* (London: Darton, Longman, and Todd, 2004), 116.
45. See, for example, Claire M. Renzetti and Sandra Yocum, eds., *Clergy Sexual Abuse: Social Science Perspectives* (Boston: Northeastern University Press, 2013); Mark Oppenheimer, "A Theologian's Influence, and Stained Past, Live On," *The New York Times* October 11, 2013, accessed September 7, 2016, http://www.nytimes.com/2013/10/12/us/john-howard-yoders-dark-past-and-influence-lives-on-for-mennonites.html?_r=0.
46. Beth Felker Jones, *Faithful: A Theology of Sex* (Grand Rapids: Zondervan, 2015), 14.
47. See Frederick van Fleteren, "Confessions," in Allan D. Fitzgerald, ed., *Augustine Through the Ages: An Encyclopedia* (Grand Rapids: Eerdmans, 1999), pp. 227–232.
48. Augustine, "The Excellence of Marriage," in *Marriage and Virginity* Vol. I/9, *The Works of Saint Augustine: A Translation for the 21st Century*, trans. Ray Kearney, ed. David G. Hunter (Hyde Park, NY: New City Press, 1999), §5.5.
49. Ibid., §5.5.
50. Augustine, *Confessions*, translated by Maria Boudling, O.S.B, preface by Patricia Hampl (New York: Vintage Books, 1998), II.ii.2.
51. Ibid.
52. Ibid., II.ii.4.
53. Ibid., VIII.5.12.
54. Ibid.
55. Ibid., VIII.5.10.
56. Ibid., VIII.6.13.
57. Ibid.
58. Augustine, *Contra Faustum*, XV.7.
59. Augustine, "The Excellence of Marriage," 18, 21.
60. See F. Crawford Burkitt, *The Religion of the Manichees: Donnellan Lectures 1924* (Eugene, OR: Wipf & Stock, 2009).
61. Augustine, "The Excellence of Marriage," 8.8.
62. On this point it is fascinating to see the range of patristic interpretations of Paul's letter. As David Hunter has pointed out, some like Jerome declared marriage to be evil, on his reading of scripture, while the monk Jovinian took a view that state of life mattered very little if at all. See David G. Hunter, *Marriage, Celibacy, and Heresy in Ancient Christianity: The Jovinianist Controversy* (Oxford: Oxford University Press, 2007).
63. Augustine, "The Excellence of Marriage," 4,4.
64. Ibid.
65. Augustine, "Continence," in *Marriage and Virginity* Vol. I/ 9, 12.26.
66. Augustine, "The Excellence of Marriage," 23, 30.
67. Ibid., 10, 11.

68. Ibid., 23, 30.
69. Ibid., 9, 9.
70. See John Paul II, *Man and Woman He Created Them: A Theology of the Body* (Boston: Pauline Books and Media, 2006).
71. Sarah Coakley, *God, Sexuality and the Self: An Essay on the 'Trinity'* (Cambridge: Cambridge University Press, 2013), 357.
72. This emphasis on control also leads to Augustine's view of women, subordinate to men in the hierarchical order of things.
73. Coakley, *God, Sexuality, and the Self,* 292.
74. Coakley, 310. Emphasis hers.
75. Ibid., 295.
76. Augustine, *Confessions,* IX.2.3.
77. Ibid., X.30.42.
78. Augustine, *The City of God,* trans. Marcus Dods (Peabody, MA: Hendrickson Publishers, 2009), XXII. 29.
79. C.S. Lewis, *The Four Loves* (New York: Mariner Books, 2012), 94.
80. Ibid.
81. For example, see Pope Francis, *Amoris Laetitia,* Post-Synodal Apostolic Exhortation (2016), https://w2.vatican.va/content/dam/francesco/pdf/apost_exhortations/documents/papa-francesco_esortazione-ap_20160319_amoris-laetitia_en.pdf, §153.
82. Ibid., §295.
83. Ibid., §317.

CHAPTER 4

1. On these kinds of concerns and protests, see the group Unmarried Equality. Accessed May 18, 2016, http://www.unmarried.org/about-us/.
2. Andre Borque, "Technology Profits and Pivots in the $300 Billion Dollar Wedding Space," *Huffpost Business* May 1, 2015. Accessed May 18, 2016, http://www.huffingtonpost.com/andre-bourque/technology-profit-and-piv_b_7193112.html.
3. Kelsey Borresen, "Average Wedding Cost Hits All Time High of More Than $31,000, Report Says," *The Huffington Post* March 13, 2015, http://www.huffingtonpost.com/2015/03/13/average-cost-of-wedding-2014_n_6864860.html.
4. See Pope Francis, *Amoris Laetitia,* Post-Synodal Apostolic Exhortation (2016), https://w2.vatican.va/content/dam/francesco/pdf/apost_exhortations/documents/papa-francesco_esortazione-ap_20160319_amoris-laetitia_en.pdf, §40.
5. In a recent NPR interview, Harris observes: "I'm hearing these different voices saying, here's how your book was used against me, here's how it was forced on me, or here's how I tried to—no one forced it on me, but I tried to apply it and it had this negative consequence in different ways. I'm trying to

go back and really evaluate, you know, where did my book contribute to that? Where was it too stringent?" Rachel Martin, host, "Former Evangelical Pastor Rethinks His Approach to Courtship," *Weekend Edition*, NPR June 10, 2016. Accessed September 17, 2016, http://www.npr.org/2016/07/10/485432485/former-evangelical-pastor-rethinks-his-approach-to-courtship.

6. Joshua Harris, *I Kissed Dating Goodbye: A New Attitude Toward Romance and Relationships* (Colorado Springs: Multnomah Books, 1997), 71.
7. Ibid., 21.
8. Ibid.
9. Ibid., 36.
10. Ibid., Chapter 3.
11. Ibid., 189.
12. Donna Freitas and Jason King, *Save the Date: A Spirituality of Dating, Love, Dinner, and the Divine* (Eugene, OR: Wipf and Stock, 2003), 55.
13. Jonathan Lindvall, "The Betrothal Path," in *5 Paths to the Love of Your Life: Defining Your Dating Style,* Alex Chediak, ed. (Colorado Springs: NavPress, 2005), 124.
14. Ibid., 137.
15. David and Brent Gudgel (with Danielle Fitch), *Before You Get Engaged* (Nashville: Thomsuas Nelson, 2007), xvii.
16. FOCCUS Inc. USA, "About Us," accessed May 25, 2016, http://www.foccusinc.com/about-us.aspx.
17. See, for example, Pam Schiffbauer, "Marriage Preparation is Key to a Successful Marriage." Accessed May 25, 2016, http://www.foccusinc.com/Resources/2.pdf.
18. Gudgel et al., *Before You Get Engaged*, 18.
19. See Wendy Griffith's *You Are a Prize to Be Won! Don't Settle for Less than God's Best* (Ventura, CA: Regal, 2014).
20. Jimmy Evans and Frank Martin, *The Right One: How to Successfully Date and Marry the Right Person* (Dallas, TX: *Marriage Today*, 2015)
21. Gudgel et al., *Before You Get Engaged*, 210.
22. Beth Felker Jones put me on to the present-day practice of promposals, proposals to attend high school proms, which follow the same kind of script and over-the-top public displays as engagement proposals. To quote her, "God help us!"
23. "First Premarital Cohabitation in the United States: 2006–2010 National Survey of Family Growth," *National Health Statistics Report* 64 April 4, 2013. Accessed March 18, 2016, http://www.cdc.gov/nchs/data/nhsr/nhsr064.pdf, 5.
24. Ibid.
25. Meg Jay, "The Downside of Cohabiting Before Marriage," *The New York Times* (April 14, 2012). Accessed May 24, 2016, http://www.nytimes.com/2012/04/15/opinion/sunday/the-downside-of-cohabiting-before-marriage.html?_r=0.
26. Jeff VanGoethem, *Living Together: A Guide to Counseling Unmarried Couples* (Grand Rapids: Kregel Academic and Professional, 2005), 29. VanGoethem is

here expounding on a 1992 study by R.R. Rindfuss and A. VandenHaueval, "Cohabitation: A Precursor to Marriage or an Alternative to Being Single," in *The Changing American Family: Sociological and Demographic Perspectives*, S.J. South and S.E. Tolnay, eds. (Boulder: Westview, 1992), 121–138.

27. Mike and Harriet McManus, *Living Together: Myths, Risks, and Answers* (New York: Howard Books, 2008), 38.
28. Ibid., see especially Chapter 3.
29. See Amanda J. Miller, Sharon Sassler, and Dela Kusi-Appouh, "The Specter of Divorce: Views from Working and Middle-Class Cohabitors." *Family Relations* 60.5 (2011): 602–616.
30. See Arielle Kuperberg, "Age at Coresidence, Premarital Cohabitation, and Marriage Dissolution: 1985–2009," *Journal of Marriage and Family* 76 (April 2014): 352–369.
31. Galena K. Rhoades et al., "Couples' Reasons for Cohabitation: Associations with Individual Well-Being and Relationship Quality," *Journal of Family Issues* 30.2 (February 1, 2009): 223–258.
32. Matthew 6:28.
33. Wesley offers reflection for much else besides Christian perfection; it is worth studying Wesley's theology in far more detail.
34. Thomas Langford, *Practical Divinity: Theology in the Wesleyan Tradition* (Nashville: Abingdon Press, 1983), 11.
35. John Wesley, *The Journal of the Reverend John Wesley*, Nehemiah Curnock, ed. 8 Vols. (London: R. Cully, 1909–1916), Vol. 1, pp. 475–476, cited in Langford, *Practical Divinity*, 13.
36. Was Wesley's warming of the heart a conversion, or simply a spiritual deepening of his relationship with God, or something else? I have named it a conversion because it did effect a change in his life, but it is not a conversion in the sense that he became a Christian where previously he had not been.
37. Randy L. Maddox, *Responsible Grace: John Wesley's Practical Theology* (Nashville: Kingswood Books, 1994), 192.
38. *Minutes of the Methodist Conferences* (Vol. 1, 1744–1798) (London: John Mason, 1862), 713. Cited in Richard Heitzenrater, *Wesley and the People Called Methodists* (Nashville: Abingdon Press, 1995).
39. John Wesley, "Christian Perfection," in *Sermons on Several Occasions* (London: Epworth Press, 1977), 459.
40. Thomas A. Langford, "Wesley and Theological Method," in *Rethinking Wesley's Theology for Contemporary Methodism*, Randy L. Maddox, ed. (Nashville: Kingswood Books, 1998): 35.
41. W. Reginald Ward and Richard P. Heitzenrater, eds., *The Works of John Wesley*, Vol. 18 (Nashville: Abingdon Press, 1988), p. 482. Cited in Kenneth Collins,

"John Wesley's Relationship With His Wife as Revealed in His Correspondence," *Methodist History* 32:1 (1993), 5.

42. This was despite many apparent openings for such proposals that Sophey's aunt and uncle arranged during the conversations between Wesley, Sophey, and themselves. See Bufford W. Coe, *John Wesley and Marriage* (Bethlehem: Lehigh University Press, 1996), 77–78. Some scholars suggest that Wesley's treatment of Sophey after her engagement (for example, he refused her communion) led to Wesley's exit from Georgia, especially given that Sophey's uncle was the magistrate of the colony. Other scholars point out that there were several issues in question in Georgia, including the uncle's mismanagement of funds and Wesley's close relationships with other women (though these didn't appear to be engagement-worthy). See Geordan Hammond, *John Wesley in America: Restoring Primitive Christianity* (New York; Oxford: Oxford University Press, 2014).
43. Coe, *John Wesley and Marriage*, 58.
44. Ibid., 59
45. Ibid.
46. Ibid.
47. Ibid., 60.
48. Ibid.
49. Cited in Coe, *John Wesley and Marriage*, 62.
50. Ibid., 65.
51. Ibid., 66.
52. Kenneth Collins, "John Wesley's Relationship With His Wife as Revealed in His Correspondence," *Methodist History* 32:1 (1993): 6.
53. See Richard P. Heitzenrater, *The Elusive Mr. Wesley*, 2nd ed. (Nashville: Abingdon Press, 2003), 172–174; see also Coe, *John Wesley and Marriage*, 58.
54. Wesley's parents' relationship was by no means "perfection," however!
55. Heitzenrater, *The Elusive Mr. Wesley*, 172.
56. See Henry D. Rack's discussion in *Reasonable Enthusiast: John Wesley and the Rise of Methodism*, 3rd ed. (London: Epworth Press, 2002), especially Chapter VI.
57. Coe, *John Wesley and Marriage*, 66.
58. Curnock, *The Journal of the Reverend John Wesley*, 3, 517
59. J.P. Briggs and John Briggs, "Unholy Desires, Inordinate Affections: A Psychodynamic Inquiry Into John Wesley's Relationship With Women," *Connecticut Review* 13:1 (1990): 6.
60. John Wesley, The Works of John Wesley, ed, Frank Baker, vol. 26 (Nashville: Abingdon Press, 1987):451–452.
61. Kenneth Collins, "John Wesley's Relationship With His Wife as Revealed in His Correspondence." *Methodist History* 32:1 (October 1993), 17.
62. Rack, *Reasonable Enthusiast*, 268.

63. Lauren Winner, "The Countercultural Path," In *5 Paths to the Love of Your Life: Defining Your Dating Style,* Alex Chedak, ed. (Colorado Springs: NavPress, 2005).
64. Freitas and King, *Save the Date,* 93.
65. Thatcher, *Living Together and Christian Ethics,* 46. Thatcher's argument extends to permitting premarital sex in limited cases of betrothed couples who have commitments far beyond those described in Chapter 2.
66. See an example of the liturgy as a whole at Greek Orthodox Archdiocese of America, "The Service of Betrothal." Accessed September 17, 2016, http://www.goarch.org/chapel/liturgical_texts/betrothal,
67. Ibid.
68. Stephanie Coontz, *Marriage, A History: How Love Conquered Marriage* (New York: Penguin Books, 2005).

CHAPTER 5

1. For example, The US Catholic bishops state, "Generally, homosexual orientation is experienced as a given, not as something freely chosen. By itself, therefore, a homosexual orientation cannot be considered sinful, for morality presumes the freedom to choose." In the 1997 "Always Our Children: A Pastoral Message to Parents of Homosexual Children and a Message to Pastoral Ministers," http://www.usccb.org/issues-and-action/human-life-and-dignity/homosexuality/. The *Catechism of the Catholic Church* describes lesbian, gay, and bisexual orientation as something that individuals often feel as a "trial" precisely because it is not chosen (§2358).
2. An additional question many churches are facing is about ordination, which also serves to highlight the tensions and crises existing in Christian theology about same-sex attraction.
3. As I write this chapter, I am awash in news about the United Methodist General Conference of 2016, at which marriage and ordination have become crisis points, even to some raising the idea of schism.
4. There is vast literature on the question of same-sex marriage from many points of view. This list does not include arguments that people have made in favor of *alternatives* to marriage, because I shall address these later in the chapter. The books I have found most engaging, deeply reflective, and aware of other peoples' arguments to the point that the authors are engaging in genuine, heartfelt, and respectful conversations are: Michael Vasey, *Strangers and Friends: A New Exploration of Homosexuality and the Bible* (London: Hodder and Stoughton, 1995); Christopher Roberts, *Creation and Covenant: The Significance of Sexual Difference in the Moral Theology of Marriage* (New York: T&T Clark, 2007); Mark Jordan, *Blessing Same-Sex Unions* (Chicago: The University of Chicago Press, 2005); Matthew Vines, *God and the Gay Christian: The Biblical Case in Support of*

Same-Sex Relationships (New York: Convergent Books, 2014); James V. Brownsen, *Bible, Gender, Sexuality: Reframing the Church's Debate on Same-Sex Relationships* (Grand Rapids: Eerdmans, 2013).

5. https://spiritualfriendship.org/
6. Tim Otto, *Oriented to Faith: Transforming the Conflict Over Gay Relationships* (Eugene, OR: Cascade Books, 2014).
7. James Dobson, *Preparing for Adolescence* (Santa Ana, CA: Vision House), 90.
8. Otto, *Oriented to Faith*, 4.
9. Ibid., 6.
10. John Alexander, "Playing With FIRE: Or, Narcissicism as Sacred Duty," in *The Secular Squeeze: Reclaiming Christian Depth in a Shallow World* (Downer's Grove, IL: Intervarsity, 1993), 69.
11. See, for example, Margaret Farley, *Just Love: A Framework for Christian Social Ethics*. New York: Continuum International, 2006; Michael Lawler and Todd Salzmann, *The Sexual Person: Toward a Renewed Catholic Anthropology* (Washington, DC: Georgetown University Press, 2008).
12. Otto, *Oriented to Faith*, 72.
13. Ibid., 73.
14. Robert Song, *Covenant and Calling: Toward a Theology of Same-Sex Relationships* (Norwich, UK: SCM Press, 2014), xii.
15. Ibid., xiii.
16. Ibid., xiv.
17. Rowan Williams, "The Body's Grace," in *Theology and Sexuality: Classic and Contemporary Readings*, Eugene F. Rogers, ed. (London: Blackwell, 2002), 311.
18. Ibid.
19. David Maztko McCarthy, "The Relationship of Bodies," in *Theology and Sexuality, Classic and Contemporary Readings*, Eugene F. Rogers, ed. (London: Blackwell, 2002), 210.
20. Williams, "The Body's Grace," 313.
21. Ibid., 314.
22. David Matzko McCarthy, *Sex and Love in the Home: A Theology of the Household* (Norwich, UK: Hymns Ancient and Modern LTD, 2004), 64.
23. Eugene F. Rogers, "Sanctification, Homosexuality, and God's Triune Life," in *Theology and Sexuality: Classic and Contemporary Readings*, Eugene F. Rogers, ed. (London: Blackwell, 2002), 217.
24. Williams, "The Body's Grace," 315.
25. John Paul II's work is not only on these points; he has a far more developed theological anthropology than is sometimes assumed. See Susan Windley Daoust, *Theology of the Body, Extended: The Spiritual Sign of Birth, Impairment, and Death*. John Paul II's work is *Man and Woman He Created Them: A Theology of the Body* (Boston: Pauline Books and Media, 2006).

26. Williams, "The Body's Grace," 317.
27. Christopher Roberts, *Creation and Covenant: The Significance of Sexual Difference in the Moral Theology of Marriage* (New York: Continuum, 2007), 246.
28. Aelred's writing is also influenced by Augustine of Hippo's book *Confessions*, and the Latin orator Cicero's book on friendship.
29. Aelred of Rievaulx, *Spiritual Friendship*, trans. Lawrence C. Braceland, ed. Marsha L. Dutton (Collegeville: Liturgical Press, 2010), I.19.
30. Ibid., I. 24.
31. Ibid., I.42.
32. Ibid., I.46
33. C.S. Lewis, *The Four Loves* (San Diego: Harcourt Brace and Company, 1988). On Lewis' discussion of homosexuality, see pages 57–62. On his discussion of men and women and the possibility of friendship, see pages 72–75.
34. Aelred, *Spiritual Friendship*, I.57. Aelred's reading of Genesis stands in stark contrast to a view of Genesis 2 that sees woman as inferior to man because she was made second and comes from Adam's side rather than being made a creature in her own right.
35. Ibid., I.70.
36. Ibid., II. 49.
37. Ibid., II. 10.
38. Ibid., II. 14.
39. Ibid., II. 20.
40. Ibid., II.42.
41. Ibid., II. 42.
42. See Ibid., III. 5.
43. Ibid., II. 40
44. Ibid., II.51.
45. Ibid., II. 12.
46. Ibid., III. 23.
47. Ibid., III. 32.
48. Elizabeth Stuart, *Just Good Friends: Toward a Lesbian and Gay Theology of Relationships* (London: Mowbray, 1995), 31–32.
49. Ibid., 231.
50. John Boswell, *Christianity, Social Tolerance, and Homosexuality: Gay People in Western Europe from the Beginning of the Christian Era to the Fourteenth Century* (Chicago: University of Chicago Press, 1981), 219.
51. Ibid., 222.
52. Ibid., 223.
53. See Alan Bray, *The Friend* (Chicago: University of Chicago Press, 2003). See also Pavel Florensky, *The Pillar and Ground of the Truth*, trans. Boris Jakim (Princeton: Princeton University Press, 2004).

54. I am not convinced by Song's insistence that marriage is a limited good post-resurrection. In my first book, *Water is Thicker than Blood,* I suggested that marriage and celibacy integrally needed each other post-resurrection, but were both fundamentally reshaped to be something new. Marriage and celibacy each exist in a transfigured way at the end of time as well.
55. My own reading of Boswell is that I think he is correct in suggesting that there were far more allusions to same-sex love in the medieval period and that such expressions were more widely accepted. That said, Boswell overreaches in his interpretations of Aelred on love and marriage, for he forgets that marriage and love are frequently used as theological symbols and metaphor—in both heterosexual and homosexual descriptions. So where Boswell suggests that Aelred likens Jesus' relationship with John to a marriage ("he [Jesus] allowed one, not all, to recline on his breast as a sign of his special love, so that the virgin head was supported in the flowers of the virgin breast, and the closer they were, the more copiously did the fragrant secrets of the heavenly marriage impart the sweet smell of spiritual chrism to their virgin love" (226)), while the language is clearly erotic, it is not clear that Aelred's use of heavenly marriage refers to Jesus and John, or that the heavenly marriage means anything like what Boswell implies.
56. See note 1 in Chapter 2 of Wesley Hill, *Spiritual Friendship: Finding Love in the Church as a Celibate Gay Christian* (Grand Rapids: Brazos Press, 2015), 30.
57. Ibid., 6.
58. Ibid., 6. Hill here cites Benjamin Myers, an Australian theologian with whom he corresponded and who writes on friendship.
59. Ibid., 10.
60. Ibid., 33.
61. Ibid., 69.
62. Ibid., 81.
63. Eve Tushnet, *Gay and Catholic: Accepting my Sexuality, Finding Community, Living my Faith* (Notre Dame, IN: Ave Maria Press, 2014), 102.
64. Ibid., 103.
65. Ibid.
66. Marta Kaufmann, quoted in Bethonie Butler, "Should We Forgive 'Friends' for Feeling a Little Offensive in 2016" *Chicago Tribune,* February 18, 2016. Accessed June 13, 2016, http://www.chicagotribune.com/entertainment/tv/ct-friends-offensive-20160218-story.html.
67. Kathleen Norris, *The Cloister Walk* (New York: Riverhead Books, 1996), 117.
68. Ibid., 118.
69. Ibid., 120.
70. Tushnet, *Gay and Catholic,* 107.
71. Ibid.

72. Hill, *Spiritual Friendship*, 41.
73. Ibid.

CHAPTER 6

1. A search of Christian widowhood in WorldCat yields several historical treatises on Augustine, medieval women, women in the nineteenth century, and in geographical places other than the United States (especially in the African continent), but few articles that might be considered contemporary. In my search of all Ohio libraries, a search of Christian pastoral care treatises as well as "church work with widows" yields four books from the 1990s like Wesley Teterud's book *Caring for Widows: You and Your Church Can Make a Difference* (Grand Rapids: Baker, 1994), and nothing later. A search on Christians and divorce, on the other hand, readily yields two pages of books with most results from 2012 or later. Theological discussions of cohabitation feature in most contemporary books on marriage and sexuality and are often the focus of such books, for example, Adrian Thatcher's *Living Together and Christian Ethics* (Cambridge: Cambridge University Press, 2002).
2. Miriam Neff, "The Widow's Might," *Christianity Today*, January 1, 2008, 43–48.
3. For example, see Howard Clinebell's *Basic Types of Pastoral Care and Counseling: Resources for the Ministry of Healing and Growth* (Nashville: Abingdon, 1994), 232–235.
4. This is the case in both Howard Clinebell's *Basic Types of Pastoral Care and Counseling* as well as the *Clinical Handbook of Pastoral Counseling*, 3 vols., Robert Wicks, Richard Parsons (and Donald Capps, 3rd vol.), eds. (Mahwah, NJ: Integration Books, 1985–2003).
5. Neff, *The Widow's Might*, 43.
6. I suggest that discussing widowhood is as important as considering other groups that comprise 10 percent or less of the population, including subsets of groups by race, ethnicity, and disability. US Census Bureau, "Facts and Figures: Unmarried and Single Americans Week, September 21–27, 2014." Accessed September 23, 2015, http://www.census.gov/content/dam/Census/newsroom/facts-for-features/2014/cb14ff-21_unmarried.pdf.
7. US Pew Forum, *Religious Landscape Survey* 2014. Accessed September 23, 2015, http://www.pewforum.org/religious-landscape-study/marital-status/.
8. US Census Bureau, "Marital Events of Americans: 2009," American Community Survey Reports 2011. Accessed September 23, 2015, https://www.census.gov/prod/2011pubs/acs-13.pdf.
9. Terry L. Martin and Kenneth J. Doka, *Men Don't Cry... Women Do: Transcending Gender Stereotypes of Grief* (Philadelphia: Taylor and Francis, 2000), 101.
10. www.deathcafe.com

11. Kübler-Ross made the now popular concept five stages of grief famous, especially in her book *On Death and Dying: What the Dying Have to Teach Doctors, Nurses, Clergy, and their Own Families* (London; New York: Routledge, 2009). Kubler-Ross' book has many critics, however, especially because a five-stage model of grief seems linear at the outset, a straight line that marks the beginning and end of grief, when in fact, grief doesn't work that way. A stage model may make us want to buttonhole people into stages, which limits our ability to empathize with the fact that they are individuals. See, for example, the critical essays in *Beyond Kübler-Ross: New Perspectives on Death, Dying and Grief* edited by Kenneth J. Doka and Amy S. Tucci. Washington, DC: Hospice Foundation of America, 2011.
12. Tony Walter, "Modern Death: Taboo or Not Taboo?" *Sociology* 25.2 (May 1991): 293–310. See also Glennys Howarth, *Death and Dying: A Sociological Introduction* (Cambridge: Polity Press, 2007), especially Chapter 1, for a discussion of philosophical thinking about death in Western society.
13. John Paul II, *Evangelium Vitae* (1995), http://w2.vatican.va/content/john-paul-ii/en/encyclicals/documents/hf_jp-ii_enc_25031995_evangelium-vitae.html.
14. Christians also make arguments in favor of abortion and euthanasia. The following books describe some complex arguments, and in some cases demonstrate direct argumentation between opposing sides. Sidney and Daniel Callahan, eds. *Abortion: Understanding Differences* (Braintree, MA: Pope John Center 1992); Charles Camosy, *Beyond the Abortion Wars: A Way Forward for a New Generation* (Grand Rapids: Eerdmans, 2015); Daniel Maguire, *Death by Choice* (New York: Schocken, 1975); Ron Hamel, ed., *Choosing Death: Active Euthanasia, Religion, and the Public Debate* (Philadelphia: Trinity Press International, 1991).
15. This paragraph attempts to summarize only part of Bishop's complex philosophical arguments. See *The Anticipatory Corpse: Medicine, Power, and the Care of the Dying* (Notre Dame: University of Notre Dame Press, 2011).
16. Ibid., 254.
17. Ibid., 257.
18. See one commentary on the two cases in Lenore Skenazy's blog post, "Sympathy for Gator Family Contrasts Sharply with Gorilla Mom," *Hit and Run* blog June 16, 2016. Accessed August 12, 2016, http://reason.com/blog/2016/06/16/sympathy-for-gator-family-contrasts-shar.
19. Eastern rite, Catholic Easter liturgy.
20. Some bioethicists have called for a recovery of "*ars moriendi*," (the art of dying)—that is, a recovery of bedside rituals of prayer and song and ritual. Such practices might go a ways toward changing the focus of contemporary death beds from questions like, "Should we remove life support?" to celebrating the life and witness of the person dying. Such bedside rituals may also be more inclusive of the people who are imminently about to become the bereaved. See

especially Allen Verhey, *The Christian Art of Dying: Learning with Jesus* (Grand Rapids: Eerdmans, 2011).

21. Julia Brumbaugh, "Spirituality for a Suffering Earth: Death, Grief, and Transformation," in *An Unexpected Wilderness: Christianity and the Natural World*, Colleen Mary Carpenter, ed. *College Theology Society* 61 (2015), 94.
22. Deuteronomy 14:28–29.
23. See as examples: Psalm 68:5, Deuteronomy 16:11, 14, Job 29:13.
24. Bonnie Bowman Thurston, *The Widows: A Women's Ministry in the Early Church* (Minneapolis: Fortress Press, 1989), 13.
25. Deuteronomy 24:19–20.
26. Exodus 22:22–24.
27. Mark 12:38–40.
28. Jouette Bassler maintains that the large number of widowed women Paul references might actually indicate that the circle of women had grown to include divorced and never-married women; widowhood meant "sexual abstinence, not bereavement" for Timothy's particular community. Jouette Bassler, "Limits and Differentiation: The Calculus of Widows in 1 Timothy 5.3–16," in *A Feminist Companion to the Deutero-Pauline Epistles*, Amy-Jill Levine, ed. (Cleveland: The Pilgrim Press, 2003), 138.
29. 1 Timothy 5:5–8.
30. Recently, Roman Catholic bishops alluded to an Order of Widows in their discussions on families in the contemporary period. They suggested that perhaps there might be a revival of an Order of Widows. See section 19 of the final document for the 2015 Ordinary Synod on the Family, http://www.vatican.va/roman_curia/synod/documents/rc_synod_doc_20151026_relazione-finale-xiv-assemblea_en.html.
31. Bonnie Bowman Thurston's book, *The Widows: A Woman's Ministry in the Early Church*, was a central book on this topic that led to other discussions.
32. M. Cathleen Kaveny, "The Order of Widows: What the Early Church Can Teach Us about Older Women and Health Care," in *Christian Bioethics* 11 (2005): 16.
33. Tertullian, *De virginibus velandis*, 9.3 Particular thanks to William Johnston for suggesting this reference.
34. *Didascalia Apostolorum*, trans. R. Hugh Connolly (Oxford: Clarendon Press, 1929), III.5.2.
35. Augustine, "Holy Virginity," in *Marriage and Virginity* Vol. I/9, *The Works of Saint Augustine: A Translation for the 21st Century*, trans. Ray Kearney, ed. David G. Hunter (Hyde Park, NY: New City Press, 1999), §47.47.
36. Augustine, "On the Good of Widowhood," Ibid., § 24.
37. Ibid.

38. *Explanation of the Psalms* 131.15, cited in Thomas Oden, *The Good Works Reader* (Grand Rapids: Eerdmans, 2007), 66.
39. Katherine Clark, "Putting on the Garment of Widowhood: Medieval Widows, Monastic Memory, and Historical Writing," *Quidditas* 31:1 (2010): 22–76.
40. Ibid., 68.
41. It should be noted that understanding of widows and their treatment varies quite a bit from place to place. This section provides only a brief synopsis of a subject that has a great many more details. For discussion of variations on medieval and early modern practices of widowhood, see Sandra Cavallo and Lyndon Warner, eds., *Widowhood in Medieval and Early Modern Europe* (Harlow: Longman, 1999).
42. Elizabeth Ann Seton, *Collected Writings* Volumes 1–5, Regina Bechtle, ed. (Chicago: New City Press, 2000), Vol. 3b, 1. http://via.library.depaul.edu/vincentian_ebooks/9/. Elizabeth Ann Seton's writings have all been placed online via DePaul University's Vincentian Heritage Collection. I am most grateful to the many people who made that collection of writings possible. Interested readers will find reading Seton's journals to be well worth the time.
43. Ibid., March 5, 1804, Vol. I, 294.
44. Ibid., February 18, 1804, Vol. I, 292–293.
45. Ibid., November 20, 1804, Vol. I, 331.
46. Ibid., July 26, 1804, Vol. I, 316.
47. Ibid., letter 6.247, note 6, Vol. II, 345.
48. For example, Eliza Grim. See Seton, *Collected Writings*, 7.65, note 2, 452
49. A.B. Simpson, "The Still Small Voice," *The Old Testament*, vol. 1, *The Holy Spirit or Power from on High* (Harrisburg, PA: Christian Publications, n.d.), 162, cited in Patricia A. Ward, *Experimental Theology in America: Madame Guyon, Fenèlon, and their Readers*, (Waco, TX: Baylor University Press, 2009), 10. Particular thanks are due to Bill Portier for putting me on to the American reception of Quietism, and to Ward's excellent book.
50. Joseph I. Dirvin, *Mrs. Seton: Foundress of the American Sisters of Charity* (New York: Farrar, Straus, and Cudahy, 1962), 84, cited in Jenny Franchot, *Roads to Rome: The Antebellum Protestant Encounter with Catholicism* (Berkeley: University of California Press, 1994), 293.
51. Bill Portier helped me see this connection. See a discussion of Bruté's work in Joseph M. White, "Physician of Body and Soul: Simon Gabriel Bruté, Doctor... Sulpician Priest... Teacher... Pioneer Scholar... Bishop... Confidante and Friend to a Saint," http://stmaryspacast.org/project/physician-of-body-and-soul-simon-gabriel-brute/. Accessed January 27, 2017.
52. Franchot, *Roads to Rome*, 287. Franchot sets up the subjectivity/objectivity debate in relation to anti-Catholic and pro-Catholic debates.
53. Ibid., 288.

54. I think Franchot does not pay enough attention to the grief and loneliness of Seton's situation as a widow. The spiritual quest for God that Elizabeth undertakes as someone who is undergoing almost constant changes is fraught with a constant back-and-forth of her own wanting to be in control, but simultaneously wanting to be a person who could give her will to God, as she sought to follow a strand of Christian tradition that emphasizes giving everything to God. Part of a spiritual journey is exactly to be faced with jockeying between two or more points, especially as one seeks to be closer and closer to God.
55. Seton, letter to Julia Scott, September 5, 1801. Cited in Sr. Marie Celeste, *The Intimate Friendships of Elizabeth Ann Bayley Seton* (New York: Alba House, 1989), 43.
56. Letter, December 13, 1803. Cited in Sr. Marie Celeste, *The Intimate Friendships of Elizabeth Ann Bayley Seton* (New York: Alba House, 1989), 62.
57. Seton, *Collected Writings*, January, 1804, Vol. I, 285.
58. Ibid., March 26, 1810. Vol. II, 116.
59. Ibid.
60. Ibid., August 26, 1808, Vol. II, 30.
61. Ibid., October 10, 1808, Vol. II, 37.
62. Ibid.
63. *Sic.* Ibid., January 28, 1804, Vol. I, 289.
64. Ibid., April 18, 1804. Vol. I., 296.
65. Ibid., 7.323. No date. Vol. II, 708.
66. Ibid., November 8, 1809, Vol. II, 89.
67. I am thinking, for example, of statements made by leaders of churches, such as the Catholic American bishops' statement made in 1999 in "Blessings of Age: Pastoral Message on Growing Older within the Faith Community," http://www.usccb.org/issues-and-action/marriage-and-family/blessings-of-age-english.cfm. Accessed January 27, 2017. I think the bishops are correct in suggesting that elderly widows ought to stay in touch with their communities. Yet it is not clear that the communities have much to offer. An Order of Widows gives a place to belong.
68. M. Therese Lysaught, "Practicing the Order of Widows," *Christian Bioethics* 11:1 (2005), 58.
69. Ibid., 59.

CHAPTER 7

1. Pat Conroy, "Anatomy of a Divorce," *Atlanta Magazine* (November 1, 1978).
2. Several theologians comment, rather quizzically, on the lack of discussion. Julie Hanlon Rubio, "Three-in-One Flesh: A Christian Reappraisal of Divorce in Light of Recent Studies," *Journal of the Society of Christian Ethics* 23.1 (2003): 47–70;

Margaret Farley, "Marriage, Divorce, and Personal Commitments," in *Celebrating Christian Marriage*, Adrian Thatcher, ed. (Edinburgh: T&T Clark, 2001), 356–377; Richard Hays, *The Moral Vision of the New Testament: Community, Cross, New Creation: A Contemporary Introduction to New Testament Ethics* (New York: Harper San Francisco, 1996), especially Chapter 15.

3. William Mattison makes this point in *Introducing Moral Theology: True Happiness and the Virtues* (Grand Rapids: Brazos Press, 2008), 353.
4. Richard Hays, *The Moral Vision of the New Testament: Community, Cross, New Creation: A Contemporary Introduction to New Testament Ethics* (New York: Harper San Francisco, 1996), 348.
5. Lauren Winner, "Lectio Divina and Divorce: Reflections in Twelve Parts about What Divorce Has to Teach the Church," *Anglican Theological Review* 97.2 (Spring2015): 281–297, p. 282.
6. Hays notes how astounding these words are—first, that Jesus would suggest that a man who divorces his wife in order to remarry is committing adultery against his wife, since in traditional understandings, adultery could only be committed against a man, not a woman. Second, Jesus' statement that women who divorce and remarry commit adultery against their husbands testifies to the idea that women might get divorced, which is not a choice women can make under Jewish law. Mark therefore seems to be adapting Greek and Roman law in his discussion. See Hays, *The Moral Vision of the New Testament*, 352.
7. Hays, *The Moral Vision of the New Testament*, 350.
8. Ibid., 355.
9. NRSV.
10. NRSV.
11. 1 Corinthians 7:15.
12. Hays, *The Moral Vision of the New Testament*, 360.
13. Raymond F. Collins, "Marriage (NT)," in *The Anchor Bible Dictionary*, D.N. Freedman et al., eds. (New York: Doubleday, 1992), IV, 570. Cited in Peter Carrell, "Marriage, Divorce, and Remarriage in the New Testament," *Stimulus* 11.4 (November 2003), 33.
14. For example, David Instone-Brewer, *Divorce and Remarriage in the Church: Biblical Solutions for Pastoral Realities* (Milton Keynes, UK: Paternoster Press, 2003), especially Chapter 8.
15. Annulment is not "Catholic divorce"; in fact, people seeking annulments must have already obtained a legal divorce before beginning annulment proceedings. To seek a divorce is to tell a story about a relationship as it exists in the present moment. The relationship is failing, therefore divorce. To seek an annulment, on the other hand, is to tell a story about a relationship at the time a couple got married. From a Catholic point of view, the central question is whether all the right conditions existed for marriage to be a sacrament. For example, did the

couple both freely consent to being married as the church understands marriage: as a union involving both faithfulness and openness to children?

16. See Pope Francis, *Amoris Laetitia*, Post-Synodal Apostolic Exhortation on the Family (2016), https://w2.vatican.va/content/dam/francesco/pdf/apost_exhortations/documents/papa-francesco_esortazione-ap_20160319_amoris-laetitia_en.pdf, especially Chapter 8.
17. Henry and Ella Mitchell, "Divorce and Remarriage for Christians," in *Transitions: Leading Churches through Change* (Louisville: Westminster John Knox Press, 2011), 94.
18. Ibid., 98.
19. Ibid.
20. Hays, *The Moral Vision of the New Testament*, 374.
21. Ibid., 349.
22. Ibid., 372.
23. Ibid., 372.
24. Bernard Cooke, "Sacramentality of Second Marriages," in *Divorce and Remarriage: Religious and Psychological Perspectives*, William P. Roberts, ed. (Kansas City: Sheed and Ward, 1990), 70.
25. Ibid., 72.
26. Anna Canon, "Marriage and Divorce: Telling Our Stories: A Very Faithful Rebel," in *Catholic Women Speak: Bringing Our Gifts to the Table, Catholic Women Speak Network* (New York: Paulist, 2015), 83.
27. Mary Rose D'Angelo, "Remarriage and the Divorce Sayings Attributed to Jesus," in *Divorce and Remarriage: Religious and Psychological Perspectives*, William P. Roberts, ed. (Kansas City: Sheed and Ward, 1990), 99.
28. Ibid.
29. Carrell, "Marriage, Divorce and Remarriage," 34.
30. Howard Clinebell, *Basic Types of Pastoral Care and Counseling: Resources for the Ministry of Healing and Growth* (Nashville: Abingdon Press, 1984), 232.
31. Ibid., 234.
32. A Google search offers an astounding array of etiquette tips for divorce parties, fun games and decorations for divorce parties, and so on.
33. John Shelby Spong, "Can the Church Bless Divorce?" *The Christian Century* 101:1126–1127, cited in Richard Hays, *The Moral Vision of the New Testament*, 371.
34. Michael Lawler, *What Is and What Ought to Be: The Dialectic of Experience, Theology, and Church* (New York: Continuum, 2005), 152.
35. Stephanie Coontz, *The Way We Really Are: Coming to Terms with America's Changing Families* (New York: Harper Collins/Basic Books, 1997), especially Chapter 2.
36. Ibid., 98.
37. Ibid.

38. See, for example, Judith Wallerstein and Sandra Blakeslee, *The Unexpected Legacy of Divorce: A 25 Year Landmark Study* (New York: Hyperion, 2005).
39. Ibid., 25.
40. See Ross A. Thompson and Paul R. Amato, eds., *The Postdivorce Family: Children, Parenting, and Society* (Thousand Oaks: Sage Publications, 1999).
41. See further Wallerstein's chapters recounting very sad interviews with children in violent and/or chaotic households, especially Part II of *The Unexpected Legacy of Divorce*.
42. Wallerstein, *The Unexpected Legacy of Divorce*, 307.
43. Stanley Hauerwas, "Christianity: It's an Adventure," in *The Hauerwas Reader*, John Berkman and Michael Cartwright, eds. (Durham: Duke University Press, 2001), 526.
44. Lawler, *What Is and What Ought to Be*, 32.
45. Ibid., 33, citing Alasdair MacIntyre, *After Virtue: A Study of Moral Theory* (London: Duckworth, 1985), 252.
46. The Catholic term is *sensus fidei*, the faith of the people.
47. As one of many examples, one need only read MacIntyre's introductory story in his best-known work *After Virtue* to see, very quickly, that a fragmented moral universe is not therefore a good moral universe.
48. Charles Pinches and Stanley Hauerwas, "Courage Exemplified," cited in *The Hauerwas Reader*, Michael Cartwright and John Berkman eds. (Durham: Duke University Press, 2001), 295.
49. Ibid., 300.
50. Ibid, 302.
51. Stanley Hauerwas, "The Radical Hope in the Annunciation," in *The Hauerwas Reader*, John Berkman and Michael Cartwright, eds. (Durham: Duke University Press, 2001), 512.
52. Ibid., 514.
53. Ibid.
54. Katie Grimes, "Breaking the Body of Christ: The Sacraments of Initiation in a Habitat of White Supremacy," *Political Theology* (May 26, 2016). Accessed September 27, 2016, http://www.tandfonline.com/doi/abs/10.1179/1743171915Y.0000000005. Grimes shows how Christians' practices of baptism and Eucharist shored up and even instigated the evils of racism and segregation. Neither of these sacraments of initiation can help the church reform, in her view, since they are racist from the beginning. Though I think Grimes is right to name the racisms involved in the church's own practices, she is wrong to do so by going after Hauerwas' theology. She suggests that Hauerwas (and his student William Cavanaugh, himself the author of several notable books and articles) overly privilege the Eucharist and the church so that it seems that racism could never happen, nor could the church be culpable. But Grimes

has clearly not read Cavanaugh's book *Torture and Eucharist* well, nor many of Hauerwas' works, if she thinks they're primarily about protecting the Church as community, and assuming that racism or other forms of injustice and suffering occur there. That said, Grimes' view is a common view of Hauerwas and his students' work.

55. Stanley Hauerwas, "Communitarians and Medical Ethicists, or Why I am None of the Above," in *Dispatches from the Front: Theological Engagements with the Secular* (Durham: Duke University Press, 1994), 157.
56. Stanley Hauerwas, *Hannah's Child: A Theologian's Memoir* (Grand Rapids: Eerdmans, 2010), 129.
57. Ibid., 144.
58. Ibid., 176.
59. Ibid., 186.
60. Ibid.
61. Ibid.
62. Ibid., 200.
63. Ibid., 203.
64. Hauerwas, *Hannah's Child*, 2012 edition, cited in Jonathan Tran, "Anne and the Difficult Gift of Stanley Hauerwas's Church," in *The Difference Christ Makes*, Charles Collier ed. (Eugene: Cascade Books, 2015), 52.
65. Jonathan Tran, "Anne and the Difficult Gift of Stanley Hauerwas's Church," in *The Difference Christ Makes*, Charles Collier ed. (Eugene: Cascade Books, 2015), 62.
66. Ibid., 64.
67. Ibid., 65.
68. Ibid., 66.
69. Ibid., 69.
70. Stanley Hauerwas, "Making Connections," in *The Difference Christ Makes*, 90.
71. Stanley Hauerwas, "Bearing Reality: A Christian Meditation," *Journal of the Society of Christian Ethics* 33.1 (Spring/Summer 2013): 3–20; 15.
72. Lauren Winner, *Still: Notes on a Mid-Faith Crisis* (New York: Harper One, 2012), 5.
73. Ibid., 6.
74. Lauren Winner, "Lectio Divina and Divorce," 282.
75. Ibid., 282–283.
76. Ibid., 285.
77. Ibid., 297.
78. Winner, *Still*, 194.
79. See Vigen Guroian, *Incarnate Love: Essays in Orthodox Ethics* (Notre Dame, IN: University of Notre Dame Press, 1989), Chapter 4.
80. Pope Francis, *Amoris Laetitia*, §297.

CHAPTER 8

1. Quiverfull as a movement was given the public eye in TLC's television show, "Eighteen and Counting..." about a Quiverfull family.
2. Emily McGowin, once a student of mine at the University of Dayton, wrote a dissertation on the Quiverfull movement that explores the themes of gender, parenting, homeschooling, and discipleship. She incisively links Quiverfull with broader Christian movements. Her insights are guiding some of my own views in this chapter. See "As for Me and My House: The Theology of the Family in the American Quiverfull Movement," unpublished dissertation (Dayton, OH: University of Dayton, 2015).
3. See, for example, John Witte and M. Christian Green, eds., *The Equal-Regard Family and its Friendly Critics: Don Browning and the Practical Theological Ethics of the Family* (Grand Rapids: Eerdmans, 2007).
4. One discussion of changing attitudes is Barbara Kantrowitz and Pat Wingert, "Unmarried, With Children," *Newsweek* May 28, 2001. Accessed October 26, 2015, http://www.newsweek.com/unmarried-children-152695.
5. Sarah DeJean, et al., "Attitudes Toward Never-Married Single Mothers and Fathers," *Journal of Feminist Family Therapy* 24 (2012): 121–138. The authors posit several possible reasons for this clear discrepancy, including that there may be an associated stigma related to being unmarried and pregnant, and the idea that mothers are the nurturers of their children and have failed their children if a relationship fails.
6. "Single Mother Statistics," Single Mother Guide, https://singlemotherguide.com/single-mother-statistics/. This website collates statistics from the most recent US Census Bureau data, the CDC, the USDA, the US Department of Labor, and other governmental agencies that collect data on households.
7. Ibid.
8. Ibid.
9. For example, Y. Sun and Y. Li, "Effects of Family Structure Type and Stability on Children's Academic Performance Trajectories," *Journal of Marriage and Family*, 73 (2011): 541–556.
10. See "Issues Facing Children with Special Needs," *Jill's House*, accessed December 8, 2015, http://jillshouse.org/wp-content/uploads/2013/05/Issues-Facing-Families-of-Children-with-Special-Needs.pdf.
11. For example, Gustavo Gutierrez, *A Theology of Liberation: History, Politics, and Salvation*, edited and translated by C. Inda and J. Eagleson (Maryknoll, N.Y.: Orbis Books, 1973; London: SCM Press, 1974); James Cone, *A Black Theology of Liberation* (Philadelphia: Lipincott, 1970); see also Pope Francis, "Evangelii Gaudium," Apostolic Exhortation (November 24, 2013), http://

w2.vatican.va/content/francesco/en/apost_exhortations/documents/papa-francesco_esortazione-ap_20131124_evangelii-gaudium.html

12. Mollie Ziegler Hemingway, "White Flag in the Mommy Wars: The Theology that Many Parents are Missing," *Christianity Today* (September 2009): 76.
13. The question of whether to allow children to walk home alone became the subject of 2015 debates in news and social media, and concluded with the passing of a federal law that allows children to walk home alone. Lenore Skenazy provides one commentary on the law and the many events that led to its passing in "Your Kids Can Walk to School Alone Again," *New York Post*, December 16, 2015, accessed September 1, 2016, http://nypost.com/2015/12/16/your-kids-can-walk-to-school-alone-again/.
14. Sandra Tsing Loh, "Rhymes With Rich: One Woman's Conscientious Objection to Mommy Wars," *The Atlantic Monthly*, May 2006, 110.
15. See Amy Laura Hall, *Conceiving Parenthood: American Protestantism and the Spirit of Reproduction* (Grand Rapids: Eerdmans, 2007).
16. Kathryn Lofton, "Willing Children," *Fides et Historia* 45:2 (Summer/Fall 2013): 68.
17. Though her work reflects an earlier decade, Julie Hanlon Rubio has also described a dichotomous atmosphere for parents in her book, *A Christian Theology of Marriage and Family* (New York: Paulist Press, 2003), especially in Chapter 1. The view of parenting as moral force has been prevalent for several decades.
18. Hemingway, "White Flag in the Mommy Wars," 76.
19. Ibid.
20. See Emily McGowin, "As for Me and My House: The Theology of the Family in the American Quiverfull Movement," (Doctoral dissertation, University of Dayton, 2015), especially Chapter 1.
21. R.L. Stollar, "The Child as Viper: How Voddie Baucham's Theology of Children Promotes Child Abuse," (2015), as cited in Emily McGowin, unpublished dissertation, 313.
22. Heidi Schlumpf, "Stand Alone Moms: Catholic Single Parents Tell Their Stories," *US Catholic* 78.1, January 2013. Accessed December 7, 2015, http://www.uscatholic.or/articles/201211/stand-alone-moms-catholic-single-parents-tell-their-stories-26588.
23. Heidi Schlumpf, "Shame, Shame: When Catholic Institutions Fire Single Moms," *US Catholic* 78.1, January 2013. Accessed December 7, 2015, http://www.uscatholic.org/articles/201211/shame-shame-when- catholic- institutions-fire-single-moms-26591.
24. David Miller, "Single Parenting in the Christian Community," in Kenneth O. Gangel and James C Wilhoit, eds., *The Christian Educator's Handbook on Family Life Education* (Grand Rapids: Baker Books, 1996), 127.

25. Jennifer Maggio, "The Church and the Single Mom," CBN, accessed December 7, 2015, http://www1.cbn.com/churchandministry/the-church-and-the-single-mom.
26. On this point, see E.J. Dionne's 2012 column reflecting on how the mommy wars intersected with the 2012 presidential campaigns. "'Mommy Wars' and Money Worries: Ann Romney Never *Had* to Work a Day in Her Life," *Commonweal* (May 18, 2012): 6.
27. Julie A. Mavity Maddalena, "Floodwaters and the Ticking Clock: The Systematic Oppression and Stigmatization of Poor, Single Mothers in America and Christian Theological Responses," *Cross Currents* 63.2 (June 2013): 158.
28. Michael B. Katz and Lorrin R. Thomas, "The Invention of 'Welfare' in America," *Journal of Policy History* (December 1998): 399–418; cited in Joe Soss and Sanford F. Schram, "A Public Transformed? Welfare Reform as Policy Feedback," *American Political Science Review* 101.1 (February 2007): 112.
29. Soss and Schram, "A Public Transformed?," 112, citing Harold Meyerson, "Whither the Democrats?" *The American Prospect Online* March 1, 1996, http://www.prospect.org/web/page.ww?section=root&name=ViewPrint&articleId=4945.
30. Eric Morath, "Get a Job? Most Welfare Recipients Already Have One," *The Wall Street Journal*, April 13, 2015. Accessed December 7, 2015, http://blogs.wsj.com/economics/2015/04/13/get-a-job-most-welfare-recipients-already-have-one/.
31. Jason DeParle and Steven A. Holmes, "A War on Poverty Subtly Linked to Race," *New York Times* (December 26, 2000): A1; cited in Soss and Schram, "A Public Transformed?," 113.
32. Soss and Schram, "A Public Transformed?," 117.
33. Linda Gordon, *Pitied But Not Entitled: Single Mothers and the History of Welfare* (Cambridge, MA: Harvard University Press, 1998).
34. H. Luke Schaefer and Marci Ybarra, "The Welfare Reforms of the 1990s and the Stratification of Material Well-Being Among Low-Income Households with Children," *Children and Youth Services Review* 34 (2012): 1811.
35. Maddalena, "Floodwaters and the Ticking Clock," 158.
36. Dionne, "Mommy Wars and Money Worries," 6.
37. H. Richard Niebuhr, *Christ and Culture* (San Francisco: Harper Collins, 1951). See especially Chapter 2. Niebuhr's five types are inadequate, especially because they presume to fit everyone into monolithic categories of "Christ" and "culture" as though those were uncontested terms. Who is Christ? Which culture? These are debates still had today.
38. Kristin Heyer, *Prophetic and Public: The Social Witness of U.S. Catholicism* (Washington, DC: Georgetown University Press, 2006), 90, cited in Benjamin Peters, *Called to Be Saints: John Hugo, the Catholic Worker, and a Theology of Radical Christianity* (Milwaukee: Marquette University Press, 2016), 228.

39. Peters, *Called to Be Saints*, 230.
40. David O'Brien, *Public Catholicism*, 2nd edition (New York: Orbis Books, 1996), 246.
41. Peters, *Called to Be Saints*, 231.
42. Michael Emerson, "A New Day for Multiracial Congregations," *Reflections: A Magazine of Theological and Ethical Inquiry from Yale Divinity School* (2013), http://reflections.yale.edu/article/future-race/new-day-multiracial-congregations.
43. Alana Semuels, "White Flight Never Ended," *The Atlantic*, July 30, 2015. Accessed September 3, 2016, http://www.theatlantic.com/business/archive/2015/07/white-flight-alive-and-well/399980/.
44. Dorothy Day, *The Long Loneliness: The Autobiography of the Legendary Catholic Social Activist* (San Francisco: Harper and Row, 1952), 235.
45. Ibid., 116.
46. Ibid., 134.
47. Dorothy Day, *Therese: A Life of Therese of Lisieux* (Springfield, IL: Templegate Publishers, 1979), vi.
48. Day, *The Long Loneliness*, 137.
49. Dorothy Day, *From Union Square to Rome* (New York: Orbis Books, 2006), 132.
50. Day, *The Long Loneliness*, 165.
51. Juliana Baggott, "Dorothy Day's Daughter, Pregnant with Her Ninth Child, Begs Her Mother for Charity: A Bedtime Prayer," *Lizzie Borden in Love: Poems in Women's Voices* (Carbondale, IL: Southern Illinois University Press, 2006), 59.
52. Larry Holben, "Day Wasn't a Good Role Model for Parenting," *National Catholic Reporter* 29 October 1999: 4.
53. Ibid.
54. Katherine Yohe, "Dorothy Day: Love for One's Daughter and Love for the Poor." *Horizons* 31.2 (Fall 2004): 287.
55. Margot Patterson, "An Extraordinary Difficult Childhood," *National Catholic Reporter* (March 7, 2003): 14.
56. Ibid.
57. Ibid.
58. Ibid.
59. Dorothy Day, *The Long Loneliness*, 139
60. Ibid., 149.
61. John J. Hugo, *A Sign of Contradiction As the Master, So the Disciple*, cited in Day (Published by Author, 1947), 137.
62. Rosalie G. Riegle, *Dorothy Day: Portraits of Those Who Knew Her* (New York: Orbis, 2003), 84.
63. Benjamin Peters, *Called to Be Saints: John Hugo, The Catholic Worker, and a Theology of Radical Christianity*, with appendix, Dorothy Day's Retreat Notebooks

(Milwaukee: Marquette University, 2016) 73. I am indebted to Ben Peters' writing and personal conversations with me in drafting this chapter.

64. Dorothy Day uses Hugo's images of pruning and sowing often in *The Long Loneliness*. See Day, *Long Loneliness*, 274.
65. Peters, *Called to Be Saints*, 81.
66. Ibid., 91.
67. Ibid., 72.
68. The Second Vatican Council (1962–1965) importantly emphasized that Christians have a "universal call to holiness."
69. Stanley Vishnewski, *Meditations: Dorothy Day* (New York: Paulist Press, 1970), 214.
70. Riegle Troester, *Voices From the Catholic Worker* (Philadelphia: Temple University Press, 1993), 20.
71. Dorothy Day, *On Pilgrimage* (Grand Rapids: Eerdmans, 1999), 123.
72. Day, *Therese*, 31.
73. Day, *The Long Loneliness*, 259.
74. Ibid., 261.
75. Dorothy Day, "House of Hospitality," *Catholic Worker Online*, Chapter 9, accessed September 2, 2016, http://www.catholicworker.org/dorothyday/articles/444-plain.htm.
76. Day, *The Long Loneliness*, 235.
77. Ibid., 236.
78. Ibid., 243.
79. Ibid., 286.
80. Day, *On Pilgrimage*, 192.
81. See Benjamin Peters' excellent essay that discusses the so-called liberal/conservative political divide among Catholics and how, because of that divide, people misunderstand and misread Dorothy Day's work. "'Apocalyptic Sectarianism': The Theology at Work in Critiques of Catholic Radicals," *Horizons* 39:2 (September 2012): 208–229.
82. Day, *On Pilgrimage*, 133.
83. Laura A. Smith, *Loves Me, Loves Me Not: The Ethics of Unrequited Love* (Grand Rapids: Baker Academic, 2005), 31.

CHAPTER 9

1. John Santelli, et al., "Abstinence and abstinence-only education: A review of U.S. policies and programs," *Journal of Adolescent Health* 38.1 (January 2006): 72–81.
2. This is a point numerous authors make. See Kate Bolick, *Spinsters: Making a Life of One's Own* (New York: Penguin Books, 2015), for example, Chapter 1.

3. Gender and singleness is occasionally discussed. See special editions of the following journals: Susan Cotts Watkins, ed., *Journal of Family History* 9.4 (1984); Katherine Holden, Amy Froide, and June Hannam, eds., *Women's History Review* 17.3 (July 2008).
4. Augustine, *The Confessions*, trans. Maria Boulding (New York: Vintage Books, 1997), IX.4,7.

Select Bibliography

Abbott, Elizabeth. *A History of Celibacy*. New York: Scribner, 2000.

Aelred of Rievaulx. *Spiritual Friendship*. Edited by Marsha L. Dutton. Translated by Lawrence C. Braceland. Collegeville: Liturgical Press, 2010.

Alexander, John. "Playing With FIRE: Or, Narcissicism as Sacred Duty." In *The Secular Squeeze: Reclaiming Christian Depth in a Shallow World*, pp. 197–219. Downer's Grove, IL: Intervarsity, 1993.

Allestree, Richard. *The Ladies Calling*. Project Cambridge. http://anglicanhistory.org/women/calling/virgins.html.

Augustine, *Confessions*. Second Edition. Edited with notes by Michael P. Foley. Translated by F.J. Sheed. Indianapolis/Cambridge: Hackett Publishing Company, 2006.

———. *Contra Faustum*. Translated by Richard Stothert. From Nicene and Post-Nicene Fathers, First Series, Vol. 4. Edited by Philip Schaff. Buffalo, NY: Christian Literature Publishing Co., 1887. Revised and edited for New Advent by Kevin Knight. <http://www.newadvent.org/fathers/1406.htm>.

———. "The Excellence of Marriage." In *Marriage and Virginity* Vol. I/9, *The Works of Saint Augustine: A Translation for the 21st Century*. Edited by David G. Hunter. Translated by Ray Kearney, 33–61. Hyde Park, New York: New City Press, 1999.

———. "Holy Virginity." In *Marriage and Virginity*. Edited by David G. Hunter. Translated by Ray Kearney, pp. 65–110. Hyde Park, NY: New City Press, 1999.

Baggott, Juliana. *Lizzie Borden in Love: Poems in Women's Voices*. Carbondale, IL: Southern Illinois University Press, 2006.

Banks, Ralph Richard. *Is Marriage for White People?: How the African American Marriage Decline Affects Everyone*. New York: Dutton, 2011.

Band-Winterstein, Tova et al. "The Experience of Being an Old Never-Married Single: A Life Course Perspective." *International Journal of Aging and Human Development* 78.4 (2014): 379–401.

Bassler, Jouette M. "Limits and Differentiation: The Calculus of Widows in 1 Timothy 5:3–16." In *A Feminist Companion to the Deutero-Pauline Epistles*. Edited by Amy-Jill Levine, 122–146. Cleveland: The Pilgrim Press, 2003.

Benedict XVI, Pope. *Deus Caritas Est*. Encyclical Letter, December 25, 2005.

Bennett, Jana Marguerite. "Singular Christianity: Marriage and Singleness as Discipleship." In *Leaving and Coming Home: New Wineskins for Catholic Sexual Ethics*. Edited by David Cloutier, pp. 85–100. Eugene, OR: Cascade Books, 2010.

_____. *Water is Thicker than Blood: An Augustinian Theology of Marriage and Singleness*. New York: Oxford, 2008.

Berkman, John and Michael Cartwright., eds. *The Hauerwas Reader*. Durham: Duke University Press, 2001.

Berry, Wendell. *Sex Economy, Freedom, and Community*. New York: Parthenon Books, 1993.

Bishop, Jeffery. *The Anticipatory Corpse: Medicine, Power, and the Care of the Dying*. Notre Dame: University of Notre Dame Press, 2011.

Bilinkoff, Jodi. "Elite Widows and Religious Expression in Early Modern Spain." In *Widowhood in Medieval and Early Modern Europe*. Edited by Sandra Cavallo and Lyndon Warner, pp. 181–192. Edinburgh: Longman, 1999.

Bird, Michael F., ed. *Four Views On The Apostle Paul*. Grand Rapids: Zondervan, 2012.

Bonhoeffer, Dietrich. *Life Together*. Translated and with an Introduction by John W. Doberstein. San Francisco: Harper SanFrancisco, 1954.

Bolick, Kate. *Spinster: Making a Life of One's Own*. New York: Crown Publishing, 2015.

Boswell, John. *Christianity, Social Tolerance, and Homosexuality: Gay People in Western Europe from the Beginning of the Christian Era to the Fourteenth Century*. Chicago: University of Chicago Press, 1981.

Boyarin, Daniel. *A Radical Jew: Paul and the Politics of Identity*. Los Angeles: University of California Press, 1994.

Braithwaite, Scott R., et al. "Is Pornography Consumption Associated with Condom Use and and Intoxication During Hookups?" *Culture, Health, and Sexuality* 17.10 (November 2015): 1155–1173.

Bray, Allen. *The Friend*. Chicago: University of Chicago Press, 2003.

Briggs, J.P. and John. "Unholy Desires, Inordinate Affections: A Psychodynamic Inquiry Into John Wesley's Relationship With Women." *Connecticut Review* 13:1 (Spring 1991): 1–18.

Brownsen, James V. *Bible, Gender, Sexuality: Reframing the Church's Debate on Same-Sex Relationships*. Grand Rapids: Eerdmans, 2013.

Brumbaugh, Julia. "Spirituality for a Suffering Earth: Death, Grief, and Transformation." In *An Unexpected Wilderness: Christianity and the Natural World*. Edited by Colleen Mary Carpenter. *College Theology Society* 61 (2015): 93–100.

Callahan, Sidney and Daniel, eds. *Abortion: Understanding Differences*. Braintree, MA: Pope John Center, 1992.

Camosy, Charles. *Beyond the Abortion Wars: A Way Forward for a New Generation.* Grand Rapids: Eerdmans, 1975.

Canon, Anna. "Marriage and Divorce: Telling Our Stories: A Very Faithful Rebel." In *Catholic Women Speak: Bringing Our Gifts to the Table.* Edited by Catholic Women Speak Network. New York: Paulist, 2015.

Carpenter, Colleen Mary, ed. *An Unexpected Wilderness: Christianity and the Natural World. College Theology Society* 61, 2015.

Carrell, Peter. "Marriage, Divorce, and Remarriage in the New Testament." *Stimulus* 11.4 (November 2003): 22–76.

Cavallo, Sandra and Lyndon Warner, eds. *Widowhood in Medieval and Early Modern Europe.* Harlow: Longman, 1999.

Cavanaugh, William T. *Being Consumed: Economics and Christian Desire.* Grand Rapids: Eerdmans, 2008.

Caudill, Whitney. "Being Single: How to Handle Loneliness." *The Huffington Post,* August 6, 2013. http://www.huffingtonpost.com/whitney-caudill/being-single-how-to-handle-loneliness_b_3461062.html.

———. "I'm Lonely and Other Things that Suck about Being Single," *Your Tango,* January 28, 2016. http://www.yourtango.com/233213/10-heartbreaking-truths-about-loneliness-single-people-dont-say.

Chediak, Alex, ed. *5 Paths to the Love of your Life: Defining Your Dating Style.* Colorado Springs: NavPress, 2005.

Chudacoff, Howard. *The Age of the Bachelor: Creating an American Subculture.* Princeton, NJ: Princeton UP, 1999.

Clark, Katherine. "Putting on the Garment of Widowhood: Medieval Widows, Monastic Memory, and Historical Writing." *Quidditas* 31.1 (2010): 22–76.

Clinebell, Howard. *Basic Types of Pastoral Care and Counseling: Resources for the Ministry of Healing and Growth.* Nashville: Abingdon, 1994.

———. *Clinical Handbook of Pastoral Counseling,* 3 vols. Edited by Robert Wicks, Richard Parsons (and Donald Capps, 3rd vol.). Mahwah, NJ: Integration Books, 1985-2003.

Coakley, Sarah. *God, Sexuality and the Self: An Essay 'On the Trinity'.* Cambridge: Cambridge University Press, 2013.

Cobb, Michael. *Single: Arguments for the Uncoupled.* New York: New York University Press, 2012.

———. "The Supreme Court's Lonely Hearts Club." *The New York Times,* June 30, 2015. Accessed November 20, 2015. http://www.nytimes.com/2015/06/30/opinion/the-supreme-courts-lonely-hearts-club.html?_r=0.

Coe, Bufford W. *John Wesley and Marriage.* Bethlehem: Lehigh University Press, 1996.

Cohn, De'Vera. "Love and Marriage," Pew Research Center, February 13, 2013. Accessed September 10, 2016http://www.pewsocialtrends.org/2013/02/13/love-and-marriage/.

Collier, Charles, editor. *The Difference Christ Makes*. Eugene: Cascade Books, 2015.

Collins, Kenneth. "John Wesley's Relationship With His Wife as Revealed in His Correspondence." *Methodist History* 32:1 (October 1993): 4–18.

Collins, Raymond F. "Marriage (NT)." In *The Anchor Bible Dictionary*. Edited by D.N. Freedman et al., 569–57.2 New York: Doubleday, 1992.

Colón, Christine A. and Bonnie E. Field. *Singled Out: Why Celibacy Must be Reinvented in Today's Church*. Grand Rapids: Brazos Press, 2009.

Cone, James H. *A Black Theology of Liberation*. Philadelphia: Lipincott, 1970.

Conroy, Pat. "Anatomy of a Divorce." *Atlanta Magazine*, November 1, 1978.

Cook, Hera. *The Long Sexual Revolution: English Women, Sex, and Contraception*. Oxford: Oxford UP, 2004.

Cooke, Bernard. "Sacramentality of Second Marriages." In *Divorce and Remarriage: Religious and Psychological Perspectives*. Edited by William P. Roberts, pp. 70–77. Kansas City: Sheed and Ward, 1990.

Coontz, Stephanie. *Marriage, A History: How Love Conquered Marriage*. New York: Penguin Books, 2005.

_____. *The Way We Really Are: Coming to Terms with America's Changing Families*. New York: Basic Books, 1997

Cornell, Laurel. "Why are There No Spinsters in Japan?" *Journal of Family History* (Winter 1984): 326–339.

Crouch, Andy. "Family Values." In *Called to the Community: The Life Jesus Wants for His People*. Edited by Charles E. Moore, pp. 229–234. Walden, New York: Plough Publishing House, 2016.

Cruz, Jessica. "Marriage: More than a Century of Change." National Center for Family and Marriage Research (2013).

Curnock, Nehemiah, ed. *The Journal of the Reverend John Wesley*, 8 vols. London: R. Cully, 1909-1916.

D'Angelo, Mary Rose. "Remarriage and the Divorce Sayings Attributed to Jesus." In *Divorce and Remarriage: Religious and Psychological Perspectives*. Edited by William P. Roberts, pp. 78–106. Kansas City: Sheed and Ward, 1990.

Danylak, Barry. *Redeeming Singleness: How the Storyline of Scripture Affirms the Single Life*. Wheaton, IL: Crossway, 2010.

Day, Dorothy. "House of Hospitality." *Catholic Worker Online*: Chapter 9. Accessed September 2, 2016. http://www.catholicworker.org/dorothyday/articles/444-plain.htm.

_____. *On Pilgrimage*. Grand Rapids: Eerdmans, 1999.

_____. *From Union Square to Rome*. New York: Orbis Books, 2006.

_____. *The Long Loneliness: The Autobiography of the Legendary Catholic Social Activist*. San Francisco: Harper and Row, 1952.

_____. *Therese: A Life Of Therese Of Lisieux*. Springfield, IL: Templegate Publishers, 1979.

DeJean, Sarah et al. "Attitudes Toward Never-Married Single Mothers and Fathers." *Journal of Feminist Family Therapy* 24 (2012): 121–138.

DePaulo, Bella. *Singled Out: How Singles Are Stereotyped, Stigmatized, and Ignored, and Still Live Happily Ever After.* New York: St. Martin's Press, 2006.

Dionne, E.J. "'Mommy Wars' and Money Worries: Ann Romney Never *Had* to Work a Day in Her Life." *Commonweal*, May 18, 2012.

Dirvin, Joseph I. *Mrs. Seton: Foundress of the American Sisters of Charity.* New York: Farrar, Straus, and Cudahy, 1962.

Dobson, James. *Preparing for Adolescence: How to Survive the Coming Years of Change.* Santa Ana, CA: Vision House, 2005.

Doka, Kenneth J. and Amy S. Tucci, eds. *Beyond Kübler-Ross: New Perspectives on Death, Dying and Grief.* Washington, D.C.: Hospice Foundation of America, 2011.

Dormor, Duncan. *Just Cohabitating? The Church, Sex, and Getting Married.* London: Darton, Longman, and Todd, 2004.

Eden, Dawn. *My Peace I Give You: Healing Sexual Wounds with the Help of the Saints.* Notre Dame, IN: Ave Maria Press, 2012.

Emerson, Michael. "A New Day for Multiracial Congregations." In *Reflections: A Magazine of Theological and Ethical Inquiry from Yale Divinity School*, 11–15, 2013.

Engels, Friedrich. *Origins of the Family, Private Property, and the State.* Translated by Ernest Untermann. Chicago: Charles H. Kerr & Co., 1909.

Evans, Jimmy and Frank Martin. *The Right One: How to Successfully Date and Marry the Right Person.* Dallas, TX: Marriage Today, 2015.

Evans, Tony. *Living Single.* Chicago: Moody Publishers, 2013.

Farley, Margaret. *Just Love: A Framework for Christian Social Ethics.* New York: Continuum International, 2006.

———. "Marriage, Divorce, and Personal Commitments." In *Celebrating Christian Marriage.* Edited by Adrian Thatcher, pp. 356–377. Edinburgh: T&T Clark, 2001.

Felker Jones, Beth. *Faithful: A Theology of Sex.* Grand Rapids: Zondervan, 2014.

First Premarital Cohabitation in the United States: 2006–2010 National Survey of Family Growth. *National Health Statistics Report* 64. April 4, 2013. Accessed March 18, 2016. http://www.cdc.gov/nchs/data/nhsr/nhsr064.pdf, 5.

Florensky, Pavel. *The Pillar and Ground of the Truth.* Translated by Boris Jakim. Princeton: Princeton UP, 2004.

Flores, Nicole M. "Latina/o Families: Solidarity and the Common Good," *The Journal of the Society of Christian Ethics* 33.2 (2013): 57–72.

Foucault, Michel. *The History of Sexuality: An Introduction*, Vol 1. New York: Vintage Books, 1990.

Franchot, Jenny. *Roads to Rome: The Antebellum Protestant Encounter with Catholicism.* Berkely, CA: University of California Press, 1994.

Francis, Pope. *Amoris Laetitia*. Apostolic Exhortation, March 19, 2016. (https://w2.vatican.va/content/dam/francesco/pdf/apost_exhortations/documents/papa-francesco_esortazione-ap_20160319_amoris-laetitia_en.pdf.

_____. *Evangelii Gaudium*. Apostolic Exhortation, November 24, 2013. http://w2.vatican.va/content/francesco/en/apost_exhortations/documents/papa-francesco_esortazione-ap_20131124_evangelii-gaudium.html.

Freeman, D.N., et al. *The Anchor Bible Dictionary*. New York: Doubleday, 1992.

Freitas, Donna. *The End of Sex: How Hookup Culture is Leaving a Generation Unhappy, Sexually Unfulfilled, and Confused about Intimacy*. New York: Basic Books, 2013.

Freitas, Donna and Jason King. *Save the Date: A Spirituality of Dating, Love, Dinner, and the Divine*. Eugene, OR: Wipf and Stock, 2003.

Freud, Sigmund. *Three Contributions to the Sexual Theory*. New York: Bartleby.com, 2010.

Gangel, Kenneth O. and James C. Wilhoit, eds. *The Christian Educator's Handbook on Family Life Education*. Grand Rapids: Baker Books, 1996.

Gillihan, Yonder Moynihan. "Jewish Laws on Illicit Marriage, the Defilement of Offspring, and the Holiness of the Temple: A New Halakic Interpretation of 1 Corinthians 7:14." *Journal of Biblical Literature* 121 (2002): 711–744.

Gordon, Linda. *Pitied But Not Entitled: Single Mothers and the History of Welfare*. Cambridge, MA: Harvard UP, 1998.

Grant, Robert. *Paul in the Roman World: The Conflict at Corinth*. Louisville: Westminster John Knox Press, 2001.

Grimes, Katie M. "Breaking the Body of Christ: The Sacraments of Initiation in a Habitat of White Supremacy." *Political Theology* (July 2015): http://www.tandfonline.com/doi/abs/10.1179/1743171915Y.0000000005.

Griffith, Wendy. *You Are a Prize to Be Won! Don't Settle for Less than God's Best*. Ventura, CA: Regal, 2014.

Grosheide, F.W. *Commentary on the First Epistle to the Corinthians: The English Text with Introduction, Exposition and Notes*. Grand Rapids: Eerdmans Publishing Company, 1953.

Gudgel, Brent and David Gudgel, with Danielle Fitch. *Before You Get Engaged*. Nashville: Thomas Nelson, 2007.

Guroian,Vigen. *Incarnate Love: Essays in Orthodox Ethics*. Notre Dame, IN: University of Notre Dame Press, 1989.

Gutierrez, Gustavo. *A Theology of Liberation: History, Politics, and Salvation*. Edited and Translated by C. Inda and J. Eagleson. Maryknoll, NY: Orbis Books, 1973; London: SCM Press, 1974.

Hafner, Katie. "Researchers Confront an Epidemic of Loneliness." In *The New York Times*, September 5, 2016. Accessed September 27, 2016. http://www.nytimes.com/2016/09/06/health/lonliness-aging-health-effects.html?_r=1.

Hall, Amy Laura. *Conceiving Parenthood: American Protestantism and the Spirit of Reproduction*. Grand Rapids: Eerdmans, 2007.

Hamel, Ron, ed. *Choosing Death: Active Euthanasia, Religion, and the Public Debate*. Philadelphia: Trinity Press International, 1991.

Hammond, Geordan. *John Wesley in America: Restoring Primitive Christianity*, New York; Oxford: Oxford University Press, 2014.

Harris, Joshua. *I Kissed Dating Goodbye: A New Attitude Toward Romance and Relationships*. Colorado Springs: Multnomah Books, 1997.

Harrison, Stephanie, ed. *The Cambridge Companion to Horace*. Cambridge: Cambridge University Press, 2007.

Hauerwas, Stanley. Bearing Reality: A Christian Meditation." *Journal of the Society of Christian Ethics* 33.1 (Spring/Summer 2013): 3–20.

———. "Christianity: It's Not a Religion, It's an Adventure." In *The Hauerwas Reader*. Edited by John Berkman and Michael Cartwright, pp.522–538. Durham: Duke University Press, 2001.

———. *Hannah's Child: A Theologian's Memoir*. Grand Rapids: Eerdmans, 2010.

———. "Making Connections: By Way of a Response to Wells, Herdt, and Tran." In *The Difference Christ Makes*. Edited by Charles Collier, pp. 77–94. Eugene: Cascade Books, 2015.

———. "Sex in Public: How Adventurous Christians are Doing It." In *The Hauerwas Reader*. Edited by John Berkman and Michael Cartwright, pp. 481–504. Durham: Duke University Press, 2001.

———. "The Radical Hope in the Annunciation: Why Both Single and Married Christians Welcome Children." In *The Hauerwas Reader*. Edited by John Berkman and Michael Cartwright, pp. 505–518. Durham, NC: Duke University Press, 2001.

Hays, Richard B. *The Moral Vision of the New Testament: Community, Cross, New Creation: A Contemporary Introduction to New Testament Ethics*. New York: Harper San Francisco, 1996.

Heitzenrater, Richard P. *The Elusive Mr. Wesley*. 2nd edition. Nashville: Abingdon Press, 2003.

———. *Wesley and the People Called Methodists*. Nashville: Abingdon Press, 1995.

Hemingway, Mollie Ziegler. "White Flag in the Mommy Wars: The Theology that Many Parents are Missing." *Christianity Today*, September 2009.

Heyer, Kristin. *Prophetic and Public: The Social Witness of U.S. Catholicism*. Washington, DC: Georgetown University Press, 2006.

Hill, Wesley. *Spiritual Friendship: Finding Love in the Church as a Celibate Gay Christian*. Grand Rapids: Brazos Press, 2015.

Hobart, Chris. "A Single-Minded Focus on Loneliness." *The (Hobart) Mercury*, March 30, 2011.

Holben, Larry. "Day Wasn't a Good Role Model for Parenting." *National Catholic Reporter,* October 29, 1999.

Holden, Katherine, Amy Froide, and June Hannam. "Introduction," *Women's History Review* 17.3 (July 2008).

Hooker, Morna D. *Paul: A Short Introduction*. Oxford: One World Publications, 2003.

Hopper, Briallen. "On Spinsters," LA Review of Books (July 15, 2015). Accessed July 26, 2016. https://lareviewofbooks.org/article/on-spinsters/#!.

Horace, *Odes and Epodes.* Edited by Jeffrey Henderson, Translated by Niall Rudd. LCL Vol. 33. Cambridge MA: Harvard University Press, 2004.

Howarth, Glennys. *Death and Dying: A Sociological Introduction.* Cambridge: Polity Press, 2007.

Hsu, Albert. *Singles at the Crossroads: A Fresh Perspective on Christian Singleness.* Downer's Grove, IL: Intervarsity Press, 1997.

Hugo, John J. *A Sign of Contradiction: As the Master, So the Disciple.* Published by author, 1947.

Hunter, David G. "Asceticism, Priesthood, and Exegesis: 1 Corinthians 7:5 in Jerome and His Contemporaries." In *Asceticism and Exegesis in Early Christianity: The Reception of New Testament Texts in Ancient Ascetic Discourses.* Edited by Hans-Ulrich Weidemann, pp. 413–427. Gottlingen, Germany: Vandenhoeck & Ruprecht, 2013.

______. *Marriage Celibacy, and Heresy in Ancient Christianity: The Jovinianist Controversy.* Oxford: Oxford UP, 2007.

Jay, Meg. "The Downside of Cohabiting Before Marriage." *The New York Times* April 14, 2012. Accessed May 24, 2016. http://www.nytimes.com/2012/04/15/opinion/sunday/the-downside-of-cohabiting-before-marriage.html?_r=0.

Jerome. *Against Jovinianus.* Translated by W.H. Fremantle, G. Lewis, and W.G. Martley. In *Nicene and Post-Nicene Fathers, Second Series,* Vol. 6. Edited by Philip Schaff and Henry Wace. Buffalo, NY: Christian Literature Publishing Co., 1893. Revised and edited for New Advent by Kevin Knight. <http://www.newadvent.org/fathers/3009.htm>.

John Paul II, Pope. *Familiaris Consortio.* Apostolic Exhortation, November 22, 1981. http://w2.vatican.va/content/john-paul-ii/en/apost_exhortations/documents/hf_jp-ii_exh_19811122_familiaris-consortio.html.

______. *Man and Woman He Created Them: A Theology of the Body.* Boston: Pauline Books and Media, 2006.

Johnson, Luke Timothy. "Catholic View." In *Four Views On The Apostle Paul,* edited by Michael F. Bird et al., pp. 65–113. Grand Rapids: Zondervan, 2012.

Jordan, Mark. *Blessing Same-Sex Unions.* Chicago: The University of Chicago Press, 2005.

Kahan, Benjamin. *Celibacies: American Modernism and Sexual Life.* Durham: Duke University Press, 2013.

Katz, Michael B. and Lorrin R. Thomas. "The Invention of 'Welfare' in America." *Journal of Policy History* (December 1998): 399–418.

Kaveny, M. Cathleen. "The Order of Widows: What the Early Church Can Teach Us about Older Women and Health Care." *Christian Bioethics* 11 (2005): 11–34.

Keating, Jessica. "Single By Default: When a Vocation is Not a Vocation." *America Magazine*, September 2016. Accessed September 16, 2016. http://americamagazine.org/issue/single-default.

Keck, Leander. *Paul and His Letters*, Second edition, revised and enlarged. Minneapolis: Fortress Press, 1988.

Kipnis, Laura. *Against Love: A Polemic*. New York: Pantheon, 2003.

Kozlowska, Hanna. "Yes Means Yes: The Big Consent Debate." *New York Times*, October 15, 2014. Accessed November 24, 2015. http://op-talk.blogs.nytimes.com/2014/10/15/yes-means-yes-the-big-consent-debate/?_r=0.

Knust, Jennifer. *Unprotected Texts: The Bible's Surprising Contradictions about Sex and Desire*. New York: Harper Collins, 2012.

Kristoff, Nicholas. "Every Parent's Nightmare," *The New York Times*, March 10, 2016. Accessed March 11, 2016, http://www.nytimes.com/2016/03/10/opinion/every-parents-nightmare.html.

Kübler-Ross, Elizabeth. *On Death and Dying: What the Dying Have to Teach Doctors, Clergy, and their Own Families*. London; New York: Routledge, 2009.

Kuperberg, Arielle. "Age at Coresidence, Premarital Cohabitation, and Marriage Dissolution: 1985–2009." *Journal of Marriage and Family* 76 (April 2014): 352–369.

Langford, Thomas A. *Practical Divinity: Theology in the Wesleyan Tradition*. Nashville: Abingdon Pres, 1983.

_____. "Wesley and Theological Method." In *Rethinking Wesley's Theology for Contemporary Methodism*. Edited by Randy L. Maddox, pp. 35–48. Nashville: Kingswood Books, 1998.

Lawler, Michael. *What Is and What Ought to Be: The Dialectic of Experience, Theology, and Church*. New York: Continuum, 2005.

Lawler, Michael and Todd Salzmann. *The Sexual Person: Toward a Renewed Catholic Anthropology*. Washington, DC: Georgetown University Press, 2008.

Lenski, R.C.H. *The Interpretation of St. Paul's First and Second Epistles to the Corinthians*. Minneapolis: Augsburg Publishing House, 1963.

Levine, Amy-Jill, ed. *A Feminist Companion to the Deutero-Pauline Epistles*. Cleveland: The Pilgrim Press, 2003.

Levy, Ariel. *Female Chauvinist Pigs: Women and the Rise of Raunch Culture*. New York: Free Press, 2005.

Lewis, CS. *The Four Loves*. New York: Mariner Books, 2012.

Lofton, Kathryn. "Willing Children." *Fides et Historia* 45:2 (Summer/Fall 2013): 65–68.

Loh, Sandra Tsing. "Rhymes With Rich: One Woman's Conscientious Objection to the 'Mommy Wars.'" *The Atlantic Monthly*, May 2006.

Lowrie, Michèle. "Horace and Augustus." In *The Cambridge Companion to Horace*. Edited by Stephen Harrison, pp. 77–90. Cambridge: Cambridge University Press, 2007.

Lindvall, Jonathan. "The Betrothal Path." In *5 Paths to the Love of Your Life: Defining Your Dating Style*. Edited by Alex Chediak. Colorado Springs: NavPress, 2005.

Liu, Hiu and Zhenmei Zhang. "Disability Trends by Marital Status Among Older Americans, 1997–2010: An Examination by Gender and Race." *Population Research and Policy Review* 32:103 (2013): 103–127.

Lysaught, M. Therese. "Practicing the Order of Widows: A New Call for an Old Vocation." *Christian Bioethics* 11:1 (2005): 51–58.

MacDonald, Margaret and Leif E. Vaage. "Unclean by Holy Children: Paul's Everyday Quandary in 1 Corinthians 7:14c." *The Catholic Biblical Quarterly* 73 (2011): 526–546.

MacIntyre, Alasdair. *After Virtue: A Study of Moral Theory*. London: Duckworth, 1985.

MacLachlan, Bonnie. *Women in Ancient Rome: A Sourcebook*. London: Bloomsbury, 2013.

MacLennan, Reverend Scotty. *Finding Your Religion: When the Faith You Grew Up With Has Lost Its Meaning*. New York: Harper Collins, 1999.

Maddalena, Julie A. Mavity "Floodwaters and the Ticking Clock: The Systematic Oppression and Stigmatization of Poor, Single Mothers in America and Christian Theological Responses." *Cross Currents* 63.2 (June 2013): 148–173.

Maddox, Randy L. *Responsible Grace: John Wesley's Practical Theology*. Nashville: Kingswood Books, 1994.

_____. *Rethinking Wesley's Theology for Contemporary Methodism*. Nashville: Kingswood Books, 1998.

Maguire, Daniel. *Death by Choice*. New York: Schocken, 1975.

Manzano, Angie. "A Different Kind of Feminism: Feminists Resisting Pornography and Prostitution." *Off Our Backs* 35.7/8. (July 1, 2005): 24–29.

Marie Celeste, Sr. *The Intimate Friendships of Elizabeth Ann Bayley Seton*. New York: Alba House, 1989.

Martin, Dale B. *Sex and the Single Savior: Gender and Sexuality in Biblical Interpretation*. Louisville: Westminster John Knox Press, 2006.

Martin, Terry L. and Kenneth J. Doka. *Men Don't Cry... Women Do: Transcending Gender Stereotypes of Grief*. Philadelphia: Taylor and Francis, 2000.

Mattison, William. *Introducing Moral Theology: True Happiness and the Virtues*. Grand Rapids: Brazos Press, 2008.

Maybank, Amina R. *Saved, Single, and Seeking Him*. Philadelphia: Words From Heaven Publishing, 2014.

McCarthy, David Matzko. *Sex and Love in the Home: A Theology of the Household*. Norwich, UK: Hymns Ancient and Modern LTD, 2004.

_____. *The Good Life: Genuine Christianity for the Middle Class*. Grand Rapids: Brazos Press, 2004.

———. "The Relationship of Bodies." In *Theology and Sexuality, Classic and Contemporary Readings*. Edited by Eugene F. Rogers, pp. 200–216. London: Blackwell, 2002.

McGowin, Emily. "As for Me and My House: The Theology of the Family in the American Quiverfull Movement." Ph.D. Dissertation, University of Dayton, 2015.

McManus, Mike and Harriet. *Living Together: Myths, Risks, and Answers*. New York: Howard Books, 2008.

McNamara, JoAnn. *Sisters in Arms: Catholic Nuns Through Two Millennia*. Cambridge, MA: Harvard UP, 2000.

Methodist Church. *Minutes of the Methodist Conferences, Volume 1*. 1744–1798. London: John Mason, 1862.

Miller, David. "Single Parenting in the Christian Community." In *The Christian Educator's Handbook on Family Life Education*. Edited by Kenneth O. Gangel and James C. Wilhoit, pp. 127–138. Grand Rapids: Baker Books, 1996.

Mitchell, Henry and Ella. "Divorce and Remarriage for Christians." In *Transitions: Leading Churches through Change*. Edited by David N. Mosser, pp.91–99. Louisville: Westminster John Knox Press, 2011.

Mohler, Albert R. "The Mystery of Marriage." 2004 New Altitude Conference. http://albertmohler.com/audio_archive.php

Molvaer, Reidulf K. "St. Paul's Views on Sex According to 1 Corinthians 7:9 and 36–38." *Studia Theologica* 54 (2004): 45–59.

Moore, Charles E., ed., *Called to Community: The Life Jesus Wants for His People*. New York: Plough Publishing House, 2016.

Mosser, David N., ed. *Transitions: Leading Churches through Change*. Louisville: Westminster John Knox Press, 2011.

Murray, Melissa. "Black Marriage, White People, Red Herrings," *Michigan Law Review* 111.977: 977–999.

Nanos, Janelle. "Single By Choice" *Boston Magazine*, January 2012. http://www.bostonmagazine.com/2012/01/single-by-choice-why-more-of-us-than-ever-before-are-happy-to-never-get-married.

Neff, Miriam. "The Widow's Might." *Christianity Today*, January 1, 2008: 43–48.

Nicolaisen, Magnhild and Kirsten Thorsen. "Who Are Lonely? Loneliness in Different Age Groups (18–81 Years Old), Using Two Measures of Loneliness." *International Journal Of Aging & Human Development* 78, no. 3 (2014): 229–257.

Niebuhr, H. Richard. *Christ and Culture*. San Francisco: Harper Collins, 1951.

Noonan, John T., ed. *The Morality of Abortion: Legal and Historical Perspectives*. Cambridge, MA: Harvard University Press, 1970.

Norris, Kathleen. *The Cloister Walk*. New York: Riverhead Books, 1996.

Obama, Barack. *Dreams from my Father: A Story of Race and Inheritance*. New York: Three Rivers Press, 1995, 2004.

Obergefell et al v. Hodges, Ohio Director of Health et al, (US S.C. 2015). Accessed August 20, 2015. http://www.supremecourt.gov/opinions/14pdf/14-556_3204.pdf.

Obrien, David. *Public Catholicism*. 2nd Edition. New York: Orbis Books, 1996.

Oden, Thomas. *The Good Works Reader*. Grand Rapids: Eerdmans, 2007.

Oppenheimer, Mark. "A Theologian's Influence, and Stained Past, Live On." *The New York Times* October 11, 2013. Accessed September 7, 2016. http://www.nytimes.com/2013/10/12/us/john-howard-yoders-dark-past-and-influence-lives-on-for-mennonites.html?_r=0.

Synod of Bishops. "XIV Ordinary General Assembly: The Vocation and Mission of the Family in the Church and in the Contemporary World: The Final Report of the Synod of Bishops to the Holy Father, Pope Francis." Vatican City, 2015. http://www.vatican.va/roman_curia/synod/documents/rc_synod_doc_20151026_relazione-finale-xiv-assemblea_en.html.

Orenstein, Peggy. "Playing at Sexy." *New York Times Magazine*, June 13, 2010. Accessed March 11, 2016. http://www.nytimes.com/2010/06/13/magazine/13fob-wwln-t.html.

Otto, Tim. *Oriented to Faith: Transforming the Conflict Over Gay Relationships*. Eugene, OR: Cascade Books, 2014.

Paul, Pamela. *Pornified: How Pornography is Transforming our Loves, Our Relationsips and Our Families*. New York: Times/Henry Holt, 2005.

Paul VI, Pope. *Humanae Vitae*. Papal Encyclical, July 25, 1968. http://w2.vatican.va/content/paul-vi/en/encyclicals/documents/hf_p-vi_enc_25071968_humanae-vitae.htm.

_____. *Lumen Gentium, Dogmatic Constitution on the Church*, November 21, 1964. http://www.vatican.va/archive/hist_councils/ii_vatican_council/documents/vat-ii_const_19641121_lumen-gentium_en.html.

Painter, Rebecca M. "Further Thoughts on a Prodigal Son Who Cannot Come Home, on Loneliness and Grace," *Christianity and Literature* 58.3 (2009):484–492.

Paul, Pamela. *Pornified: How Pornography is Transforming our Loves, Our Relationships and Our Families*. New York: Times/Henry Holt, 2005.

Patterson, Margot. "An Extraordinary Difficult Childhood." *National Catholic Reporter*, March 7, 2003.

Peters, Benjamin. "'Apocalyptic Sectarianism': The Theology at Work in Critiques of Catholic Radicals." *Horizons* 39:2 (September 2012): 208–229.

_____. *Called to Be Saints: John Hugo, The Catholic Worker, and a Theology of Radical Christianity*. Milwaukee: Marquette University Press, 2016.

Pew Research Center. "Millennials in Adulthood." http://www.pewsocialtrends.org/2014/03/07/millennials-in-adulthood.

Pinches, Charles and Stanley Hauerwas. "Courage Exemplified." In *Christians Among the Virtues: Theological Conversations with Ancient and Modern Ethics*, pp. 149–165. South Bend, IN: Notre Dame Press, 1997.

Quast, Kevin. *Reading the Corinthian Correspondence: An Introduction.* New York: Paulist Press, 1994.

Rack, Henry D. *Reasonable Enthusiast: John Wesley and the Rise of Methodism.* London: Epworth Press, 2002.

Regnerus, Mark. "The Pornographic Double Bind." *First Things,* November 11, 2014. Accessed January, 29, 2016. http://www.firstthings.com/web-exclusives/2014/11/the-pornographic-double-bind.

Regnerus, Mark and Jeremy Uecker. *Premarital Sex in America: How Young Americans Meet, Mate, and Think About Marrying.* New York: Oxford University Press, 2011.

Reisman, David. *The Lonely Crowd, Revised Edition: A Study of the Changing American Character.* New Haven: Yale University Press, 2001.

Renzetti, Claire M. and Sandra Yocum, eds. *Clergy Sexual Abuse: Social Science Perspectives.* Boston: Northeastern University Press, 2013.

Reno, R.R. *In the Ruins of the Church: Sustaining Faith in an Age of Diminished Christianity.* Grand Rapids: Brazos, 2002.

Riegle, Rosalie G. *Dorothy Day: Portraits of Those Who Knew Her.* New York: Orbis 2003.

Rhoades, Galena, et al. "Couples' Reasons for Cohabitation: Associations with Individual Well-Being and Relationship Quality." *Journal of Family Issues* 30.2 (February 1, 2009): 223–258.

Rindfuss, R.R. and A. VandenHaueval. "Cohabitation: A Precursor to Marriage or an Alternative to Being Single." In *The Changing American Family: Sociological and Demographic Perspectives.* Edited by S.J. South and S.E. Tolnay. Boulder: Westview, 1992.

Roberts, Christopher. *Creation and Covenant: The Significance of Sexual Difference in the Moral Theology of Marriage.* New York: Continuum, 2007.

Roberts, William, ed. *Divorce and Remarriage: Religious and Psychological Perspectives.* Kansas City: Sheed and Ward, 1990.

Rodrigue, Carl, et al. "The Structure of Casual Sexual Experience Among Adults Aged 18–30 Years Old: A Latent Profile Analysis." *Canadian Journal of Human Sexuality* Vol. 24 Issue 3, (December 2015): 215–227.

Roetzel, Calvin J. *The World that Shaped the New Testament.* Atlanta: John Knox Press, 1985.

Rogers, Eugene F., ed. *Theology and Sexuality, Classic and Contemporary Readings.* London: Blackwell, 2002.

Rojas, Rick and John Surico. "A Guardian is Accused of Holding 2 Teens Captive for Years." *The New York Times* January 12, 2016. Accessed March 11, 2016. http://www.nytimes.com/2016/01/13/nyregion/a-guardian-is-charged-with-holding-2-teenagers-captive-in-queens-for-years.html.

Rosin, Hanna. *The End of Men (and the Rise of Women).* New York: Riverhead Books, 2012.

Roberts, Christopher. *Creation and Covenant: The Significance of Sexual Difference in the Moral Theology of Marriage*. New York: T&T Clark, 2007.

Rogers, Eugene F. "Sanctification, Homosexuality, and God's Triune Life." In *Theology and Sexuality: Classic and Contemporary Readings*. Edited by Eugene F. Rogers, pp. 217–248. London: Blackwell, 2002.

Rubio, Julie Hanlon. *A Christian Theology of Marriage and Family*. New York: Paulist Press, 2003.

_____. "Three-in-One Flesh: A Christian Reappraisal of Divorce in Light of Recent Studies." *Journal of the Society of Christian Ethics* 23.1 (2003): 47–70.

Schaefer, H. Luke and Marci Ybarra. "The Welfare Reforms of the 1990s and the Stratification of Material Well-Being Among Low-Income Households with Children." *Children and Youth Services Review* 34 (2012): 1810–1817.

Schiffbauer, Pam. "Marriage Preparation is Key to a Successful Marriage." Accessed May 25, 2016. http://www.foccusinc.com/Resources/2.pdf.

Schlumpf, Heidi. "Shame, Shame: When Catholic Institutions Fire Single Moms." *US Catholic* 78.1, January 2013. Accessed December 7, 2015. http://www.uscatholic.org/articles/201211/shame-shame-when-catholic-institutions-fire-single-moms-26591.

_____. "Stand Alone Moms: Catholic Single Parents Tell Their Stories." *US Catholic* 78.1, January 2013. Accessed December 7, 2015. http://www.uscatholic.org/articles/201211/stand-alone-moms-catholic-single-parents-tell-their-stories-26588.

Schwartzberg, Natalie, Kathy Berliner, and Demaris Jacob. *Single in a Married World: A Life Cycle Framework for Working With the Unmarried Adult*, 1st edition. W.W. Norton & Company, 1995.

Schworm, Peter. "Harvard's View on Consent at Issue in Sexual Assault Policy." *Boston Globe*, November 17, 2014. Accessed November 24, 2015. https://www.bostonglobe.com/metro/2014/11/17/harvard-sexual-assaults-policy-fuels-debate-about-consent/IRpfuo5MkjbHohN8ETErbK/story.html.

Semuels, Alana. "White Flight Never Ended." *The Atlantic*, July 30, 2015. Accessed September 3, 2016. http://www.theatlantic.com/business/archive/2015/07/white-flight-alive-and-well/399980/.

Seton, Elizabeth Bayley. *Collected Writings, Volumes 1-5*. Edited by Regina Bechtle. Chicago: New City Press, 2000.

"Single Mother Statistics." *Single Mother Guide*. https://singlemotherguide.com/single-mother-statistics/.

Song, Robert. *Covenant and Calling: Towards a Theology of Same-Sex Relationships*. Norwich, UK: SCM Press, 2014.

Soss, Joe and Sanford F. Schram. "A Public Transformed? Welfare Reform as Policy Feedback." *American Political Science Review* 101.1 (February 2007): 111–127.

Smit, Laura. *Loves Me, Loves Me Not: The Ethics of Unrequited Love*. Grand Rapids: Baker Academic, 2005.

Smith, Kevin L. "The Challenge of Matriarch: Family Discipleship and the African-American Experience." *Journal of Discipleship and Family Ministries* 2.2 (2012): 34–40.

Spiritual Friendship. https://www.spiritualfriendship.org/.

Spong, John Shelby. "Can the Church Bless Divorce?" *The Christian Century* 101:1126–1127.

Sprecher, Susan, et al. "Premarital Sexual Standards and Sociosexuality: Gender, Ethnicity, and Cohort Differences. *Archives of Sexual Behavior* 42 (2013): 1395–1405.

Stark, Christine and Rebecca Whisnant. *Not For Sale: Feminists Resisting Prostitution and Pornography*. North Melbourne, Australia: Spinifex Press, 2004.

Stimpson, Emily. *The Catholic Girl's Survival Guide for the Single Years: The Nuts and Bolts of Staying Sane and Happy While Waiting for Mr. Right*. Steubenville, OH: Emmaus Road Publishing, 2012.

Stollar, R.L. "The Child as Viper: How Voddie Baucham;s Theology of Children Promotes Child Abuse." January 16, 2015. Accessed September 27, 2016. https://homeschoolersanonymous.org/2015/01/16/the-child-as-viper-how-voddie-bauchams-theology-of-children-promotes-abuse/.

Stracham, Owen et al. *Whole in Christ: A Biblical Approach to Singleness*. Louisville: Danvers Press, 2015.

Strauss, Jillian. *Unhooked Generation: The Truth About Why We're Still Single*. New York: Hyperion, 2007.

Stuart, Elizabeth. *Gay and Lesbian Theologies: Repetitions with Critical Difference*. Hampshire, UK: 2003.

———. *Just Good Friends: Toward a Lesbian and Gay Theology of Relationships*. London: Mowbray, 1995.

"Survey: A Decade of Change in American Attitudes about Same-Sex Marriage and LGBT Issues." February 26, 2014. http://publicreligion.org/research/2014/02/2014-lgbt-survey/#.VlSvOHarRD9.

Sun, Y. and Y. Li. "Effects of Family Structure Type and Stability on Children's Academic Performance Trajectories." *Journal of Marriage and Family* 73 (2011): 541–556.

Synod of Bishops. "XIV Ordinary General Assembly: The Vocation and Mission of the Family in the Church and in the Contemporary World: The Final Report of the Synod of Bishops to the Holy Father, Pope Francis." Vatican City, 2015. http://www.vatican.va/roman_curia/synod/documents/rc_synod_doc_20151026_relazione-finale-xiv-assemblea_en.html.

Teterud, Wesley. *Caring For Widows: You and Your Church Can Make a Difference*. Grand Rapids: Baker Books, 1994.

Thatcher, Adrian. *Living Together and Christian Ethics*. Cambridge: Cambridge University Press, 2002

Thiselton, Anthony C. *The Living Paul: An Introduction to the Apostle's Life and Thought*. Downers Grove, IL: IVP Academic, 2009.

Thomas, Gary. *Sacred Marriage: What If God Designed Marriage to Make Us Holy More Than to Make Us Happy?* Grand Rapids: Zondervan, 2015.

Thompson, Edward H. et al. "Widows' Spiritual Journeys: Do They Quest?" *Journal of Religious Gerontology* 14.2/3 (2003): 119–138.

Thompson, Ross A. and Paul R. Amato, eds. *The Postdivorce Family: Children, Parenting, and Society*. Thousand Oaks: Sage Publications, 1999.

Thurston, Bonnie Bowman. *The Widows: A Woman's Ministry in the Early Church*. Minneapolis: Fortress Press, 1989.

Tushnet, Eve. *Gay and Catholic: Accepting my Sexuality, Finding Community, Living my Faith*. Notre Dame, IN: Ave Maria Press, 2014.

Troester, Riegle. *Voices From the Catholic Worker*. Philadelphia: Temple University Press, 1993.

Traister, Rebecca. *All the Single Ladies: Unmarried Women and the Rise of an Independent Nation*. New York: Simon and Schuser, 2016.

Tran, Jonathan. "Anne and the Difficult Gift of Stanley Hauerwas's Church." In *The Difference Christ Makes*. Edited by Charles Collier, pp.71–76. Eugene: Cascade Books, 2015.

Unmarried Equality. http://www.unmarried.org/about-us/.

US Catholic Church. *Catechism of the Catholic Church*. New York: Doubleday, 1995.

US Catholic Conference of Bishops. "Blessings of Age: Pastoral Message on Growing Older within the Faith Community." Accessed January 27, 2017. http://www.usccb.org/issues-and-action/marriage-and-family/blessings-of-age-english.cfm.

US Census Bureau, "Facts and Figures: Unmarried and Single Americans Week, September 21–27, 2014." http://www.census.gov/content/dam/Census/newsroom/facts-for-features/2014/cb14ff-21_unmarried.pdf.

US Census Bureau, "Marital Events of Americans: 2009," American Community Survey Reports 2011. Accessed September 23, 2015. https://www.census.gov/prod/2011pubs/acs-13.pdf.

US Pew Forum, *Religious Landscape Survey* 2014. Accessed September 23, 2015. http://www.pewforum.org/religious-landscape-study/marital-status/.

Van der Sypt, Liesbeth. "The Use of 1 Corinthians 7:36–38 in Early Christian Asceticism." In *Asceticism and Exegesis in Early Christianity: The Reception of New Testament Texts in Ancient Ascetic Discourses*. Edited by Hans-Ulrich Weidemann. Gottlingen, Germany: Vandenhoeck & Ruprecht, 2013.

van Fleteren, "Confessions." In *Augustine Through the Ages: An Encyclopedia*. Edited by Allan D. Fitzgerald, pp. 227–232. Grand Rapids: Eerdmans, 1999.

VanGoethem, Jeff. *Living Together: A Guide to Counseling Unmarried Couple*. Grand Rapids: Kregel Academic and Professional, 2005.

Vasey, Michael. *Strangers and Friends: A New Exploration of Homosexuality and the Bible*. London: Hodder and Stoughton, 1995.

Verhly, Allen. *The Christian Art of Dying: Learning with Jesus*. Grand Rapids: Eerdmans, 2011.

Vines, Matthew. *God and the Gay Christian: The Biblical Case in Support of Same-Sex Relationships*. New York: Convergent Books, 2014.

Vishnewski, Stanley. *Meditations: Dorothy Day*. New York: Paulist Press, 1970.

Vrangalova, Zhana. "Is Casual Sex on the Rise in America?" *Psychology Today*, April 25, 2014. Accessed March 11, 2016. https://www.psychologytoday.com/blog/strictly-casual/201404/is-casual-sex-the-rise-in-america.

Wallace-Hadrill, Andrew. *Augustan Rome*. London: Bristol Classical Press, 1993.

Wallerstein, Judith and Sandra Blakeslee. *The Unexpected Legacy of Divorce: A 25 Year Landmark Study*. New York: Hyperion, 2005.

Walter, Tony. "Modern Death: Taboo or Not Taboo?" *Sociology* 25.2 (May 1991): 293–310.

Ward, Patricia A. *Experimental Theology in America: Madam Guyon, Fènelon, and Their Readers*. Waco, TX: Baylor University Press, 2009.

Ward, W. Reginald and Richard P. Heitzenrater, eds. *The Works of John Wesley* Vol. 18, Journals of Diaries I. Nashville: Abingdon Press, 1988.

Weidemann, Hans-Ulrich, ed. *Asceticism and Exegesis in Early Christianity: The Reception of New Testament Texts in Ancient Ascetic Discourses*. Gottlingen, Germany: Vandenhoeck & Ruprecht, 2013.

Wesley, John. "Christian Perfection." In *Sermons on Several Occasions*. London: Epworth Press, 1977.

———. *The Journal of the Reverend John Wesley*. Edited by Nehemiah Curnock, 8 vols. London: R. Cully, 1909–1916.

White, James F. *The Sacraments in Protestant Practice and Faith*. Nashville: Abingdon Press, 1999.

White, Joseph M. "Physician of Body and Soul: Simon Gabriel Bruté, Doctor... Sulpician Priest... Teacher... Pioneer Scholar... Bishop... Confidan te and Friend to a Saint." Accessed January 27, 2017. http://stmaryspacast.org/project/physician-of-body-and-soul-simon-gabriel-brute/.

Wikipedia, "Freedom of Religion." Accessed November 23, 2015. http://en.wikipedia.org/wiki/Freedom_of_religion.

Williams, Rowan. "The Body's Grace," in *Theology and Sexuality: Classic and Contemporary Readings*. Edited by Eugene F. Rogers, pp. 309–321. London: Blackwell, 2002.

Williams, Russelyn. *The Single Christian Woman's Guide: Wisdom in Getting to Our God Ordained Man of Promise*. Bloomington, IN: Westbow, 2016.

Windley-Daoust, Susan. *Theology of the Body, Extended: The Spiritual Sign of Birth, Impairment, and Dying*. Hobe Sound, FL: Lectio Publishing, 2014.

Winner Lauren F. "The Countercultural Path." In 5 *Paths to the Love of Your Life: Defining Your Dating Style*. Edited by Alex Chediak, pp. 17–56. Colorado Springs: NavPress, 2005.

_____. "Lectio Divina and Divorce: Reflections in Twelve Parts about What Divorce Has to Teach the Church." *Anglican Theological Review* 97.2 (Spring 2015): 281–297.

_____. *Real Sex: The Naked Truth About Chastity*. Grand Rapids: Brazos, 2005.

_____. *Still: Notes on a Mid-Faith Crisis*. New York: Harper One, 2012.

Wheeler-Reed, David. "Paul on Marriage and Singleness: Reading 1 Corinthians 7 with the Augustan Marriage Laws." Ph.D. Dissertation, University of Toronto, 2013.

Witte, John and M. Christian Green, eds. *The Equal-Regard Family and its Friendly Critics: Don Browning and the Practical Theological Ethics of the Family*. Grand Rapids: Eerdmans, 2007.

Wuthnow, Robert. *After the Baby Boomers: How Twenty- and Thirty-Somethings are Shaping the Future of American Religion*. Princeton: Princeton University Press, 2007.

Yohe, Katherine. "Dorothy Day: Love for One's Daughter and Love for the Poor." *Horizons* 31.2 (Fall 2004): 272–301.

Index